STILL

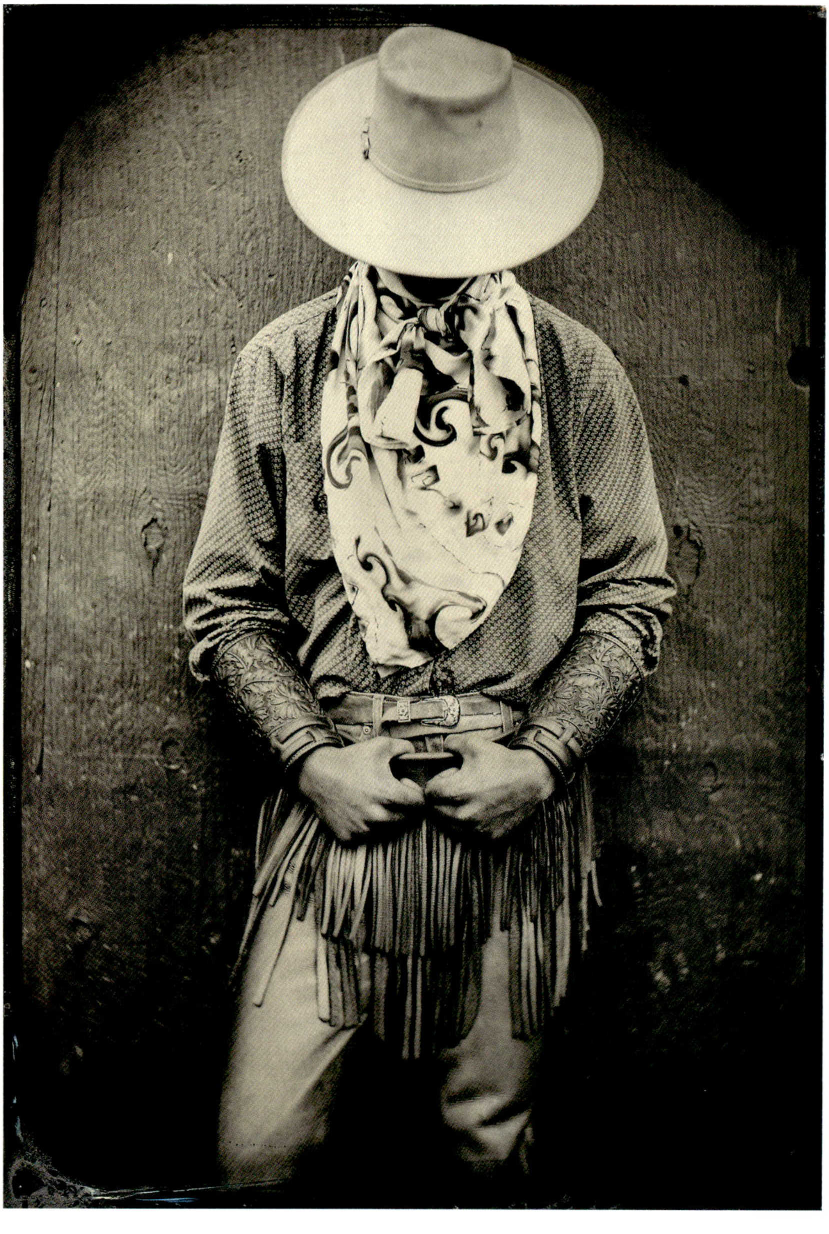

STILL

Cowboys at the Start of the Twenty-First Century

TINTYPES BY ROBB KENDRICK

ESSAY BY MARIANNE WIGGINS

AFTERWORD BY JAY DUSARD

UNIVERSITY OF TEXAS PRESS AUSTIN

NUMBER TWENTY-TWO

The M. K. Brown Range Life Series

FRONTISPIECE

Colter Schlosser

GANG RANCH, BRITISH COLUMBIA, CANADA

Printed in China
First edition, 2008

∞ The paper used in this book meets the minimum requirements of ANSI/NISO Z39.48-1992 (R1997) (Permanence of Paper).

ISBN 978-0-292-71438-0 (cl. : alk paper)
Library of Congress Cataloging Number 2007931160

For Jeannie, Gus, & Jeb, always in my heart.

A special place for Katie, a spark of life like no other,
a horse in another life, no finer best "man,"
great friend to our whole family.

CONTENTS

PURELY AMERICAN

Marianne Wiggins

I. THE NATIONAL COSTUME

For years now, every June, it has been the custom of the current reigning monarch of Great Britain, Queen Elizabeth II, to invite a privileged clutch of lesser subjects to a bash—okay, a Garden Party—in the backyard of her London digs, otherwise known as Buckingham Palace.

When the invitation arrives, as it did to the house where I was living in Islington in 1988, it reeks of money. It is larger than every other piece of mail you will receive that day, and the paper of the envelope, itself, seems to have been manufactured on a cloud by chubby *putti*. The card inside is edged in gold, the words embossed with what appears to be the real McCoy, and the inclination (if you are me) is to take a knife and scrape the fraction of an ounce of gold right off the surface of the card for future use inside a tooth.

The invitation does not issue from H.R.H., herself, but from her Household Chamberlain, and after the address and time and so forth, at the bottom of the card there is printed (in gold, of course) the suggestion, *"Lounge Wear or National Costume."*

"Lounge Wear," in England, is what we call in the United States "business attire"—a tie and suit for men, a dress or suit (but never a *pant* suit) for women. But what, I wondered, as an American, could I don that day, if I so desired, as a "National Costume"? Do we Americans *have* one? The Brits, themselves, do not (although the Scots do: *kilts*)—and this "National Costume" business was yet another trick of the Royal Household to put "foreigners" in their designated place as colorful exotics, outside the mainstream of lounge-wearing Little Englanders.

The Garden Party, when I finally got there, was all the more beautiful and vibrant for the Hindi women in their saris, Kenyans in their kente cloths, Scots in their kilts, Sikhs in their turbans, and Burmese in their silks. And, yes, they all looked *foreign*, in that setting. And part of me longed, that afternoon, as the band played "God Save the Queen," for some emblem, in my way of dressing, of my nation-hood, of my *American*-ness, beyond the mall-wear uniform we see everywhere these days—sweat pants, sneakers, t-shirt, and a baseball cap.

Is this who we *are?*

If I asked you to draw a picture in your mind of the archetypical American, what would that image be?

How would he/she look?

What would he/she be wearing?

And, more importantly, what would that costume signify, what would it say about the kind of nation that we are?

Because implicit in the idea of a "national costume" is the idea of a national identity—a national costume *suggests* a national identity. In the absence of a "national costume," can we really form a cohesive model of our ideal American?

This would all be easier if we were an homogenous nation. If, for example, we were a nation like the Zuni, Navajo, or Sioux—a tribe, by DNA and blood.

When you think of Indian nations, you think of *national costumes*—the wrapped leggings of the Zuni nation, feathers, quills, and beadwork of the Sioux.

Thomas Jefferson would recognize the costumes at a modern powwow, but what would he make of men in suits on Wall Street or in Washington, D.C., or the baggy pants and bling currently affected by teenage boys in malls from New Hampshire to Idaho? Would he even recognize the judges' robes of the Supreme Court? In his day, breeches and powdered wigs were the costume of the nation—hoop skirts and wigs for women—both fashions borrowed from the leading lights in France and England. But Revolution in the state led to revolution in the closet, and as the cramped East Coast of Jefferson's era turned West to Tennessee, Kentucky, and Missouri, a purely *American* way of dressing appeared on the frontier: durable, affordable, and utilitarian, though still with the occasional frill. A costume men could work and ride a horse in, and still be protected from the rough and tumble, from the weather.

I think it's reasonable to say that Thomas Jefferson would recognize the men and women in this book as the same kind of hard-working Americans he envisioned when he bartered with Napoleon for the Louisiana Purchase.

I think it's reasonable to say that after two hundred and thirty years Thom Jeff and the other Framers of the Constitution would recognize the dignity, nobility, and working savvy at play in the classic combo of a Stetson or Resistol hat, jeans, chaps, high boots, low spurs, and a bright bandana that constitute the elements of what I have to argue is our hands-down *national* costume.

Ask me what I think our national costume is, I'll tell you *it's a cowboy's.*

Because, as Robb Kendrick verifies in his own words, every aspect of a cowboy's clothing reflects some solution to a problem, some way to get the job done—that neckerchief pulled up around your nose keeps the traildust off your throat and lungs. That hat keeps the sun from burning off your corneas, the rain from coursing down your neck. Those chaps and boots can stop a thorn or horn from severing an artery. That strand of braided leather can snap an errant dogie back in line. A cowboy's clothes reflect the virtues we hold sacred as our national ideals: independence, duty, and unflinching courage.

A cowboy's is the one job we Americans have dreamed of doing—the one life we've all dreamed of living, if only for a little while.

I cannot imagine an America without the cowboy—no one can.

So when we look at the faces in this book, what are we seeing, if not an image of our nation, of ourselves?

II. THE NATIONAL DIET

There is no way, really, to talk about what a cowboy does and who a cowboy is, without first talking about *beef.*

Per capita, Americans consume more beef than any other country on the planet. We eat *a lot* of beef—our consumption fueling a $49-billion-a-year beef industry, making cattle rearing the most lucrative sector in the nation's agri-business. For the last decade, revenues at restaurants calling themselves "steakhouses," exclusively, have increased at a steady rate of thirteen percent per year (second only to fast-food franchises and the coffeehouse-clones of Starbucks).

Our beef consumption is an emblem of our history—our *frontier* history—but how did all this happen? How did we go from an English culinary heritage of a roast, a "joint" of beef or a beef stew, to a nation self-described as existing strictly on "steak and potatoes"?

Like most things about the history of this country (including our history of slavery, Indian internment, and land expansion), the answer can be found by following the money trail it's left behind.

Unlike our beef-consuming predecessor, England, the young United States discovered as early as the end of the eighteenth century that we had a *lot* of space, seemingly endless reaches, even near the eastern coast, in West Virginia and Tennessee, where cattle could thrive on open meadows. Beginning in the decade preceding the Civil War, the expansion of territories west of the Mississippi opened cattle farming to what appeared to be limitless sources of nutritious grasslands that didn't need seeding and mowing, didn't need fences, and required only a small labor force on horseback for tending and guarding from theft. Livestock breeding moved from the closed quarters of the East to the open range, led by the disease-resistant, hardy "Texas" longhorns, a semi-wild bastard breed descended from a herd brought here by the Spanish. Longhorns were noted for their trail endurance, capable of surviving drives of more than 1,000 miles, camel-like, with very little food or water. By the late 1880s, America had officially entered an "era of cheap beef," owing to the proliferation of the railroads through the Western territories, ending the long drives to market. Former cattle towns—Wichita, Dodge City, Abilene—were replaced on the food chain by slaughterhouses close to where the cattle could be raised, then put on refrigerated trains. Market demand to fatten cattle fast led to the rise of corn-fed herds and penned-in feed lots. But the rise of more sophisticated modern tastes has seen a renaissance in grass-fed herds and fattier, more tasteful breeds—Hereford, Angus, both Red and Black, Charolais from France, Chianina from Italy, and the Wagyu from Japan, source of Kobe-style beef.

All the cowboys Robb has photographed for this collection work on these grass-fed operations, running herds in what Robb considers more faithful to the traditional way of cattle rearing. This is a conscious decision on his part and is not meant to imply a prejudice against the industrialized feedlots (which still require working cowboys on horseback to patrol the pens), but more a commitment, just like the antiquated equipment and method he has used to make the images, to an older, less artificially enhanced way of working, living, and putting life in focus.

The emergence of the giant industrialized cattle lots seems, also, to beg the question, "What are cowboys *for?*"

Gone are the days, made famous on film, of the enormous cattle drives, John Wayne and Tommy Lee Jones at the front of several thousand head of cattle. And how come England, a great beef-eating nation for hundreds of years, has yet to produce a single cowboy? What about Japan, where Kobe beef is a national treasure?

Are cowboys universally necessary everywhere there's cattle?

(Nope. Not really. In theory, you can raise a cow or two without a cowboy. But if you need to brand or rope or cut a herd, you need a man or woman on a horse.)

So if the cowboy, as a unit of labor, is negotiable, is there something unique to our nation, to America, that's turned him into this legendary icon?

(Yep.) (Darn tootin'.)

For one thing, along with steak and hamburgers, two other favorite items on our national diet are TV and movies. Strong coffee around the campfire and lone nights beneath the stars on celluloid and in prime time have shaped the active cowboy myth far more than Zane Grey and Louie L'Amour combined. The question, "Which came first, John Wayne or the Wrangler jean?" is as thorny as its egg-or-chicken counterpart. Other nations have cowboys—Canada, Spain, Mexico, Argentina, and Australia—but no other country gave rise to John Ford, *Rawhide, Red River, Cimarron,* or *Bonanza.* Growing up in Pennsylvania, I had never been out West, but I learned all about bovine encephalitis (and how to fill a pair of jeans) from watching the star of *Hud*, Paul Newman (a dyed-in-the-wool New Yorker, no less).

Not only do the cowboy traditions of other nations deviate from ours—in Australia, for example, there's neither branding nor roping: the saddle is without a pommel, and the herd responds to audible commands, to *sound*, for cutting—other cowboy traditions aren't as widely disseminated nor as fervently romanticized at the local cineplex as ours.

So which came first—the men (and now women) of steely reserve, a squint, few words, a horse, a poncho, and endurance . . .

. . . or Clint?

. . . or Duke?

. . . or *Shane?*

III. THE TIN

Robb Kendrick first came to my attention through the magazine *Texas Monthly.*

Two years ago, I was paging through my subscription issue when I was stopped cold by a stunning photograph. *Texas Monthly* is renown for commissioning photographic work by hip, cultish artists (Keith Carter, Matt Mahurin, and Dan Winters come to mind), so I'm used to finding something visually exciting in its layout, but the image that arrested me this time was part of an *ad*, of all things. For a *bank*. It was a cleverly targeted advertising campaign, designed to hook the reader into thinking that the bank in question was as invested in the past as it was in the future. And the way it went about delivering that message was to have as its centerpiece a single eye-catching image:

A tintype.

Of a cowboy.

I ripped the page out and saved it.

The ads ran for several months, each ad using a different image, and for the first few moments that I looked at them, I could feel my mind playing tricks on me, trying to convince my eyes that I was staring at a moment from the faded past.

I could tell a large-format camera had been used, and even on the glossy magazine page I could tell that, before being reproduced, the original image had been printed on a sheet of tin, a process that went out of style in the early 1900s.

I had a selfish motive at that time for my interest in early photographic techniques, because I was in the process of writing a novel about the American photographer Edward S. Curtis, who made his career creating portraits of American Indians with a similar type of large-format camera, fixing the image on glass, instead of what we commonly call "tin" (the substance is actually iron).

Between 1856 and 1900, tintypes were common as salt—cheap to produce and relatively fast from start to finish, they were the preferred medium of itinerant photographers and usually went, depending on their size, for a mere penny a sitting.

They went out of style with the advent of negative films and photographic papers, but their lustre (owing to a surface varnish) and depth of focus (owing to the type of camera) combine to make a beauty you can hold that can elicit and solicit a jolt of true emotion.

And I like to think there was something about their name—*tin*—that reverberated in the national psyche, too, especially where they were most popular, out West.

Because it's the West that created the *tin* star, *tin* marshal and *tin*horn. Pressed tin (a form of lead, actually) was the ceiling style of choice in saloons and general stores, and if you visit Tombstone, Deadwood, or Cheyenne today, you can still sit in those high-ceilinged rooms on their tourist-attraction Main Streets and imagine the sounds of boots and spurs across the floor and the tang of cattle being driven through their streets.

Tintypes look old, because they are—even when they're modern—because they're old in the making, in the tedious and antiquated way they're created, just as a Bach cantata or a Baroque string ensemble sounds old even if the instruments are played before us in a concert hall.

In the back of my mind, I had always intended to try to get in touch with Robb Kendrick as part of my research into the hazards of large-format photography for my Edward S. Curtis novel—but one thing led to another, and I never followed up. Imagine my delight, then, when, a year later, vacationing in San Miguel de Allende, Mexico, I accepted a dinner party invitation from a Texas acquaintance and found myself standing, margarita in hand, in front of a tall, reserved, self-effacing, young (younger than I am), handsome, blue-eyed man leaning against a wall on the Texan's patio, trying to create a more inventive conversational gambit than who-are-you, where-are-you-from, what do you *do?*—when the young man tentatively explained that he had moved down to Mexico from Texas with his wife Jeannie and their two sons, that he was a photographer, and that he had just published his first book, *Revealing Character*, a collection of portraits that he had made of Texas cowboys, originally commissioned by a Texas bank.

The shoe suddenly dropped, and I guess I gushed unashamedly about how I had torn those ad pages out of *Texas Monthly* because there was something about the solitude and inner dignity of his portrait subjects that reminded me of the kind of studies Edward Curtis made of the American Indians—and Robb graciously offered to have me visit his studio in San

Miguel to look at his collection of vintage tintypes and ask him to explain how he worked.

I was there at nine o'clock the next morning.

Though he smiles easily and has a charming, even self-deprecating, humor about the mistakes he's committed pursuing his art, the one quality of Robb's that outshines all the others when he's talking about what he does for a living is his almost monastic commitment to the service of making fine pictures.

Around his vintage tintypes, he's like a boy with an enviable baseball card collection—*You have to look at* this *one,* this *one is really rare*. He admits that some bug bit him years ago, and its bite won't leave his system. As he talked me through the process, his eyes began to have that light you see in perennially happy people, and I could see how, without even trying, he must win his subjects over just by the joy he radiates, unpacking his camera and setting up his stuff to *work*.

And *work* it is, as he explains in his own words—sometimes bone-wearying, sometimes Keystone Kops hilarious, as when he tells what its like trying to haul the vast supply of suspicious-looking chemicals in coolers that he needs on hand in the field through the high-alert border crossings between the United States and Mexico.

Although he speaks of his predecessors, the nineteenth-century itinerant tintype photographers, with awe and handles each vintage tintype he's collected, especially the tiny 1/2" x 1" "gem"-sized ones, as if they were ancient religious relics, Robb is very much an artist fluently conversant in twenty-first-century high-tech visual vocabulary. His large, airy studio in San Miguel is outfitted with state-of-the-art computers, and as we spoke about the vintage process, an assistant sat at a computer, meticulously going over every micro-inch of one of Robb's scanned tintypes, removing any trace of dust on its surface. Although there is very little Robb can do to manipulate the actual tintype as it develops and is fixed (he adds surface lines, sometimes, or scratches), the full panoply of modern technology is at his disposal for perfecting the scanned, paper-printed images.

Portraiture, of course, is only one face of the edifice of American photography. We are a nation of grandiose scenery, after all, and most of our early photographers (Timothy O'Sullivan, Carleton Watkins) were *landscape* photographers. The human portrait, however beautiful and symbolic, was largely a private pursuit, the subject of well-heeled studio photographers catering to the landed classes, and itinerant jobbers servicing the poor.

Non-celebrity portraits, portraits of the un-famous, portraits of the un-named, as an elevated art form, began to flourish only in the late nineteenth century, because of their beauty and their spiritual evocation—and then ignited in the twentieth century as male artists (Steiglitz, Weston) turned to their female wives and muses (Georgia O'Keefe, Claris Weston) as sources of beautiful inspiration. Earlier, Jacob Riis and Lewis Hine were making portraits of the desperate in New York City, but it was the birth of twentieth-century photojournalism that gave rise to the American Face (think of the breadline and Dust Bowl portraits of Dorothea Lange and Walker Evans; and the "freak" documentations by Weegee and Diane Arbus).

As a documentarian of the American Face, Robb is singular in what he's done, owing to the fact that he's focused on a group defined not by blood-lines, religion, or celebrity, but by their jobs, their work, and by the way they choose to live their lives.

Finding these cowboys where they live, going out to the remote outposts of their cattle ranches, has to have exacted a physical price on the photographer—and an emotional one on his family, as well. Robb was in the field, away from home, for weeks at a time—and that is only one aspect of his working method that leads me to draw comparisons between his career and that of Edward S. Curtis.

Like Curtis, Robb has focused on a narrow demographic that evokes a legend of the past, even as it perseveres in modern times. Like Curtis, Robb exceeds the journeyman expectations of mere documentation. Like Curtis, he is an artist, first and foremost, and is not satisfied with making dull or ordinary pictures. Both his reflexes and his eye for beauty can't and won't respond until the image that he sees through his lens is something that lights up his heart.

Unlike Curtis, Robb is honest. He takes his subjects as he finds them and doesn't tart them up as Curtis did, with extra beads and feathers, for the sake of making something pretty or theatrical. His first aesthetic principle is to respect what he is seeing, to portray his subjects with dignity and honor.

Because, like them, Robb is the real deal.

A real *tin* star.

IV. STILL . . .

Curtis's work in the American West is something I've studied at length and in depth, and it's perhaps predictable that he would spring to mind as a touchstone while considering the photographs in this collection. One of his most renowned images is of a string of Indian braves on horseback, riding away from the camera toward a gathering storm on the horizon. Curtis called this photograph "The Vanishing Race," because he believed, as mainstream American society did at that time, that American Indians were doomed to extinction, that their languages, cultures, and beliefs could not survive.

He was wrong.

But his belief that he was recording a dying race led him to lard the roast, over-dramatize and romanticize the way he represented them as subjects.

The opposite is true of the way Robb Kendrick works.

Still was his first choice for the title of this book—not only because of the dictates of the large-format lens and its long exposures (the subjects had to stand real *still*), but because he believes in the historical stamina of American cowboys, in their enduring place in the national image and in the fact that a century from now these people will be part of our energetic, vital, independent spirit, *still.*

And for that, for giving us this archive, just as Edward S. Curtis gave us a document of American Indians, we owe Robb Kendrick a national debt.

We owe him our kinship and our national gratitude.

For tomorrow, for now . . . and, for *Still.*

30 JUNE 2007

LOS ANGELES

Marianne Wiggins writes extensively about photography and is the author of ten books. She has been nominated for both the National Book Award and the Pulitzer Prize. Her novel about Edward S. Curtis is *The Shadow Catcher.* She is a Professor of English at the University of Southern California.

EVOLUTION

Robb Kendrick

THE COWBOY ICON is so fixed in our collective mind that it's easy to believe that all cowboys are alike. The chaps, the spurs, the hat shadowing a sweaty, stubbly face. But after 41,000 miles driving across North America to find cowboys in their natural setting, I can tell you that cowboys have evolved differently—in subtle and substantial ways—depending on the weather, topography, vegetation, and history of diverse regions.

The cowboy family tree starts in Mexico, where the Spanish brought their steeds and their horse skills. The Spanish word for someone who tends cows is "vaquero." The vaquero style includes flat-brimmed hats, high-cantle (seatback) saddles made of flower-stamped leather, wide, slick saddle horns and large, eagle-bill tapaderos (stirrup covers)—the size and shape of which suggest prehistoric leather ski boots.

Yet the best place to see this look today is not in Mexico—since ranch hands in that country now are more influenced by the style of Texas, where many have spent time—but in Oregon, Idaho, Nevada, and parts of Canada west of the Rockies. Many vaqueros ended up in these states, after passing through California, which was after all once part of Mexico. The cowboys in these parts are called "buckaroos," which is a bastardization of "vaquero." Buckaroos are known as the pretty-boys of the cowboy world, though they wouldn't like to hear it put that way. The buckaroos' signature look is flat hats, chinks (short chaps with long fringe), braided rawhide reatas, horsehair *mecate* reins (anglicized as "McCartys"), and lots of fancy silver trimming on themselves and their horses. But the one accessory a self-respecting buckaroo would never be without is what's known as a "wild rag"—a bright silk neckerchief so large it looks as if it could easily serve as a tablecloth.

Another branch of cowboy genealogy runs through the desert south-west: Arizona, New Mexico, Texas, and Oklahoma. These ranch workers are known as "cowpunchers," a name that reflects the rough, thorny terrain they work in. Cowpunchers are no-nonsense, practical, and not about show. A typical cowpuncher in Texas might favor what's known as a "taco" hat, a hat that shoots up steeply on both sides, so as not to catch tree branches or a gust of wind. In Arizona, the hat brims are curled too, but they bend more like arcing waves than sheer cliff faces. Three types of chaps predominate in cowpuncher territory—bullhide batwings, shotgun leggings, and Arizona bellbottoms—all protect against the sharp brush. Most chaps have rings where tie-down strings can be stored—for easy access when a cow's legs need to be tied off or a gate needs to be kept open.

"Cowboys," as a regional classification, are found east of the Rockies in Kansas, Nebraska, the Dakotas, Colorado, Wyoming, and much of Montana. Cowboy style is a hybrid of traditions. It's not as flashy as the buckaroo's, but definitely not as rough and practical as the cowpuncher's. These ranch hands tend to work cattle more gently than the cowpunchers because the terrain allows it.

Because ranch hands are constantly on the move, looking for work across the West, stylistic differences have migrated too. Thirty years ago, you would never have seen chinks in Texas or a taco hat in Oregon, but today the looks are more mixed, which is why in some photos you may see a whole array of headgear at one ranch—flat-brimmed, short-brimmed, taco, or a high-crowned "Gus" hat. Each cattle worker adopts his own look and usually sticks to it tenaciously. Every element is a link to the past, a proud tradition in a far-flung culture that survives still in the midst of one of the richest and most high-tech societies in the world. Many cultures threatened by so-called progress can lose much in a matter of one or two generations. But cowboys—actual working cowboys, in all their manifestations—proudly and determinedly endure.

THE TINTYPES

I remember one time when I was about six or seven years old my dad he was startin' a colt down at the round pen out there at the JA Ranch. I just kept on pesterin' him cause I was just wantin' to see this and really thought that, you know, that I could do it myself. Daddy started and jacked a leg up on the colt and got a saddle on him and everything and kinda gypped him around that round pen and stepped up on him and that old colt did go to buckin' around there. That horse was jumpin' really high and dad was gruntin' and groanin' up there and I knew right then that, you know, that was darn sure a man's job.

I've got an eight-year-old son wants to be a cowboy so bad, you know, he'd give anything to be out ridin' horses and herdin' cattle every day, but, you know, we gotta do school and stuff. I want to pass the things that I learned from other guys on to him, cause a cowboy's kind of a dyin' breed and we all gotta pass the good stuff on and keep raisin' good cowboys cause there's just gonna be a handful of them, you know.

Everybody looks forward to the spring brandin' cause that's a fun time. You get a crew together and you get to see some friends you haven't seen in two or three months and you have a big time. In the summertime, you get the bulls gathered and put up and start some young horses and go to some ranch rodeos. Then we go into the fall and wean all our calves and get them shipped out and cut out all our keeper heifers and we all have big fun doin' that. If you're in the herd cuttin' out keeper heifers, the guys on the line will make fun of you for the one you cut out, saying you're not cuttin' out the right one. We give each other a hard time about that stuff—it's really like a pat on the back when they start makin' fun of you, is really what it is.

The relationship between all of us, every guy out here—there's not a guy that wouldn't go out of his way to help the other one out. You know, we're scattered out through the ranch, and we've got our own parts of the ranch that we have to take care of, and if you get in a bind and you call the other one, he'll come help you, and he may gripe at you and complain a little bit the whole time over there, but he's gonna go help you one way or the other.

My favorite part of bein' out here is when the crew's together and we're workin' and we're goin' out to scatter out across the pasture, and you get all your men dropped off, and you holler off to start the drive, and everybody starts out, and you ride up on a hill, lookin' out across the country there. You can see all your men ridin' through the country, and they got all them old cows and calves out in front of them, you know, comin' down out of an old long draw with a little bit of fog in there, and it's kinda cool, a little smoke blowin' out of your horse's nose. You set right up there on that hill and you see your

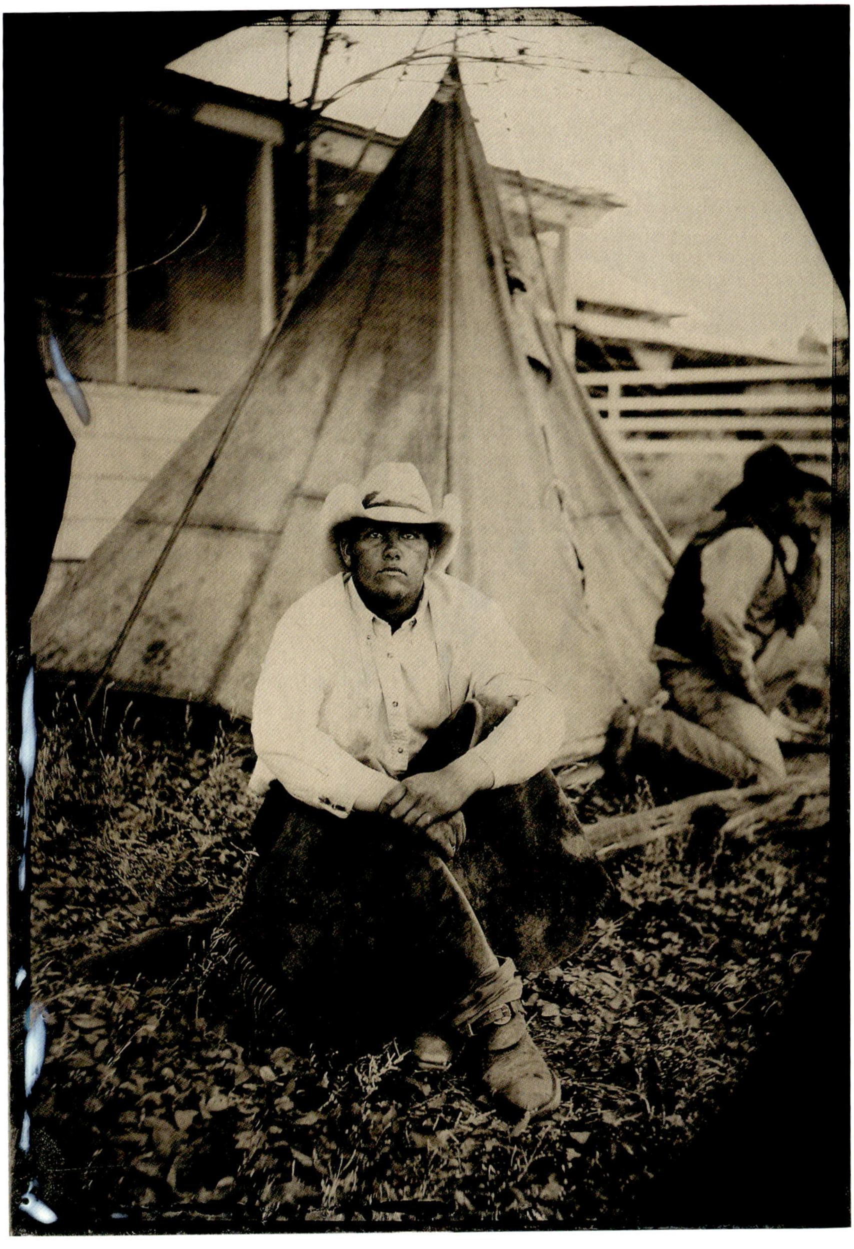

PLATE 1

Jake Rodgers (front), J. B. Kessler

DIAMOND A RANCH, ARIZONA

buddies coming down through there and you know right then that you're in the right place and you thank God you're gettin' to do this every day. You get the opportunity to step on a good horse and trot out across some good country and, you know, look at some big fat cows and pretty little baby calves and, man, you can't beat that. In my eyes you can't beat a feeling like that—just sittin' out there in the middle of nowhere. You can't have a problem out there, you know, no problems at all. All your worries are gone and it sure makes you thankful for life.

JUSTIN JOHNSON
TONGUE RIVER RANCH, TEXAS

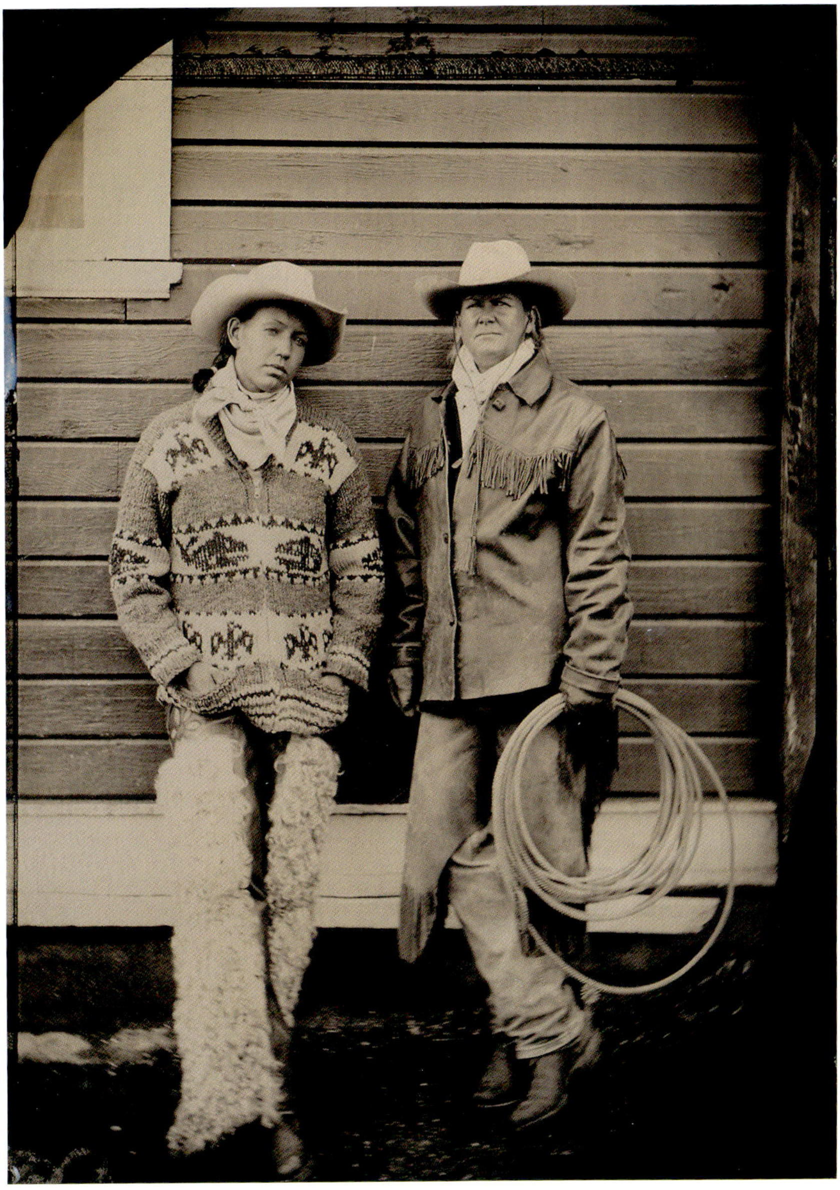

PLATE 2

Carmen Sippola, Janice Cornforth

GANG RANCH, BRITISH COLUMBIA, CANADA

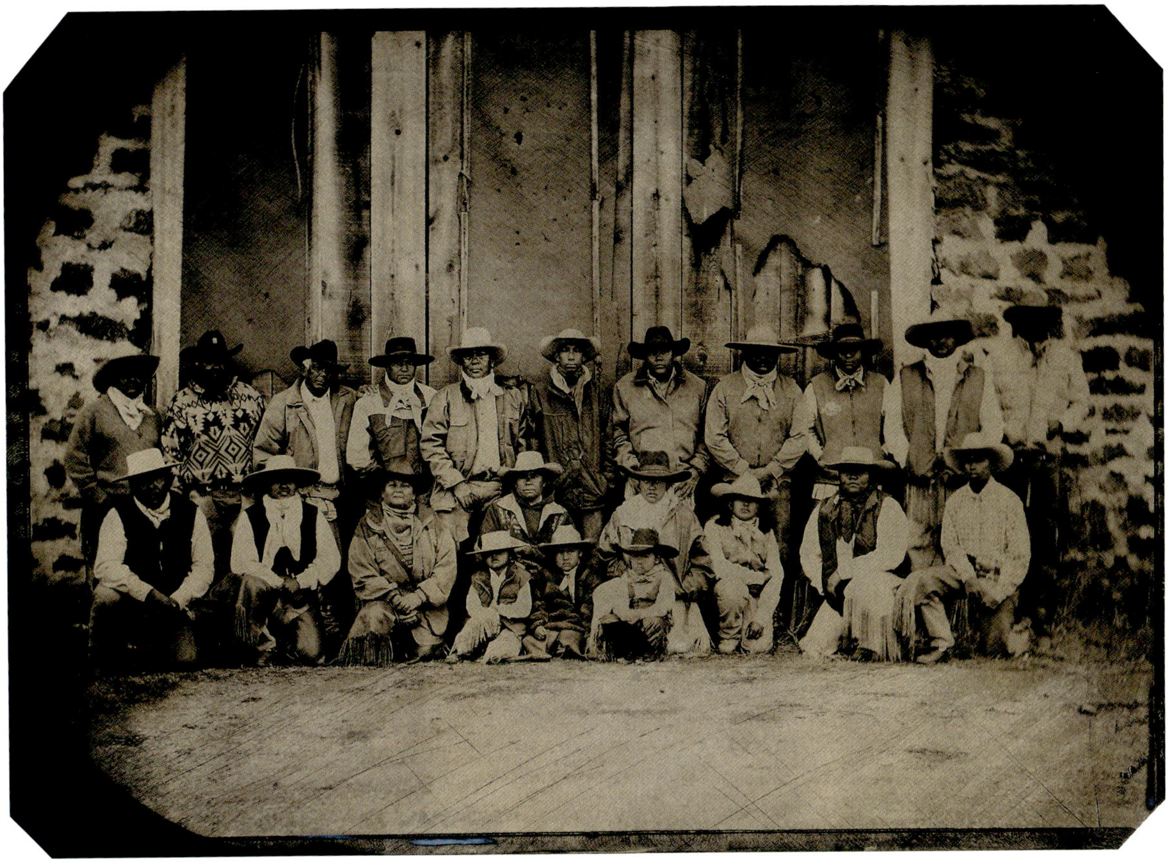

PLATE 3

(Back row, left to right) Reggie Sope, Erickson Hooper, Delbert Jim, Nathan Kelly, Jr., Jr. Knight, Gordan García, Alan Malotte, Nathan Kelly, Sr., Tyrill Knight, Will Knight, Jr., Manfred McKinney; (middle row) Steve Harney, Ashley Cota, Dolly Blossom-Paiva, Sherry Crutcher, Harli Cota, Katelyn Cota, Jessica Kelly, Dalton Jim; (kneeling) Macee McKinney, Chancie McKinney, Jenna Sope

DUCK VALLEY RESERVATION, NEVADA

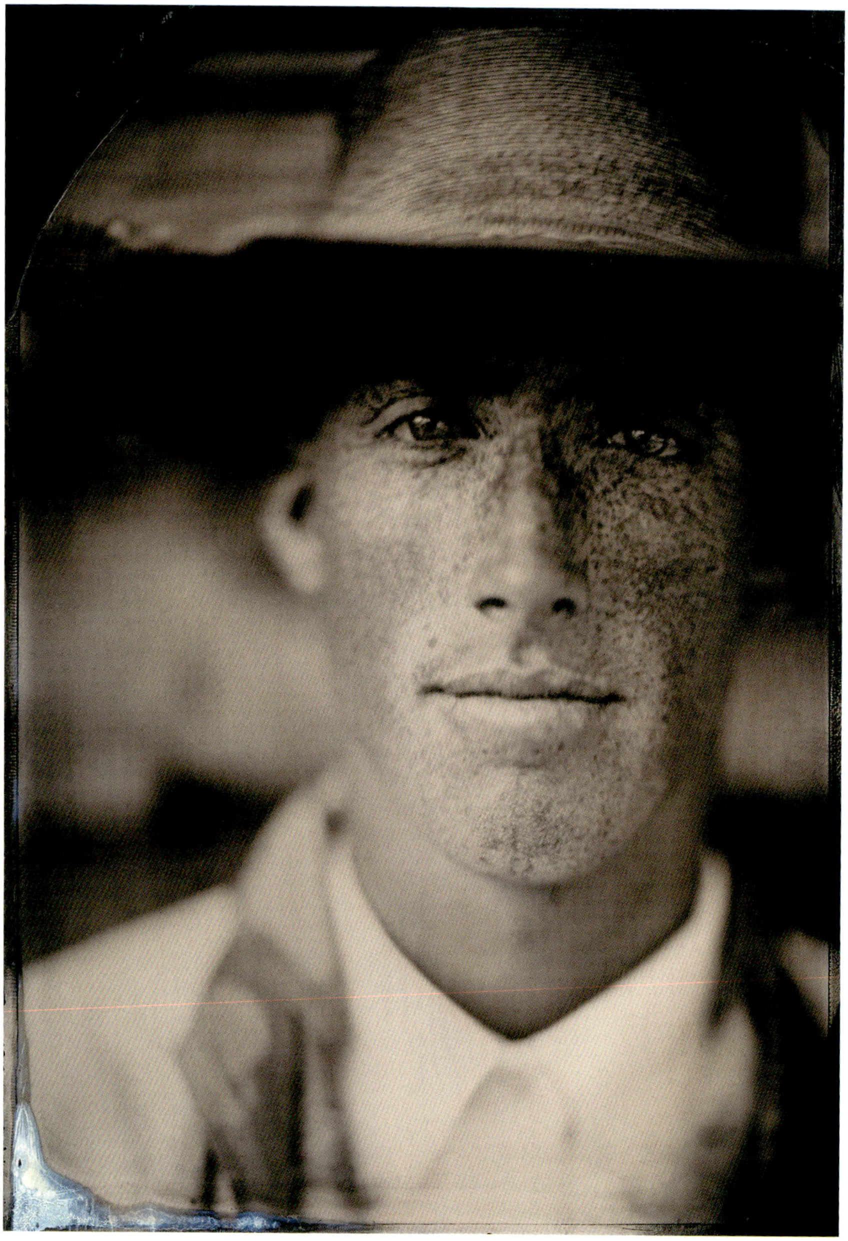

PLATE 4

Nate Patterson

SPANISH RANCH, NEVADA

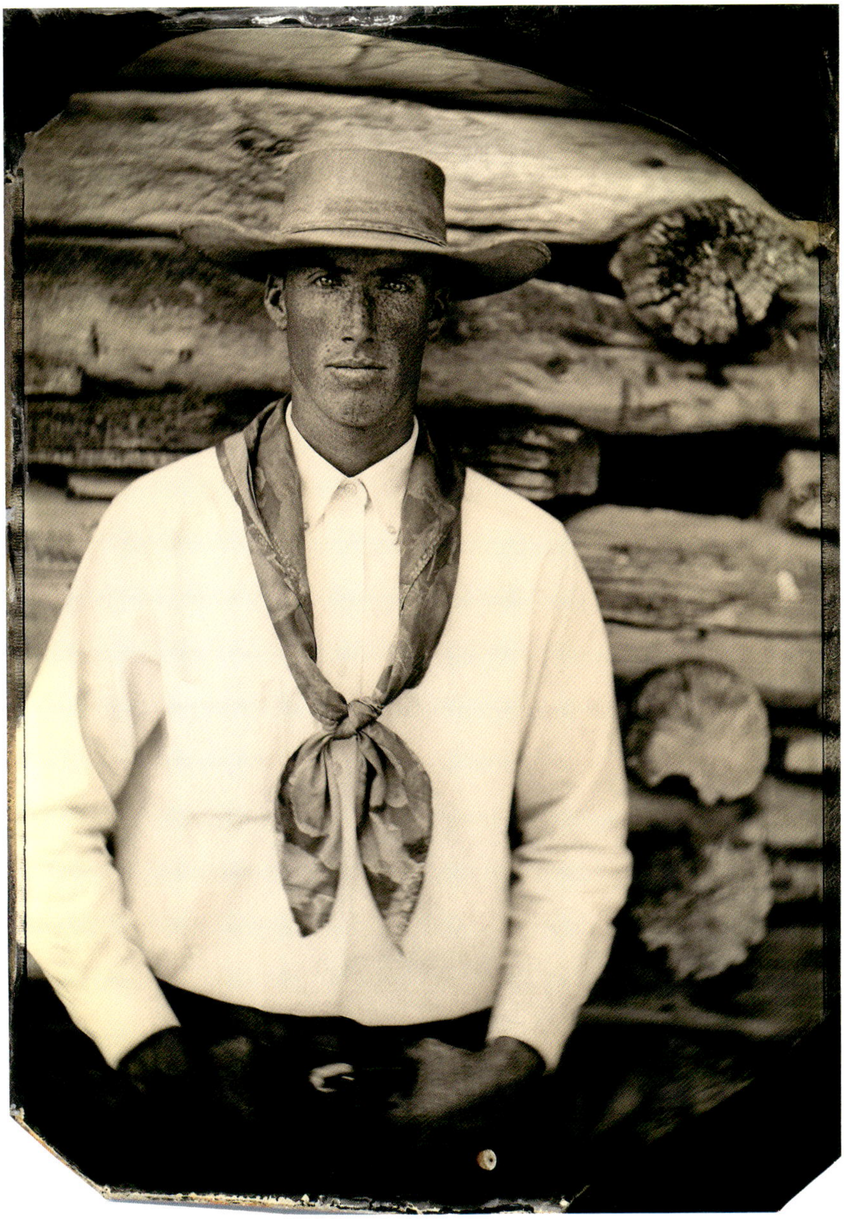

PLATE 5

Nate Patterson

SPANISH RANCH, NEVADA

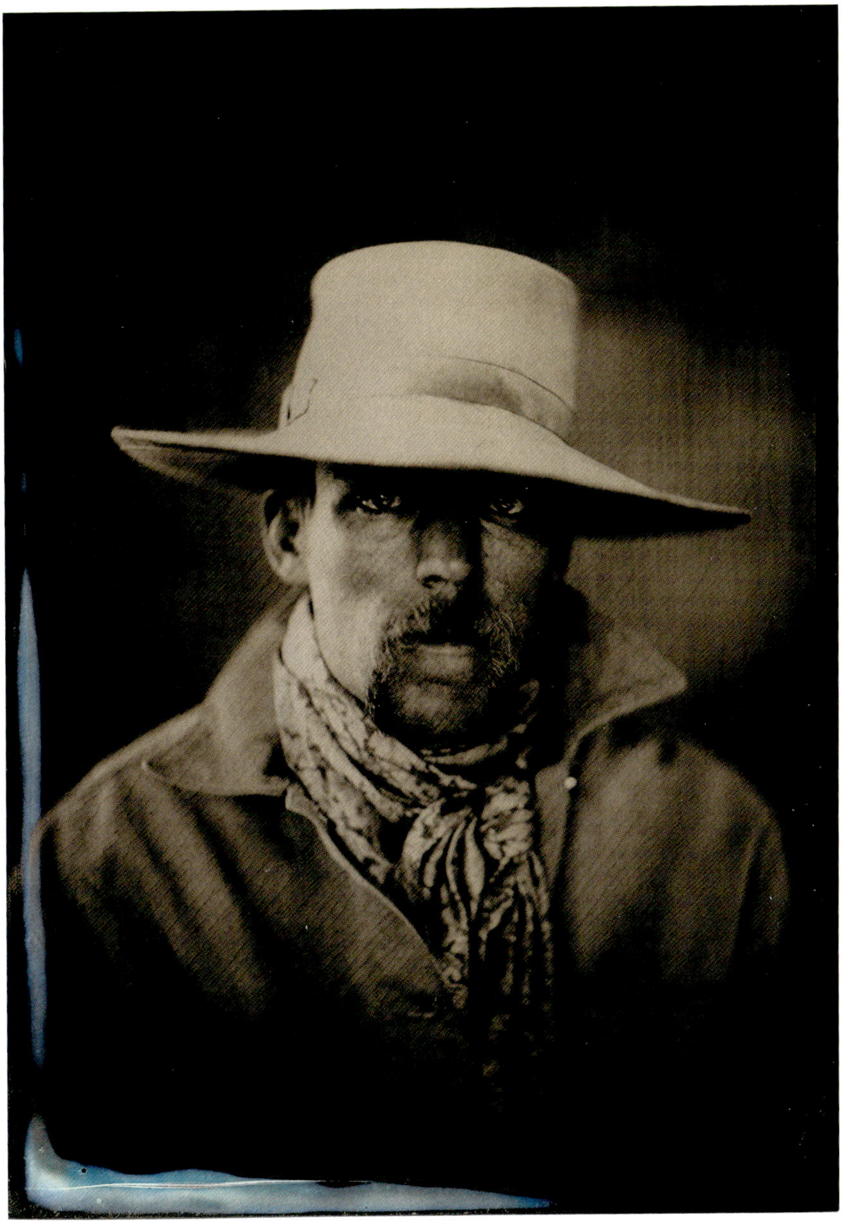

PLATE 6

Blaine Tucker

BABBITT RANCH, ARIZONA

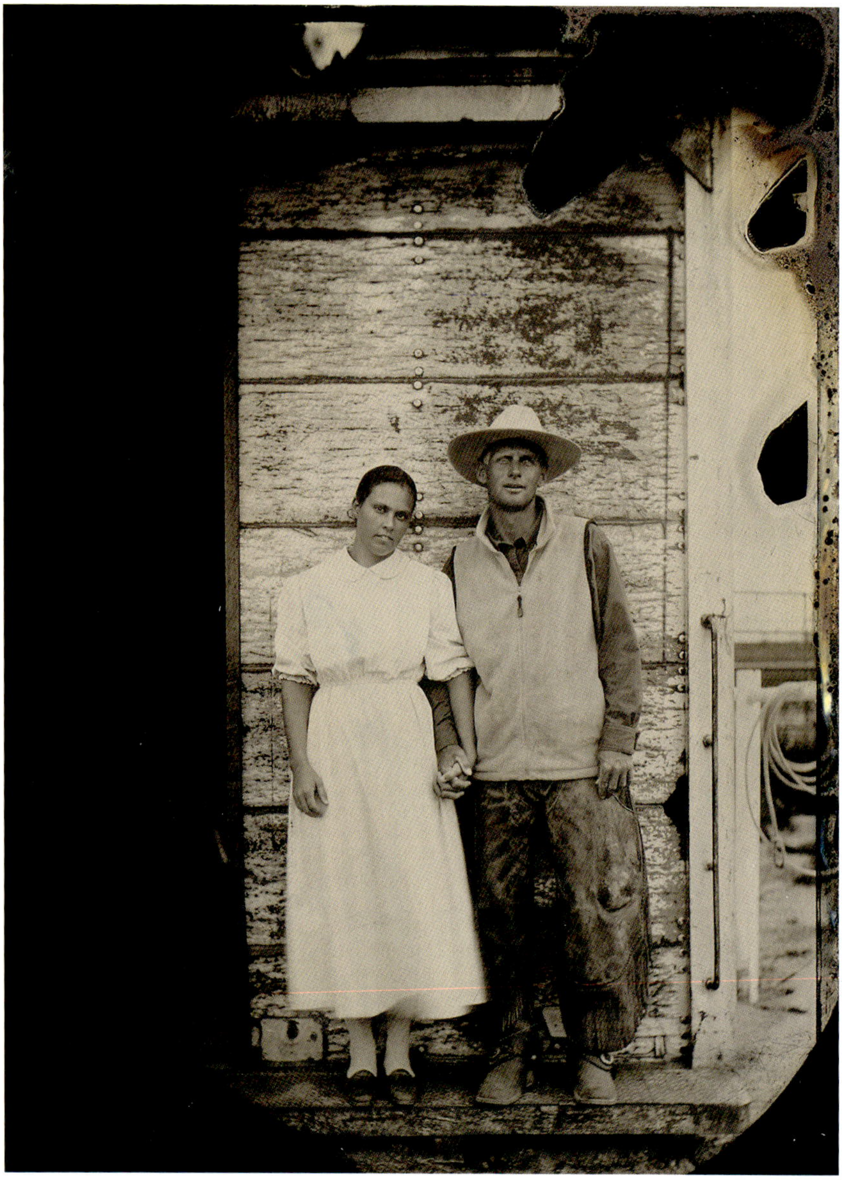

PLATE 7

Jane and Marcel Troyer

LAZY M8 RANCH, COLORADO

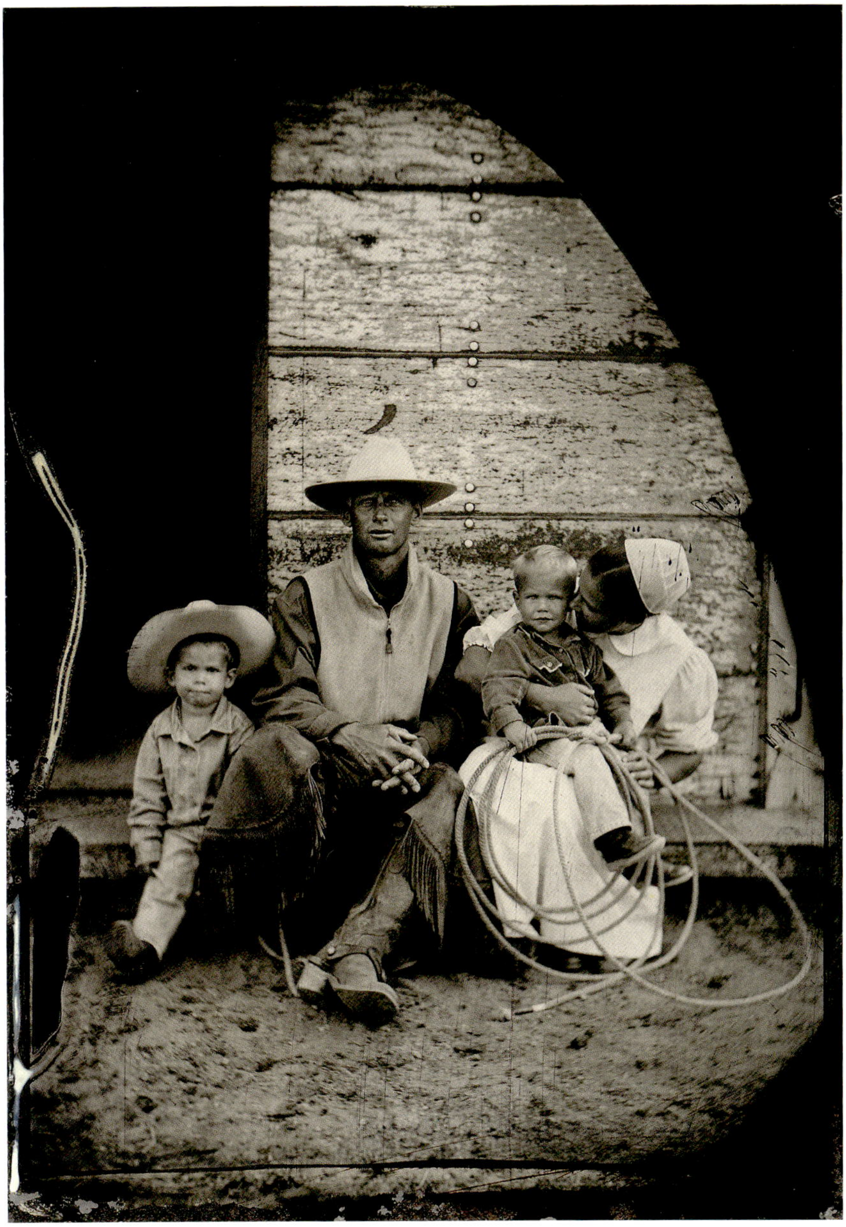

PLATE 8

Zane, Marcel, Ira, and Jane Troyer

LAZY M8 RANCH, COLORADO

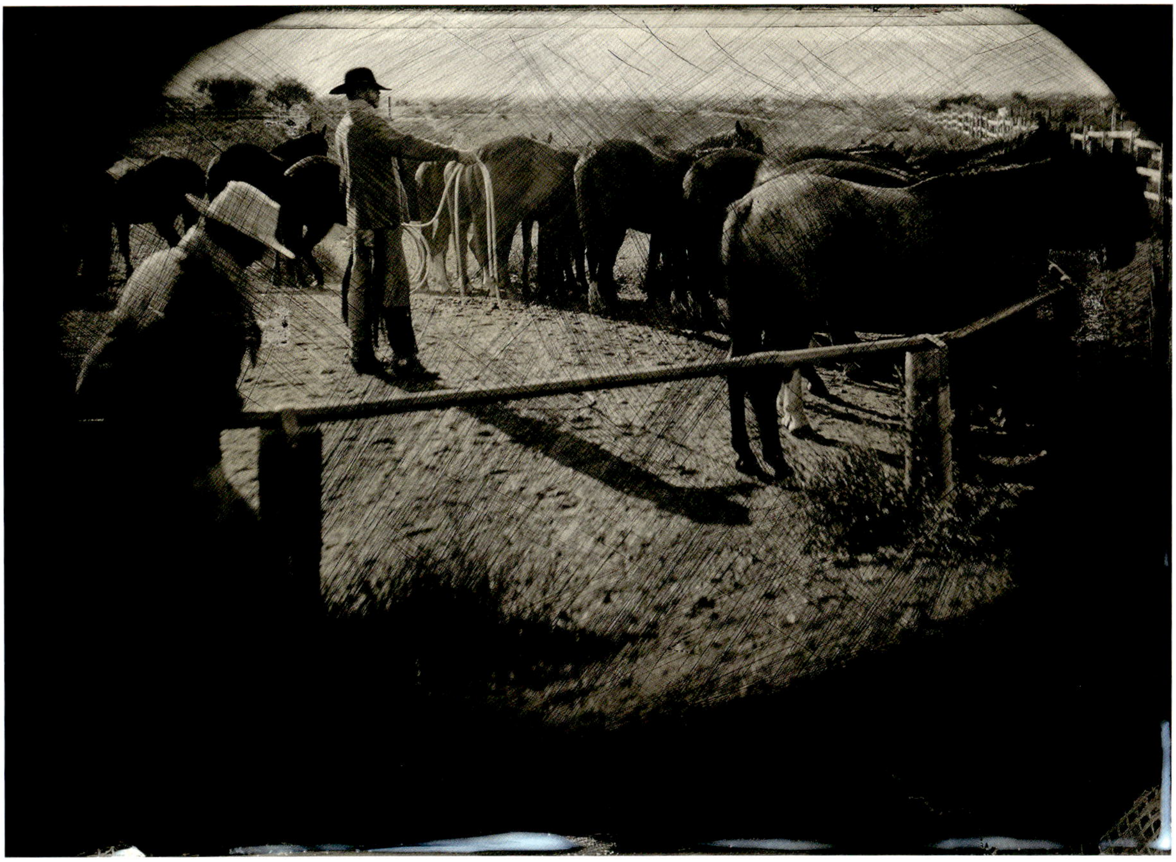

PLATE 9

Jimmy vanBelle (front), Clint Damewood

ZX RANCH, OREGON

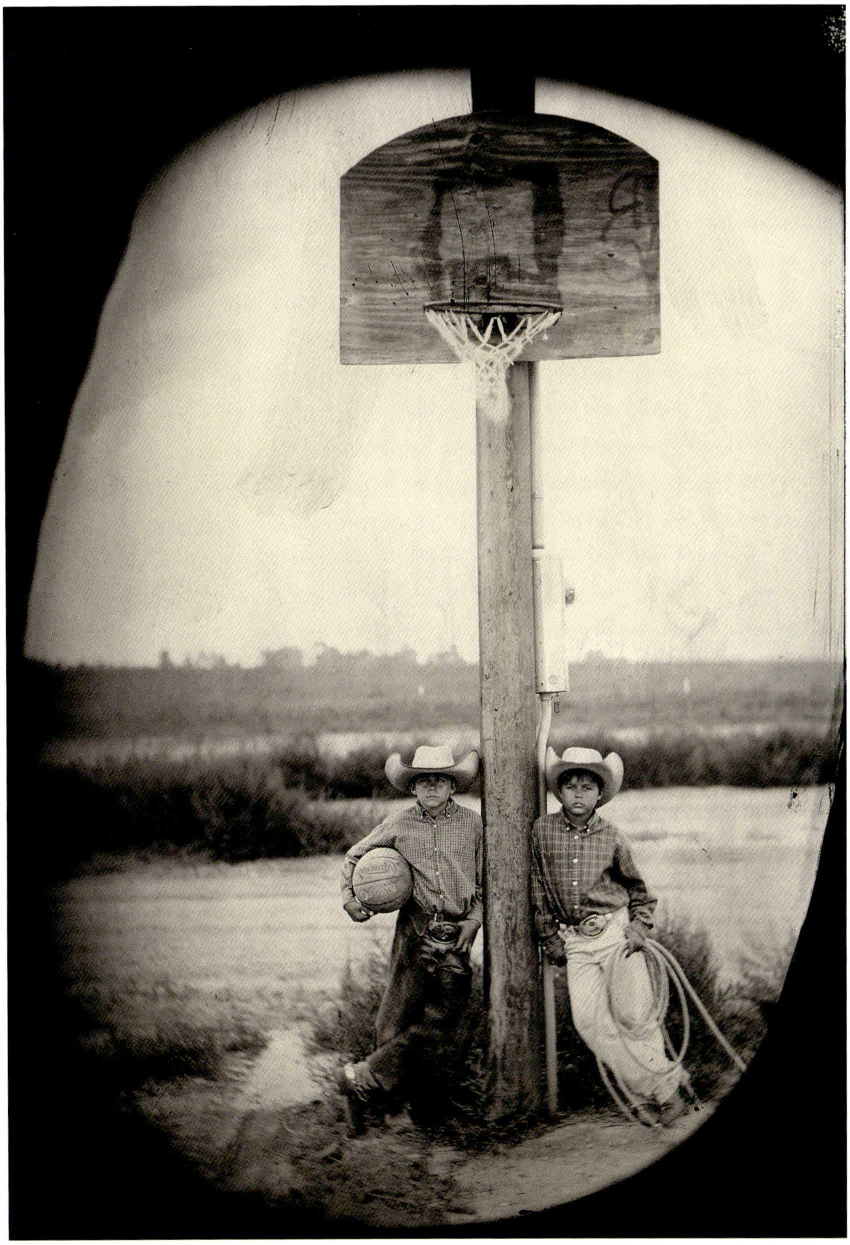

PLATE 10

Beau and Rowdy Hall

LAZY M8 RANCH, COLORADO

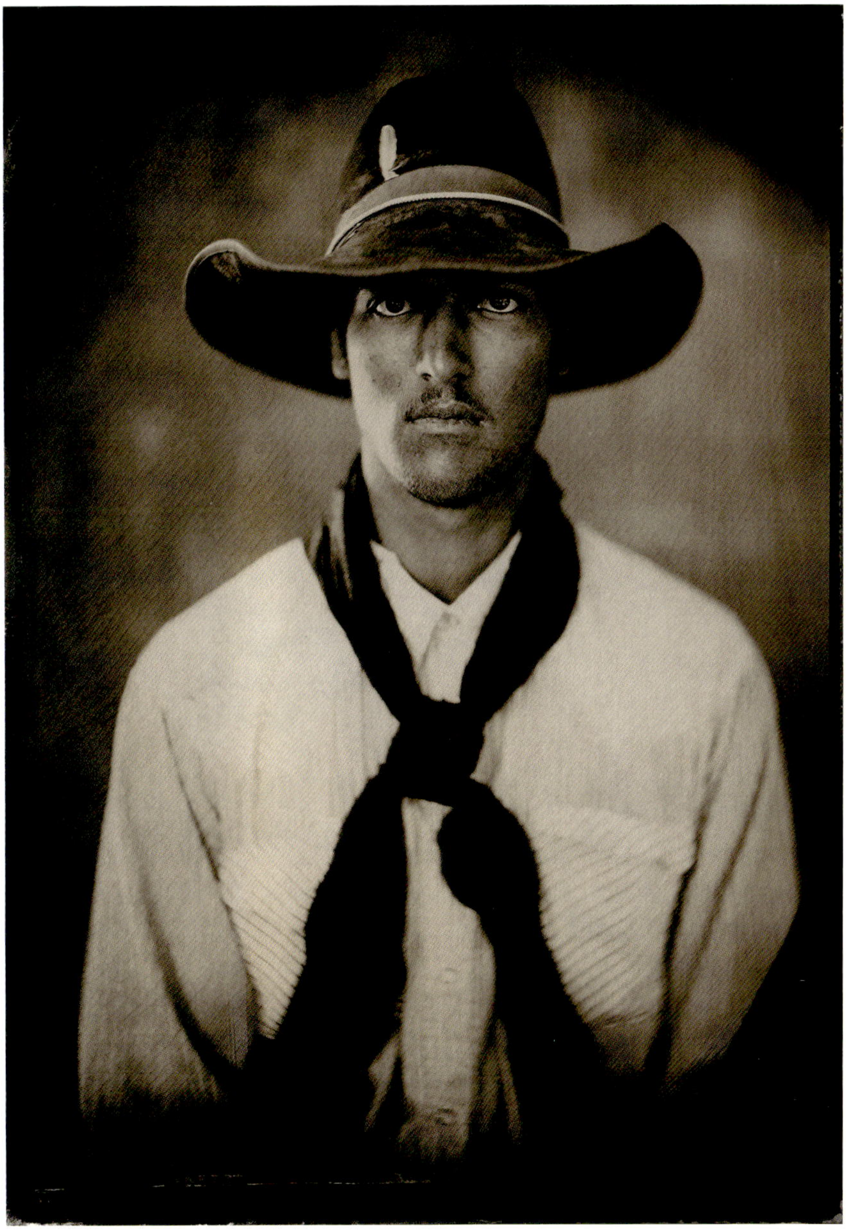

PLATE 11

Tyrel Tucker

BABBITT RANCH, ARIZONA

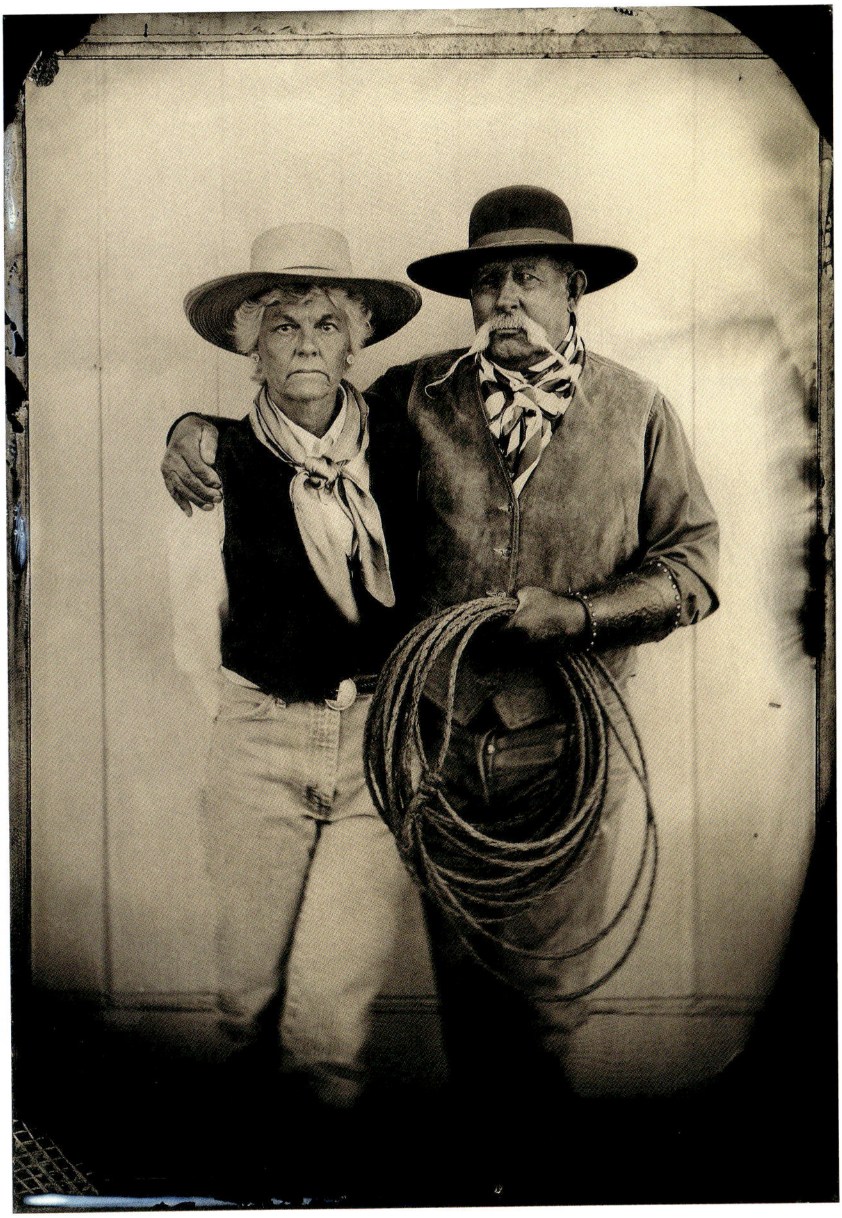

PLATE 13

Faithe and Merlin Rupp

OREGON

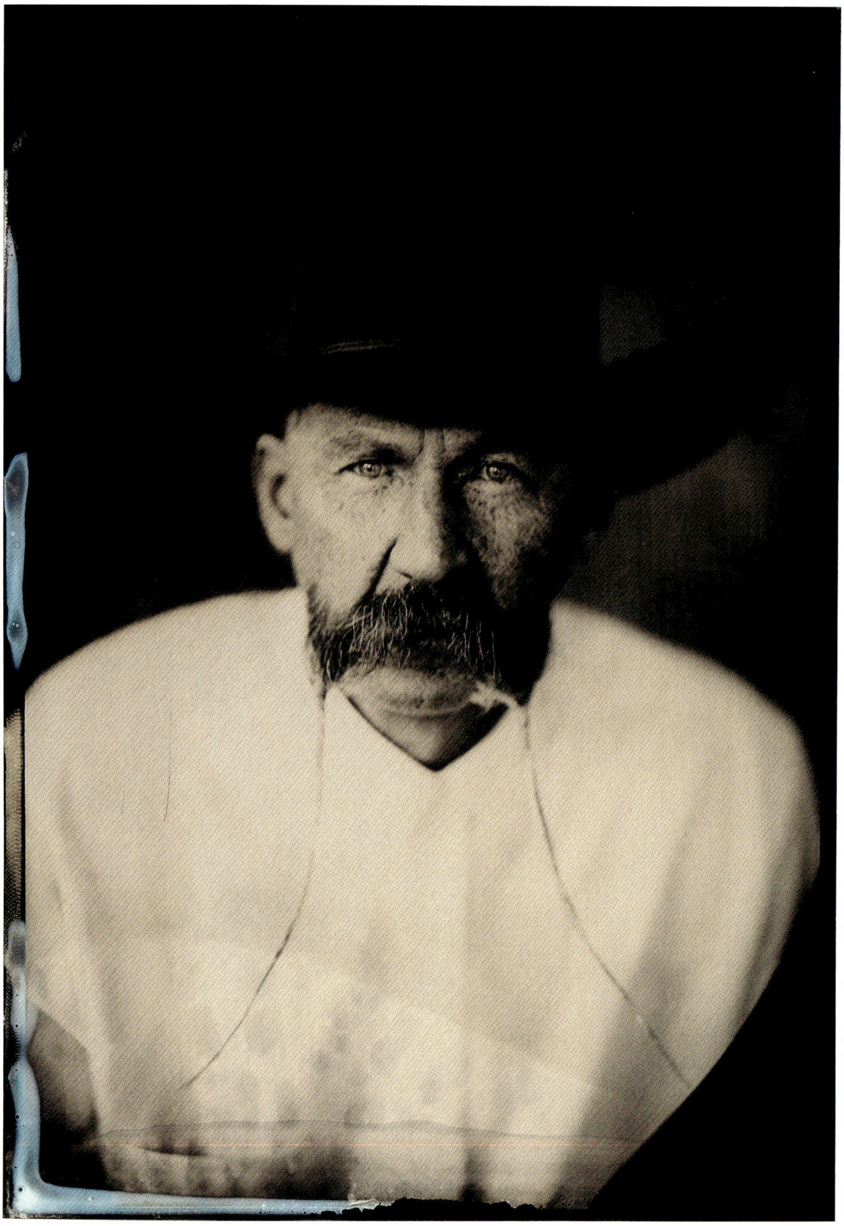

PLATE 14

Rick Tune

ROCK CREEK RANCH, COLORADO

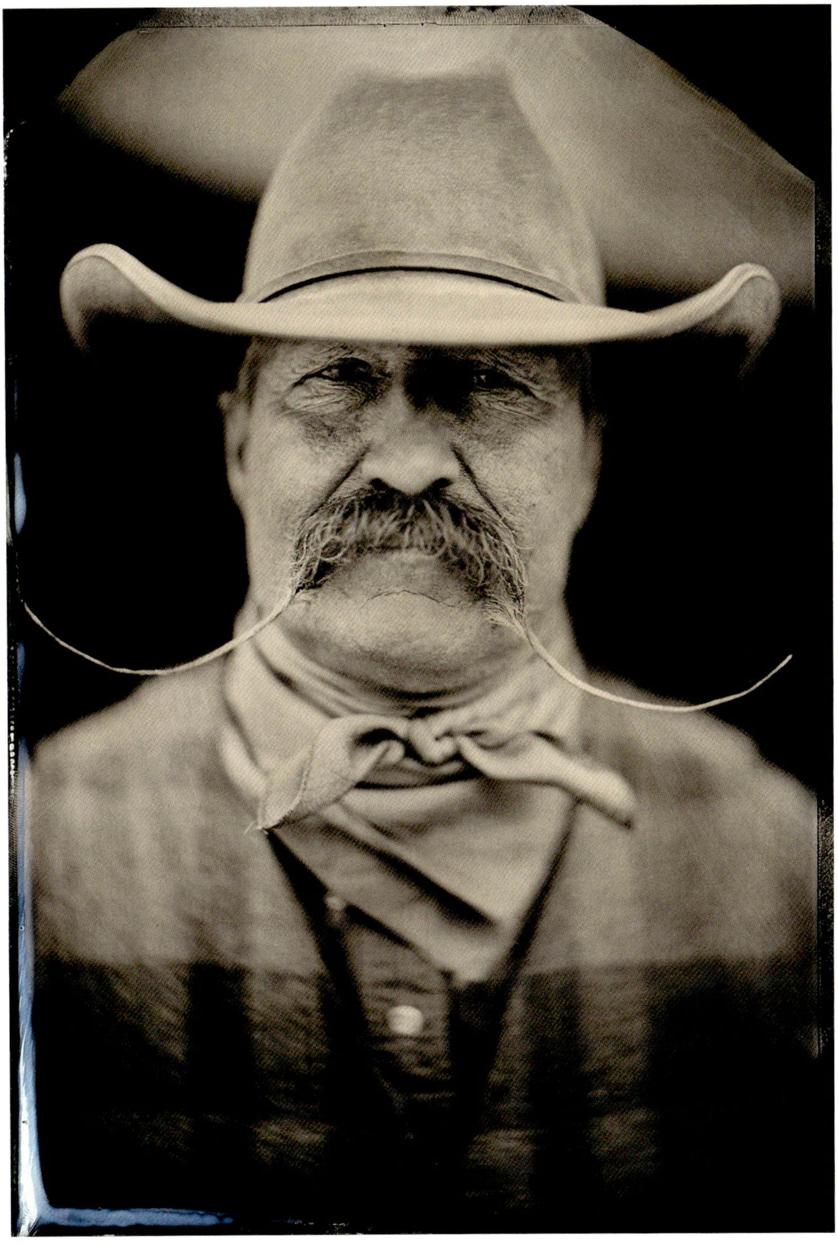

PLATE 15

Bret Reeder

REEDER RANCH, UTAH

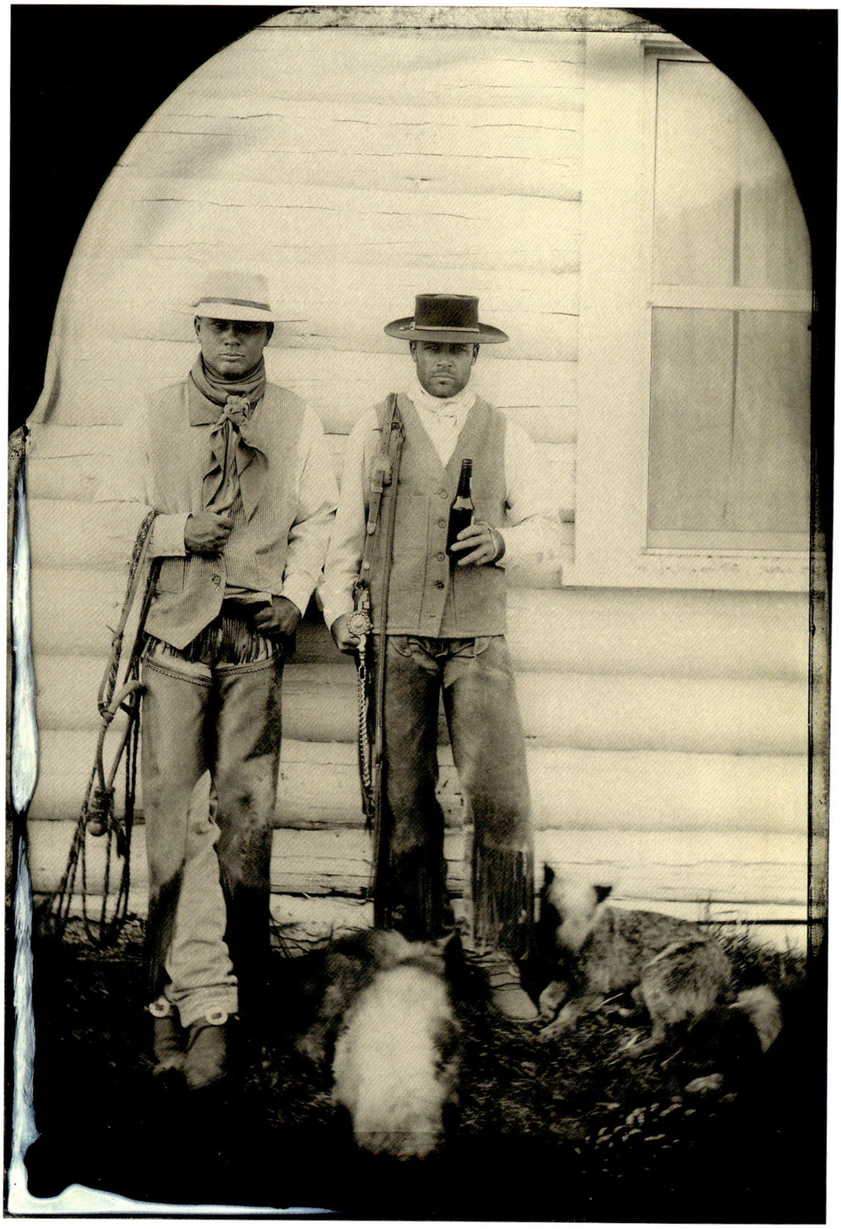

PLATE 16

Corey Northup, Blake Rainsdon

SUNLIGHT RANCH, MONTANA

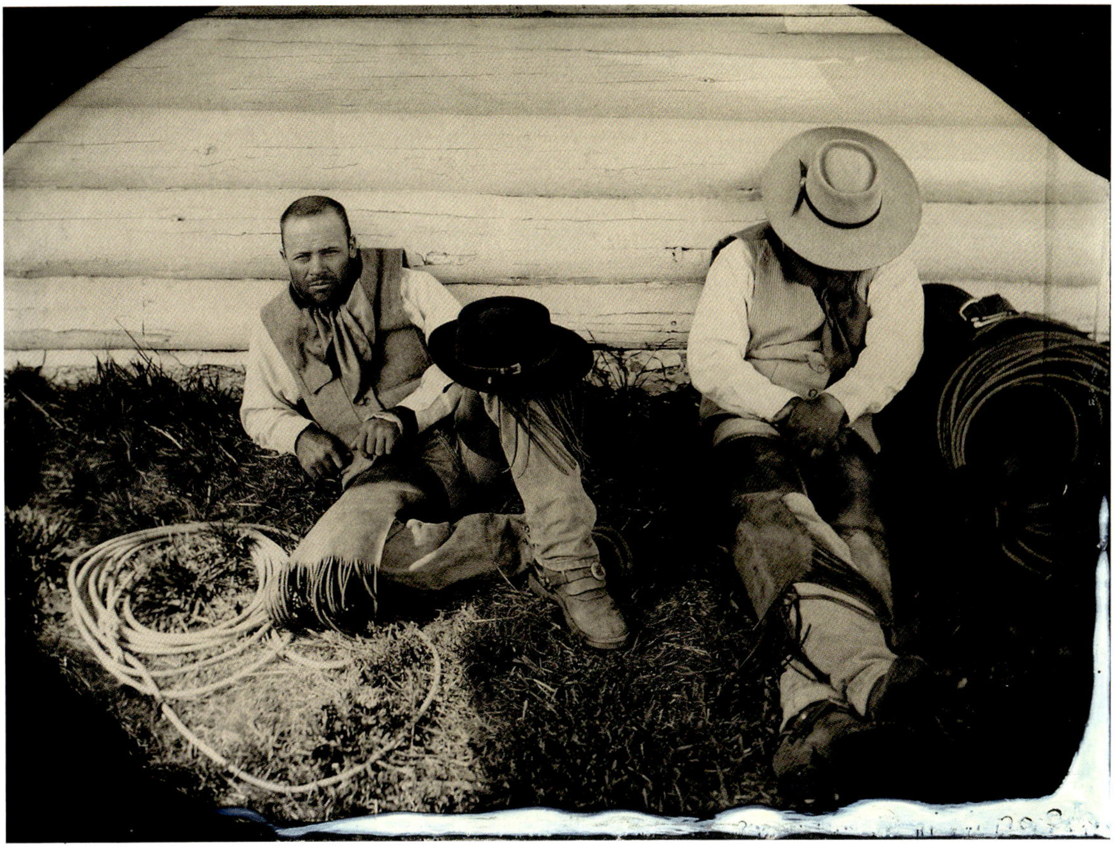

PLATE 17

Blake Rainsdon, Corey Northup

SUNLIGHT RANCH, MONTANA

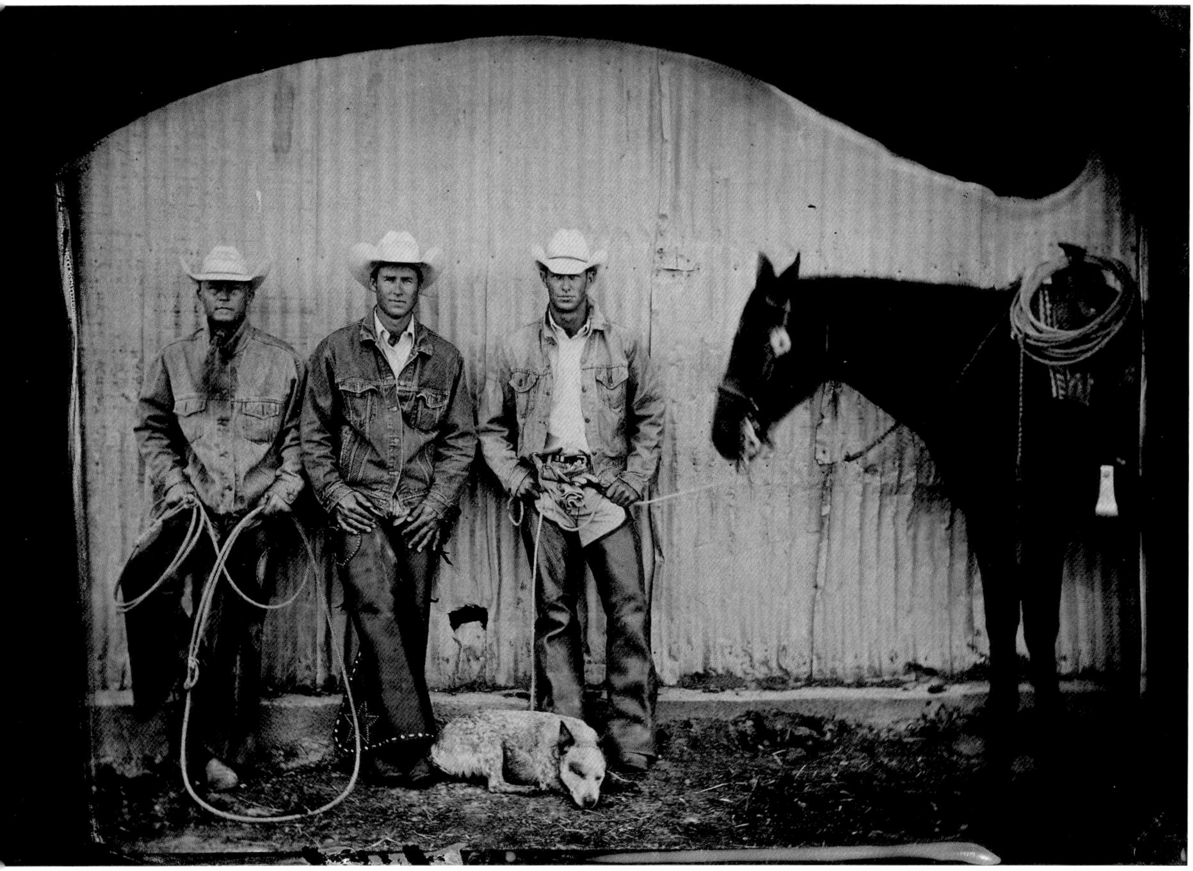

PLATE 18

Tanner Rollins, H. G. Adams V, Cooper Adams, Ruby (dog)

XI RANCH, KANSAS

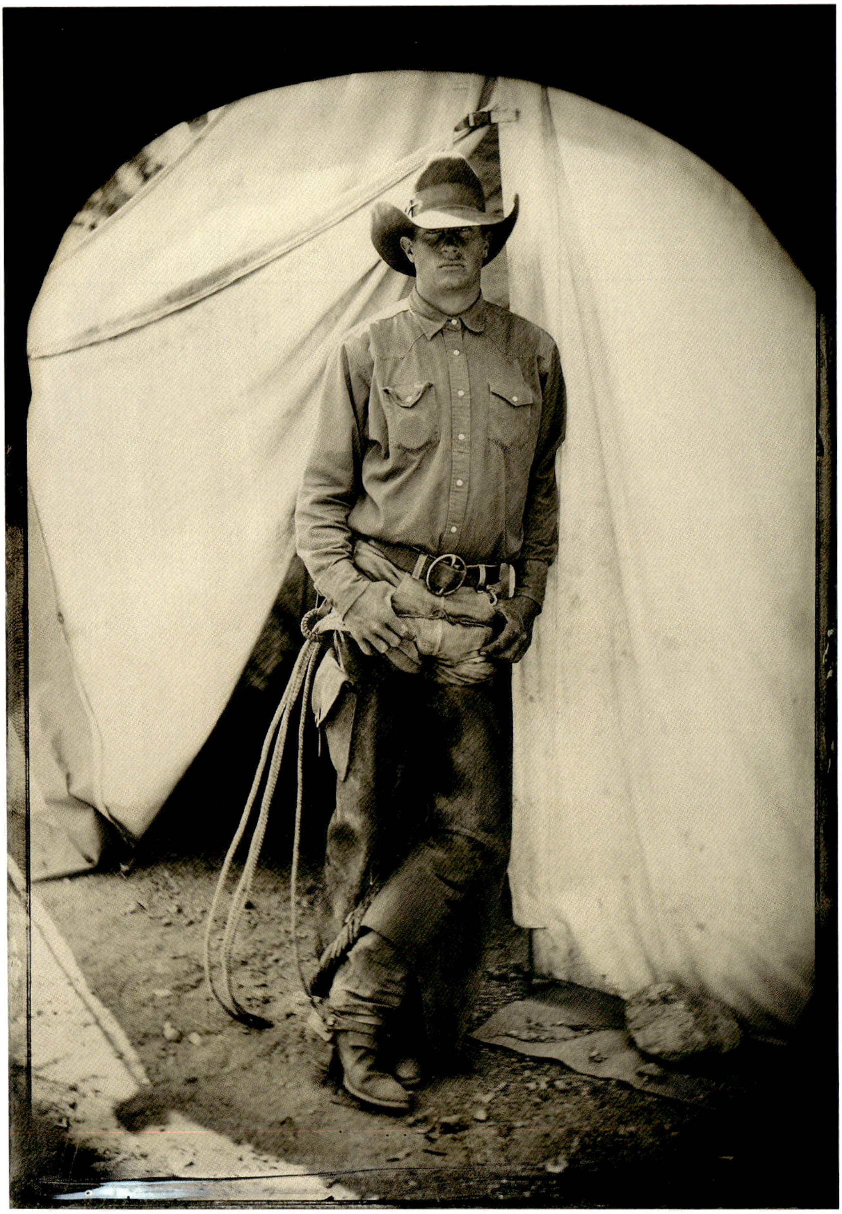

PLATE 19

Tim Mertzweiller

ORO RANCH, ARIZONA

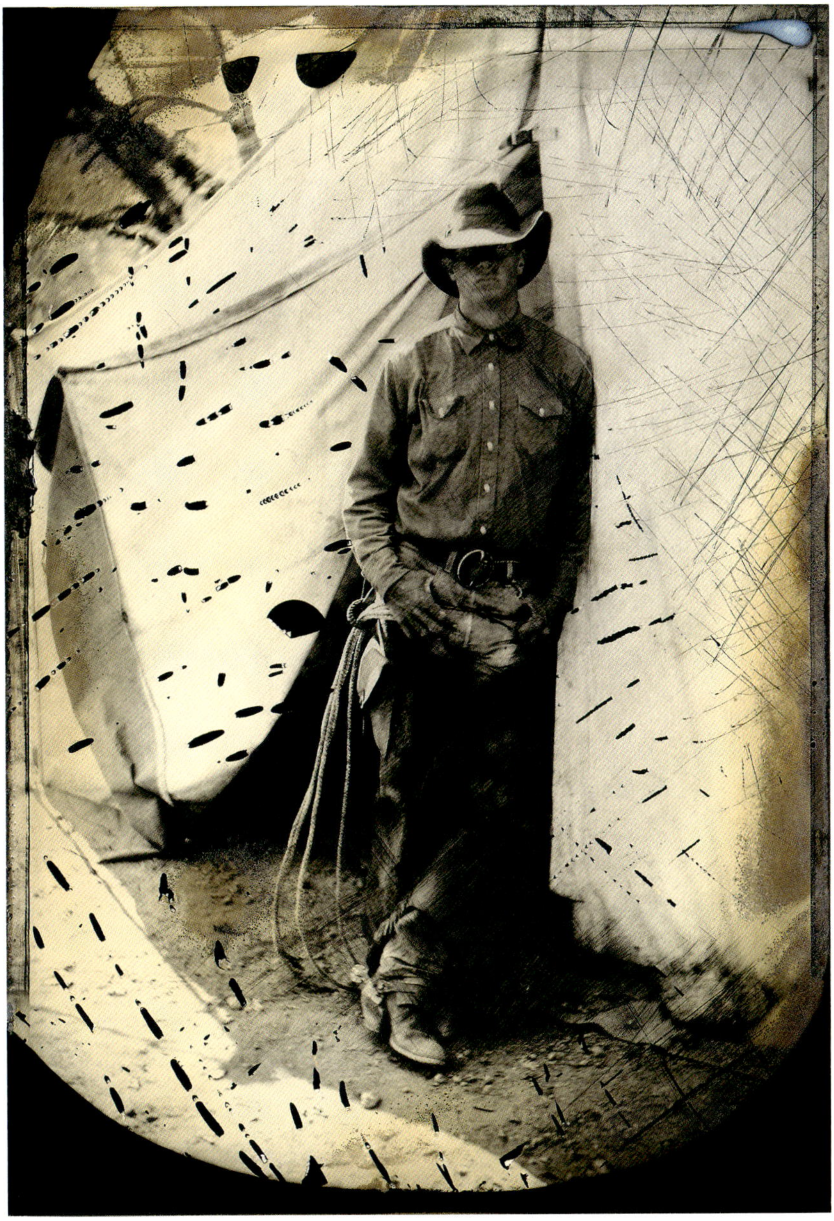

PLATE 20

Tim Mertzweiller

ORO RANCH, ARIZONA

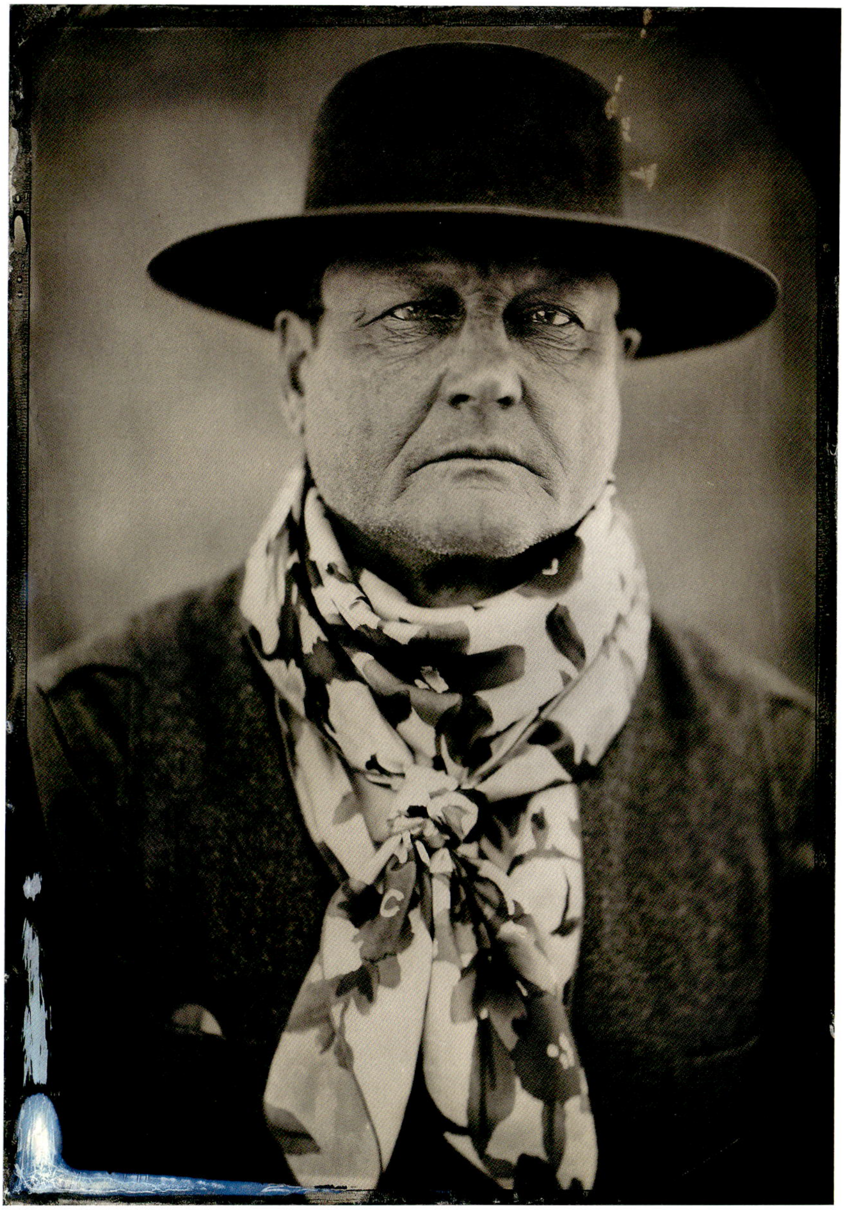

PLATE 21

Pete Wagner

LONE PINE RANCH, OREGON

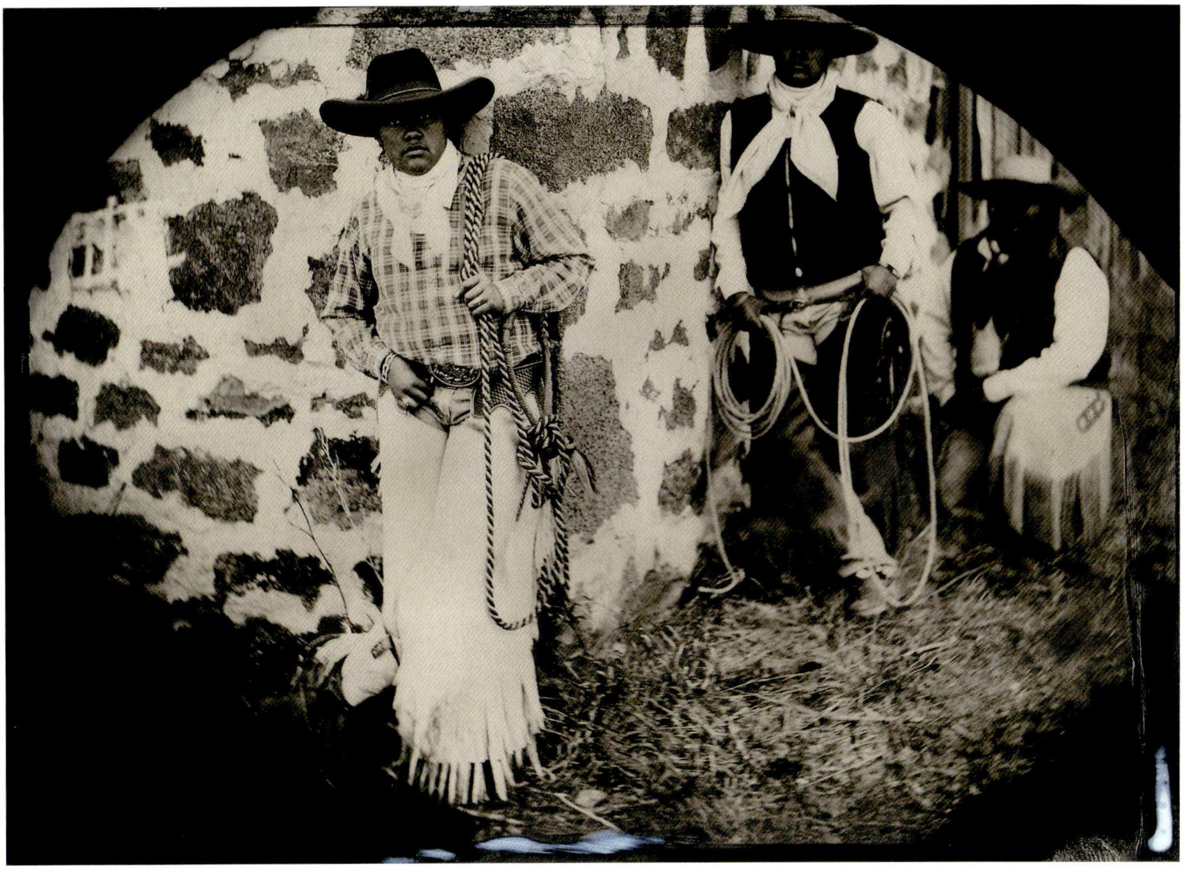

PLATE 22

Harli, Ashley, and Katelyn Cota

DUCK VALLEY RESERVATION, NEVADA

It's just a way of life that come easy. Solitude, God, nature, and animals. Raised a family, probably didn't do too good a job on that. Met a lot of good people. Very good wife. Probably ruined her with all this business, but she stood it well. I work alone, try to. Solitude. Animals. Raw land. The big country. It's just a way of life. Some people prefer it; some don't.

What makes you really feel alive, or me anyway, is gettin' caught in a big storm out there alone. It's up to you to come out and do this. It's just the vast emptiness of it, and you really feel alive, or I do, in that sort of an environment. I never been in a bad place. Every place to me that you make a living and stay horseback is a good place. I worked prairies, mountains, breaks, and desert. I guess maybe I prefer where I started. The Missouri River Breaks I think is as good as they come, but, they're all good; they really are.

I'm sure there's other things I could have done and adapted to well, but it would have to involve solitude and a big area. People wonder how you can live by yourself and not get out and not go out and so on and this and that. It's really pretty easy. If you can't live with yourself, it can't be any easier to live with a lot of people around you.

ROYCE HANSON
SUNLIGHT RANCH, MONTANA

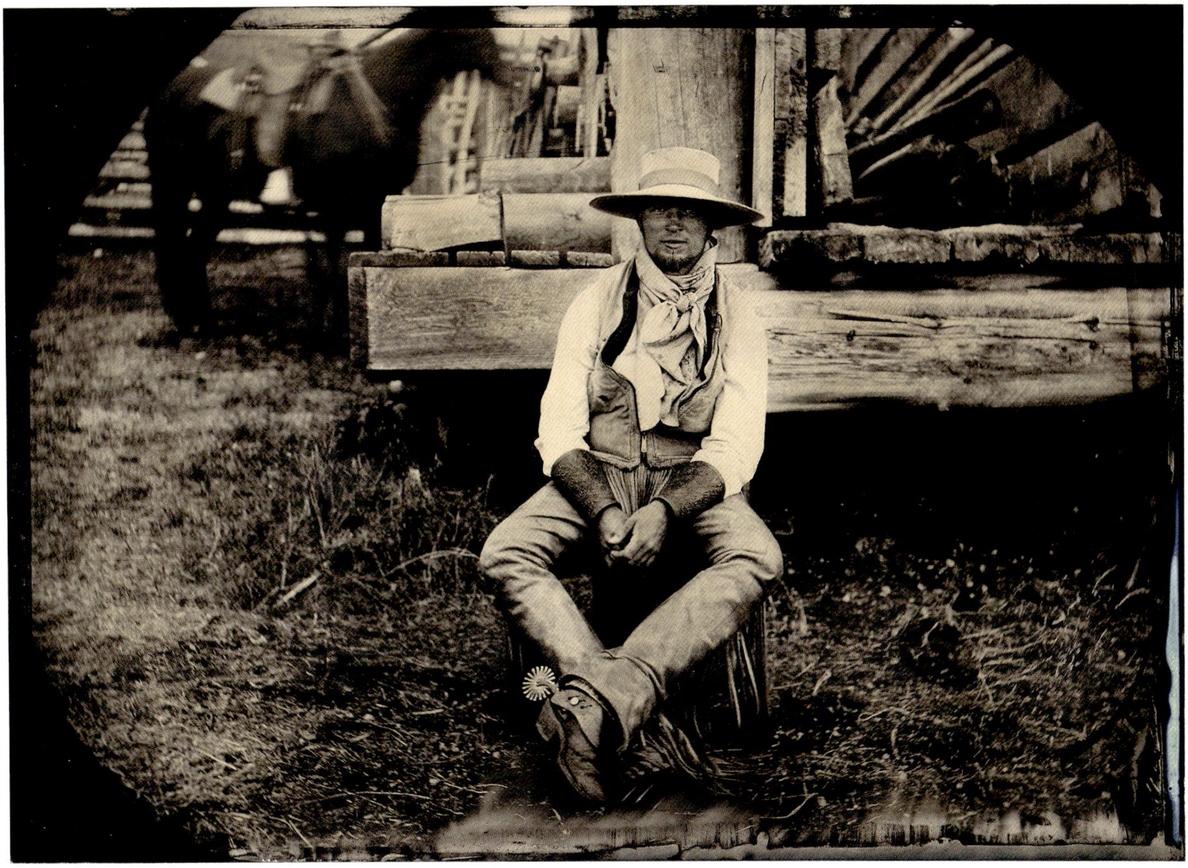

PLATE 23

Mark Elliott

DOUGLAS LAKE RANCH, BRITISH COLUMBIA, CANADA

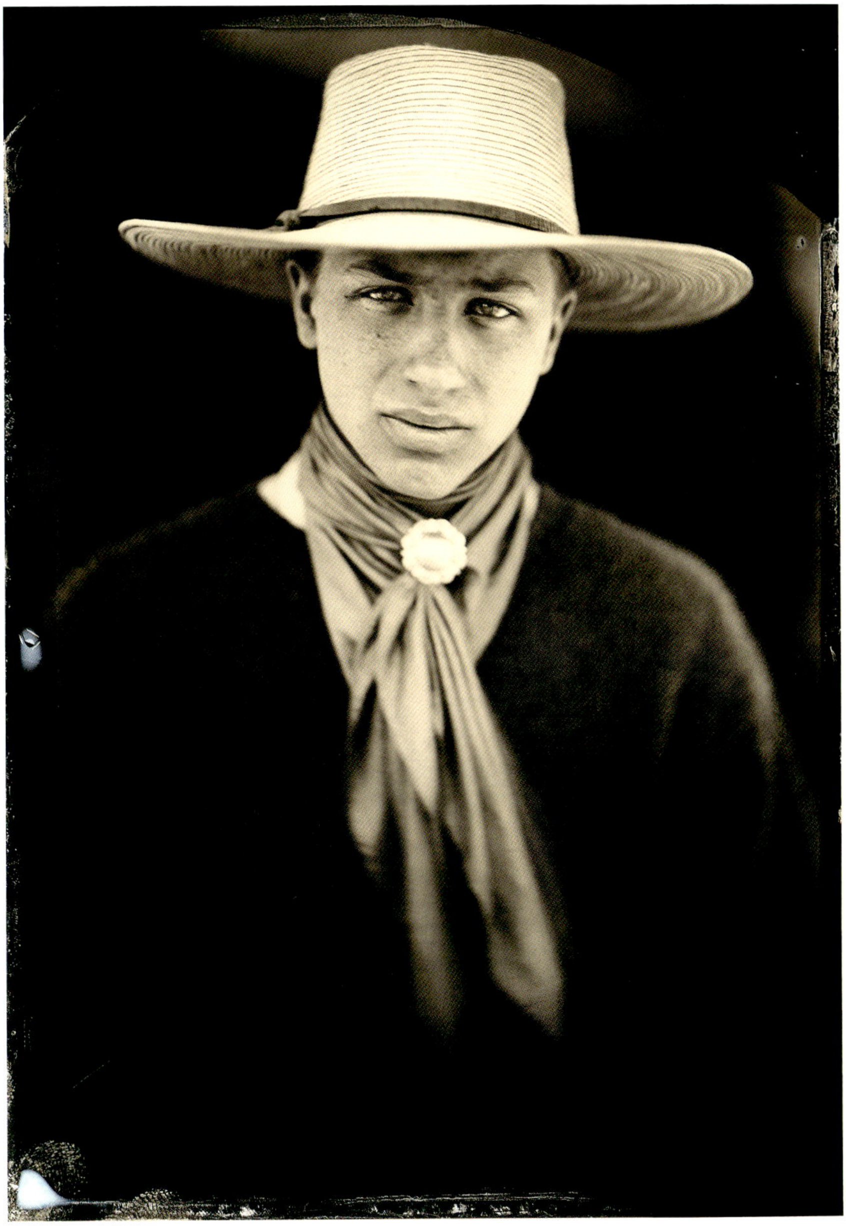

PLATE 24

Eric Witkowski

BUTTE CREEK RANCH, OREGON

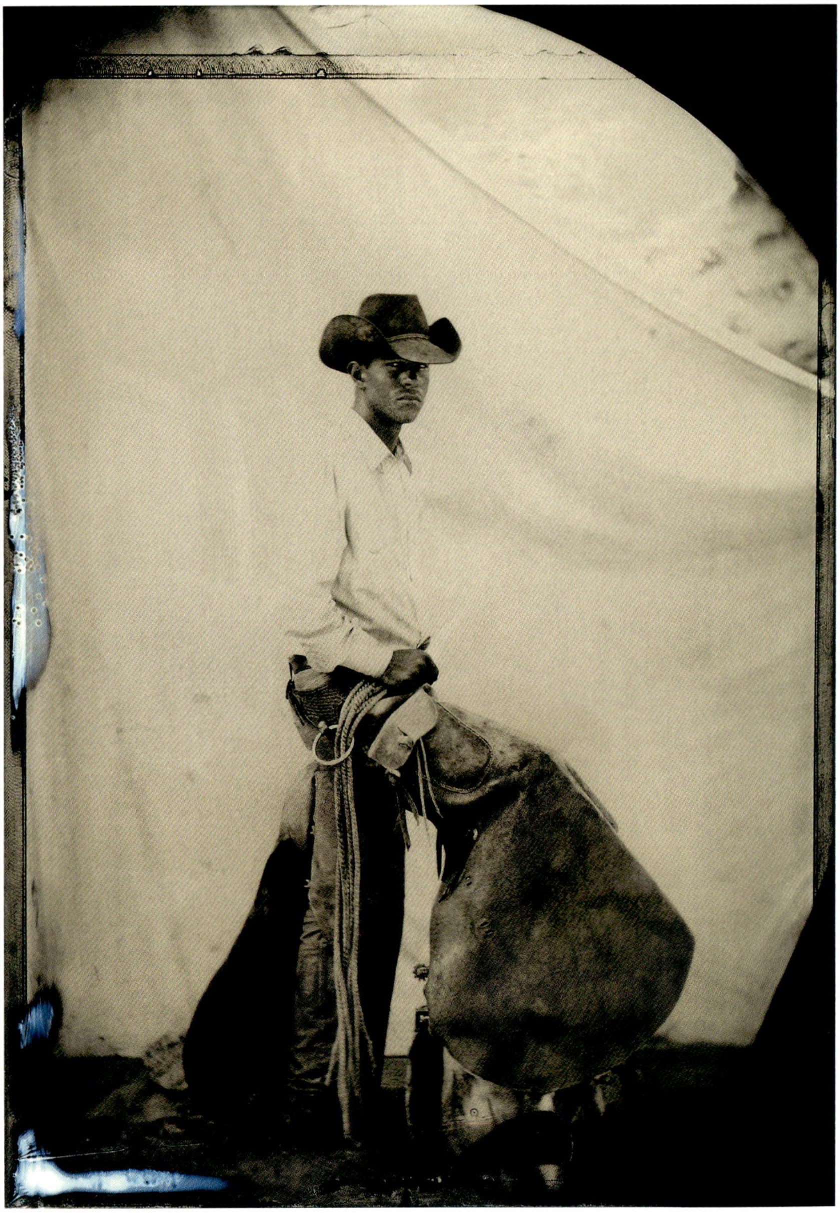

PLATE 25

Kyle Stone

ORO RANCH, ARIZONA

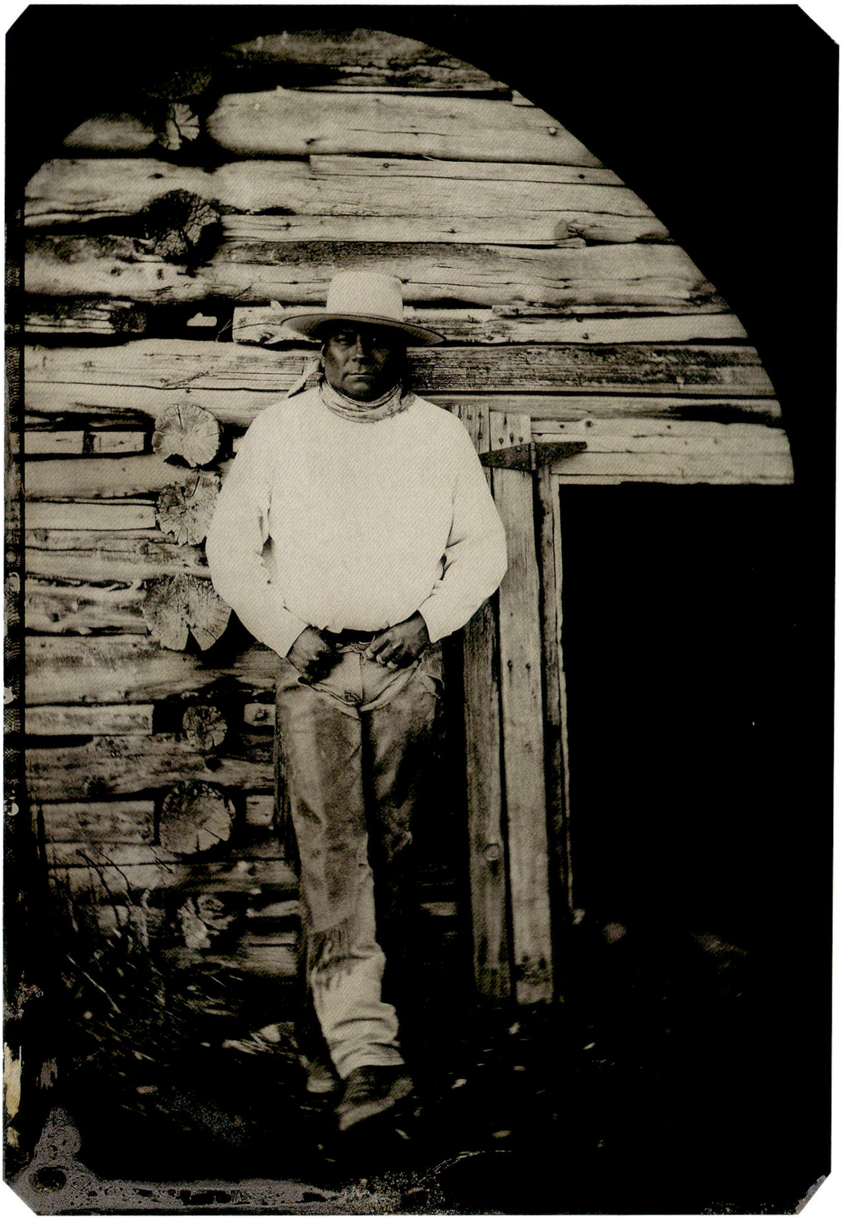

PLATE 26

Woody Harney

SPANISH RANCH, NEVADA

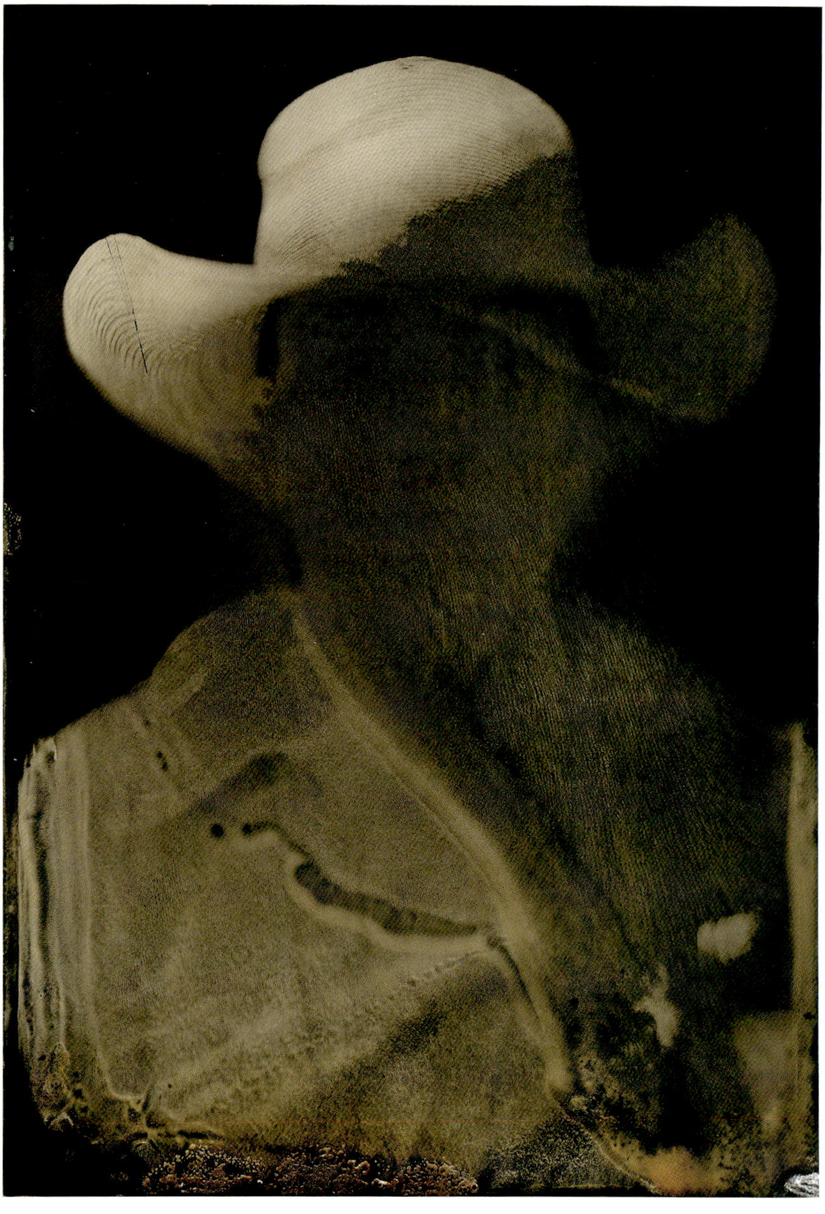

PLATE 27

Chet Bartlett

RHOADS RANCH, NEVADA

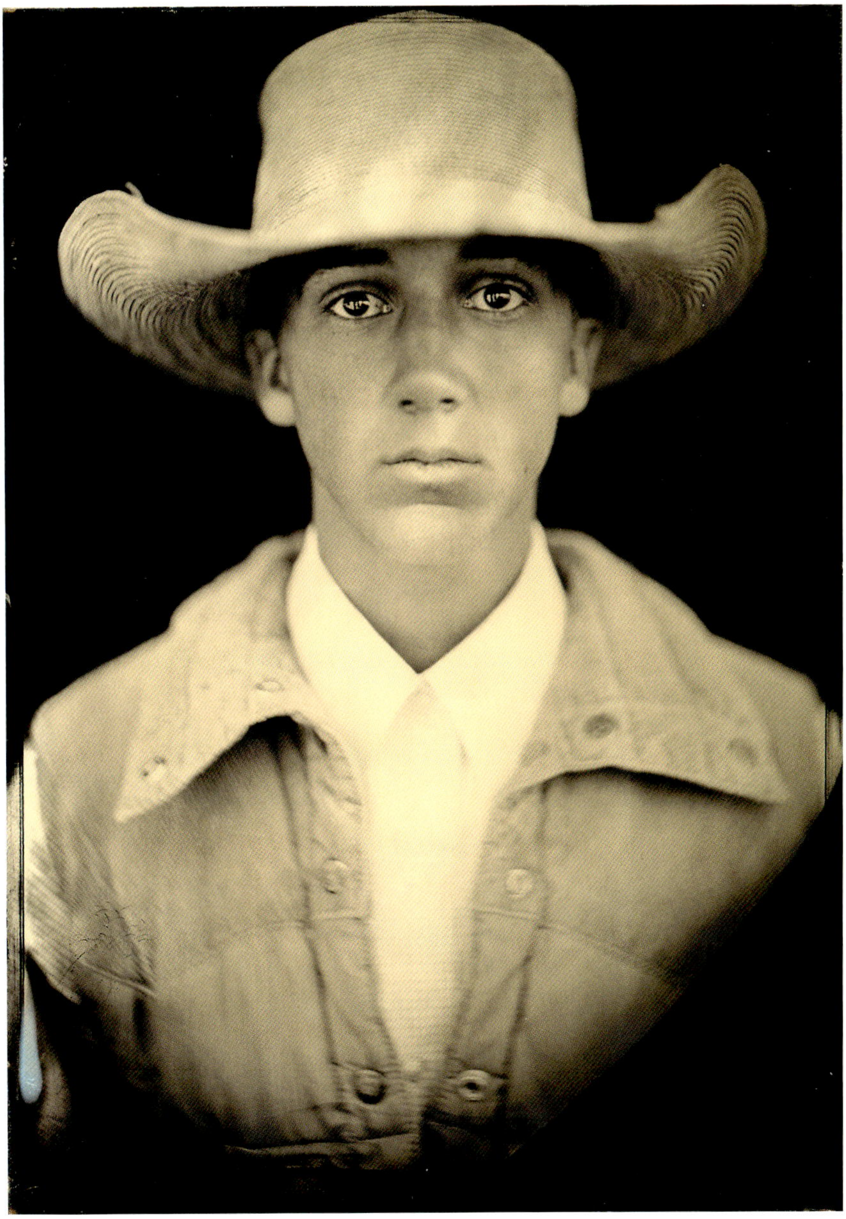

PLATE 28

Chet Bartlett

RHOADS RANCH, NEVADA

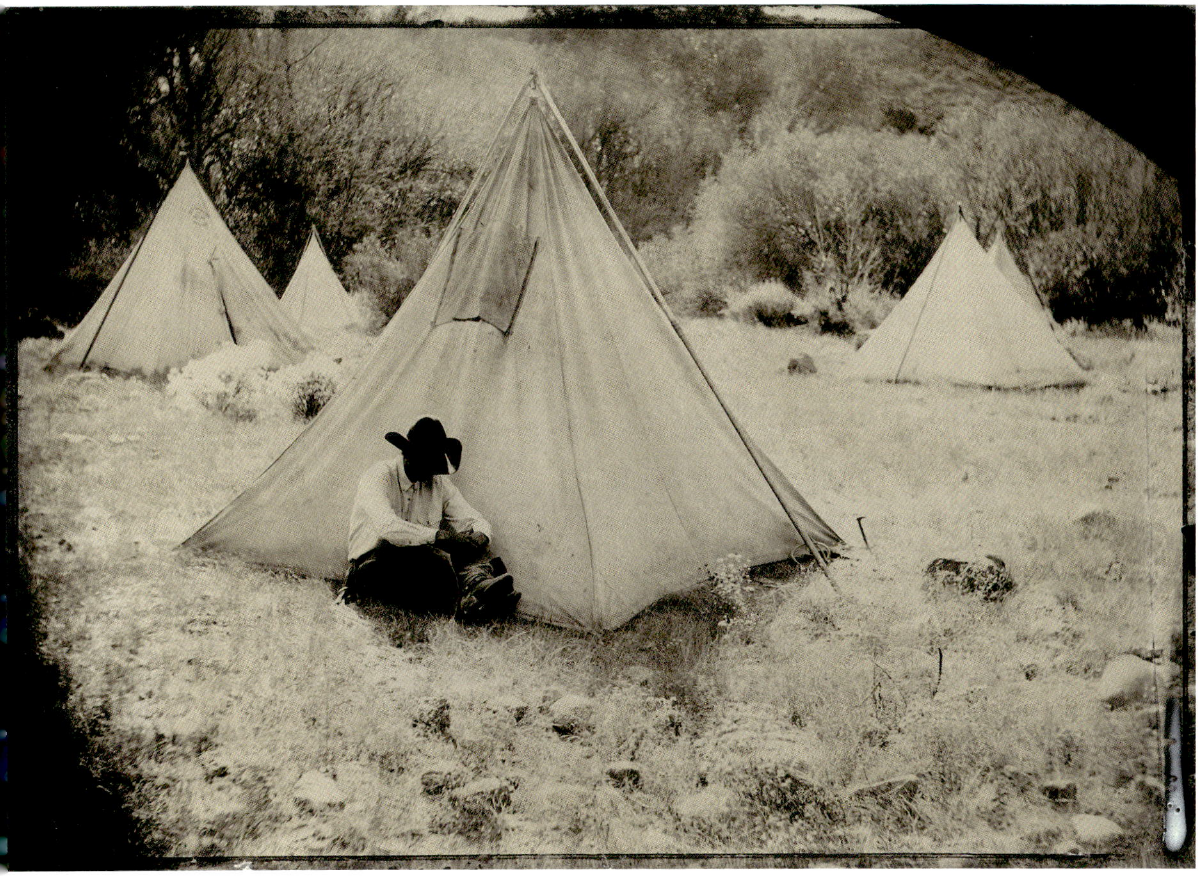

PLATE 29

Linc Bundy

ORO RANCH, ARIZONA

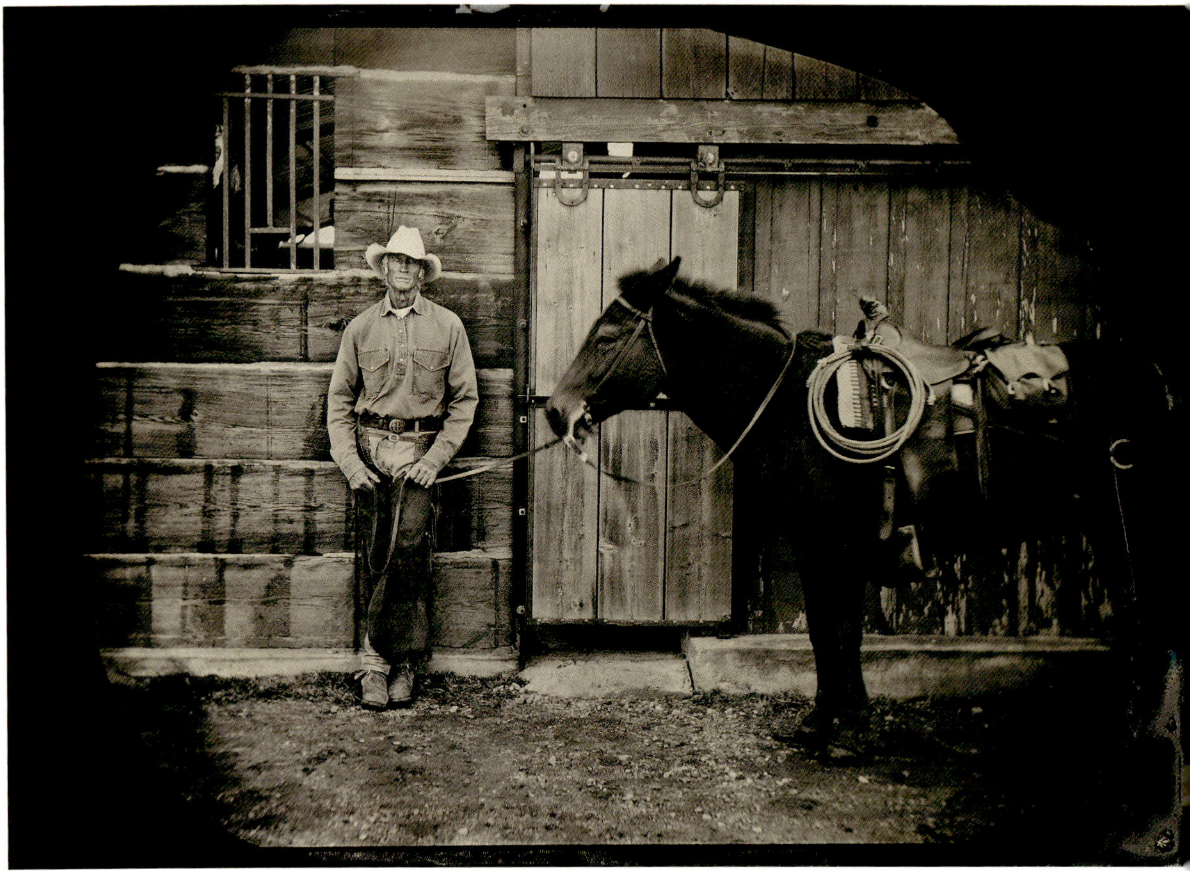

PLATE 30

Warner Glenn

MALPAI RANCH, ARIZONA

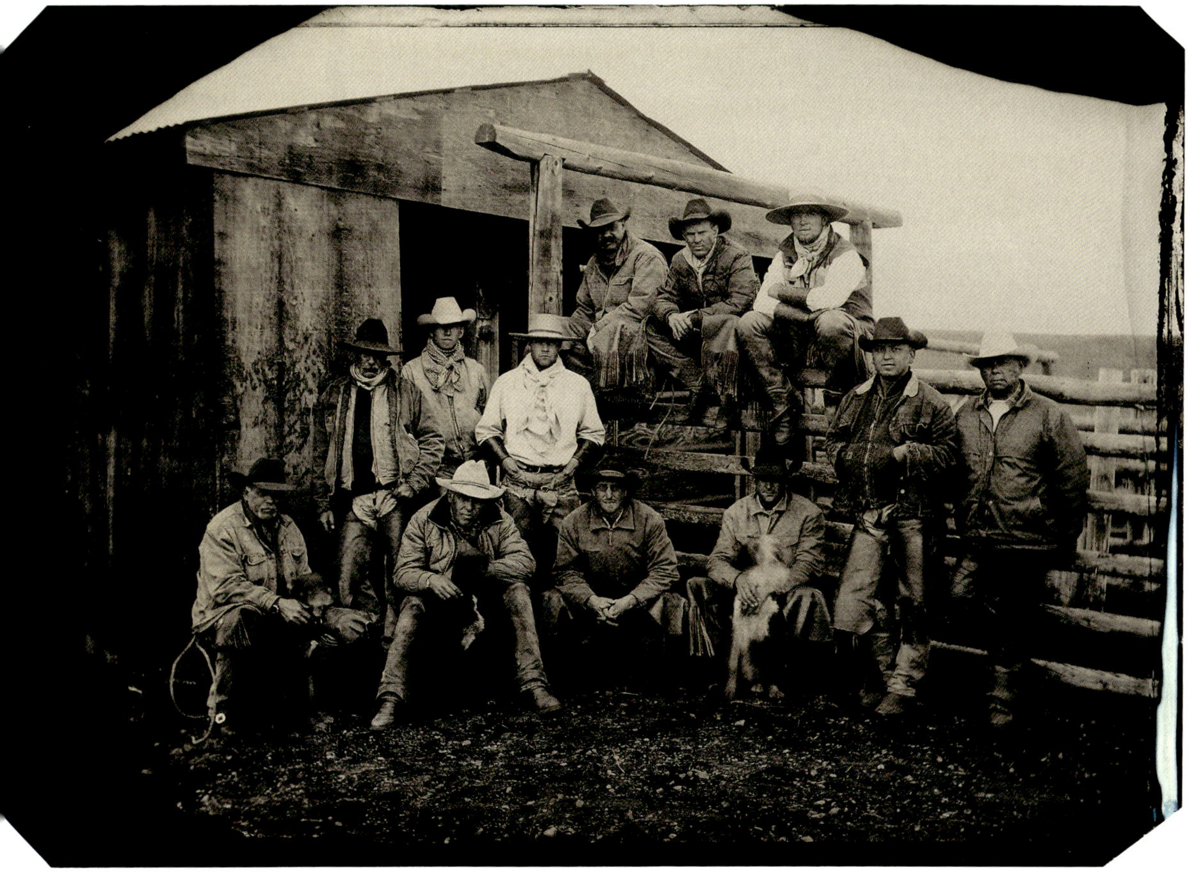

PLATE 31

(Sitting on fence) Dale Arnell, Nolan Eek, Mark Elliott; (standing) John Edwards, Cameron Jacobs, Mike McCormick, Brad Chillihitzia, Jesse Coutlee; (crouching) Stan Jacobs, Wendel Stolzfus, Ken Blackwell, Steve Brewer

DOUGLAS LAKE RANCH, BRITISH COLUMBIA, CANADA

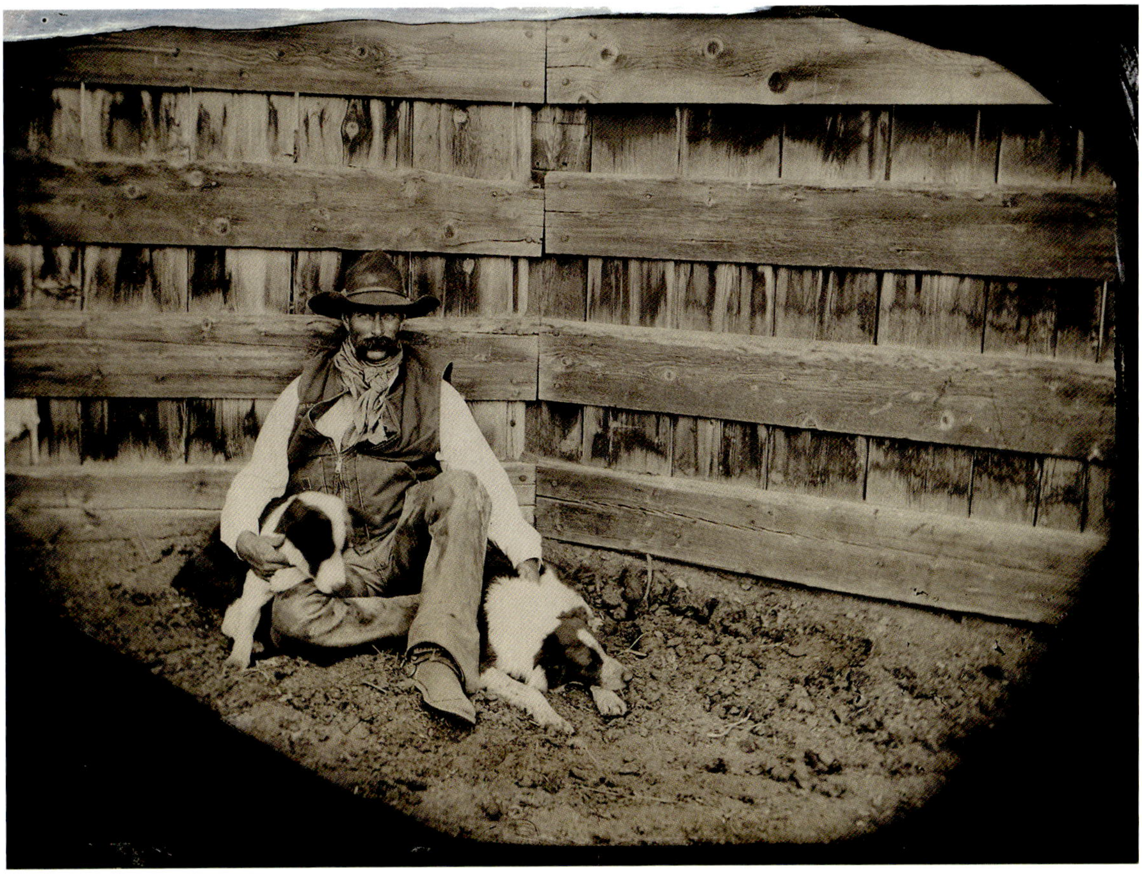

PLATE 32

Martin Anseth, with Jiggs and Patches

EZ RANCH, MONTANA

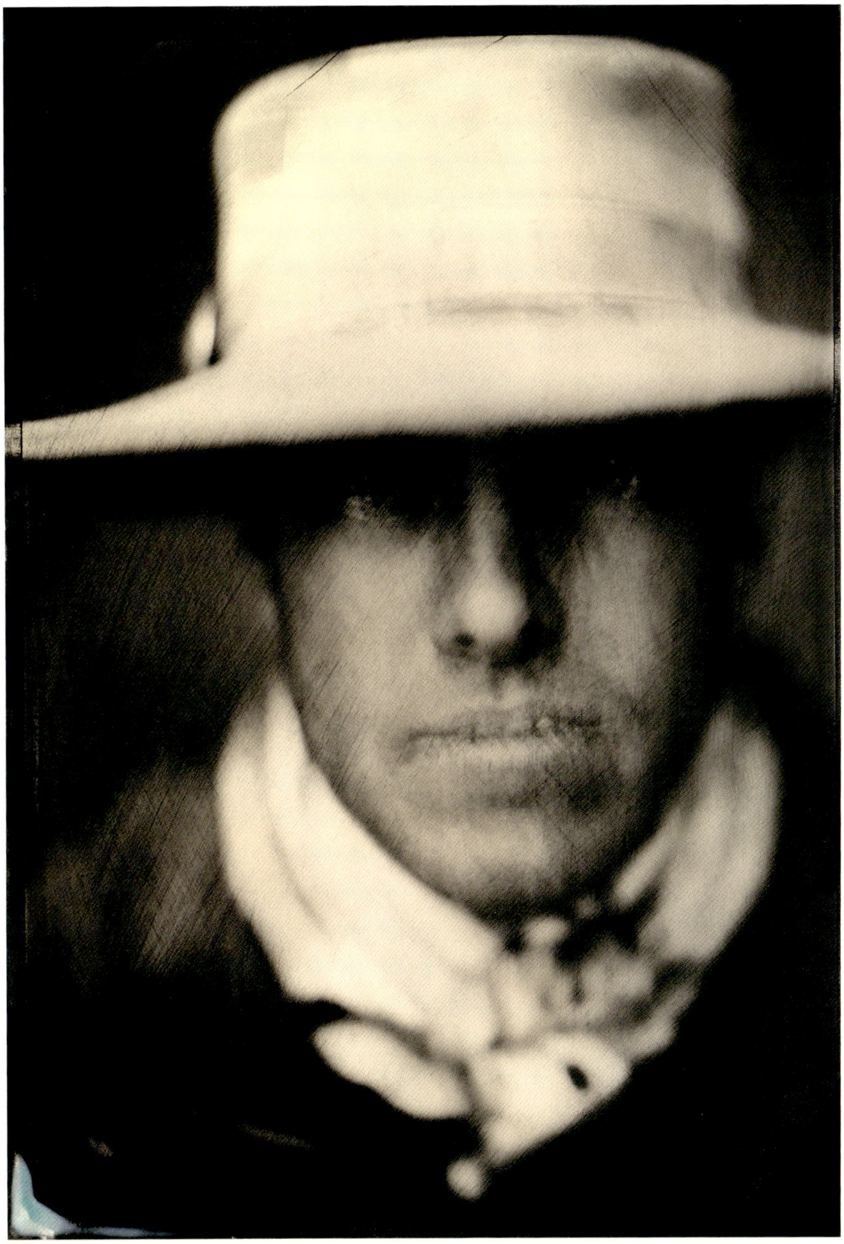

PLATE 33

Steven Patterson

SPANISH RANCH, NEVADA

I went from being a cowboss's daughter to being a cowboss's wife. I'm proud of what I do. I'm proud to be a cowboy, or a cowgirl, however you want to word it. I read a quote once that I've always remembered cause it really meant a lot to me when I read it: "The best thing about bein' a woman, or a cowgirl, is having the ability to work like a man, but the wisdom to know when to be a lady." I feel like I try to live my life kinda along those same lines.

I love being outside and I love all the seasons. Fall is my favorite, but there's definitely something about when each season begins. My favorite thing about what I do is, I know a lot of men probably have doubts as to my abilities or if I'm capable of doing a job or not, and I think the best thing for me is, when I do something well and maybe surprise them or, you know, they'll tell me "good job" or even just knowing myself that I did pretty good and I held my ground. I like that feeling a lot, that feeling of accomplishment, that I'm independent and able to do what I love and, even though it is generally a man's world, I—women—can still hold their own.

I wouldn't pick any other lifestyle. I think it's the best way to raise a family. I really do. Your kids grow up learning responsibility and respect for animals and the outdoors and the basics of life. They know where their food comes from and they know how to work hard and, you know, they learn how to always do their best and be proud of what they do. You know, there isn't always someone lookin' over their shoulder to tell them "good job" or pat them on the shoulder. They need to know in their heart that they did a job well done and that's what's important. I'm so grateful that Wes and I have the opportunity to raise our kids in this lifestyle. I pray we always will.

I don't mind only going to the grocery store once a month or once every two months. You learn to get what you need and stock up buyin' bulk, and you learn to do without, too, and, you know, you make sure you have the necessities and that's all you need. I always admire women whose husbands are always changing jobs and moving to the next ranch. That's hard at times. My mom is one of those women that has lived on several different ranches and has had to pack her family up and move to this place or that and the houses were not always very good. But wherever we lived she always made it a home. You know, they always say home is where the heart is; it's not a particular building or place and I think those women really—they know what that means.

JODI MINER
SNOWLINE RANCH, MONTANA

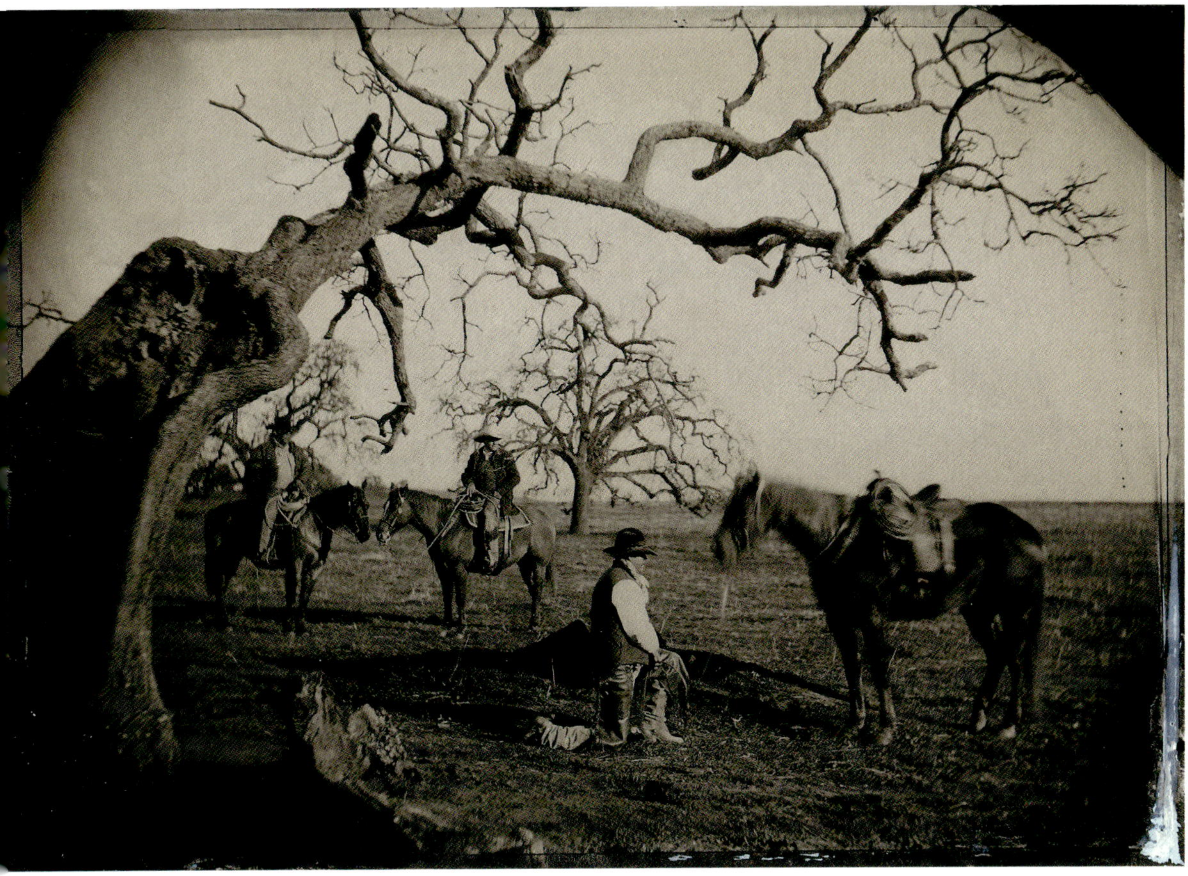

PLATE 34

Davey Towse (foreground), Bill Perez, Bruce Ryan

LACEY LIVESTOCK, CALIFORNIA

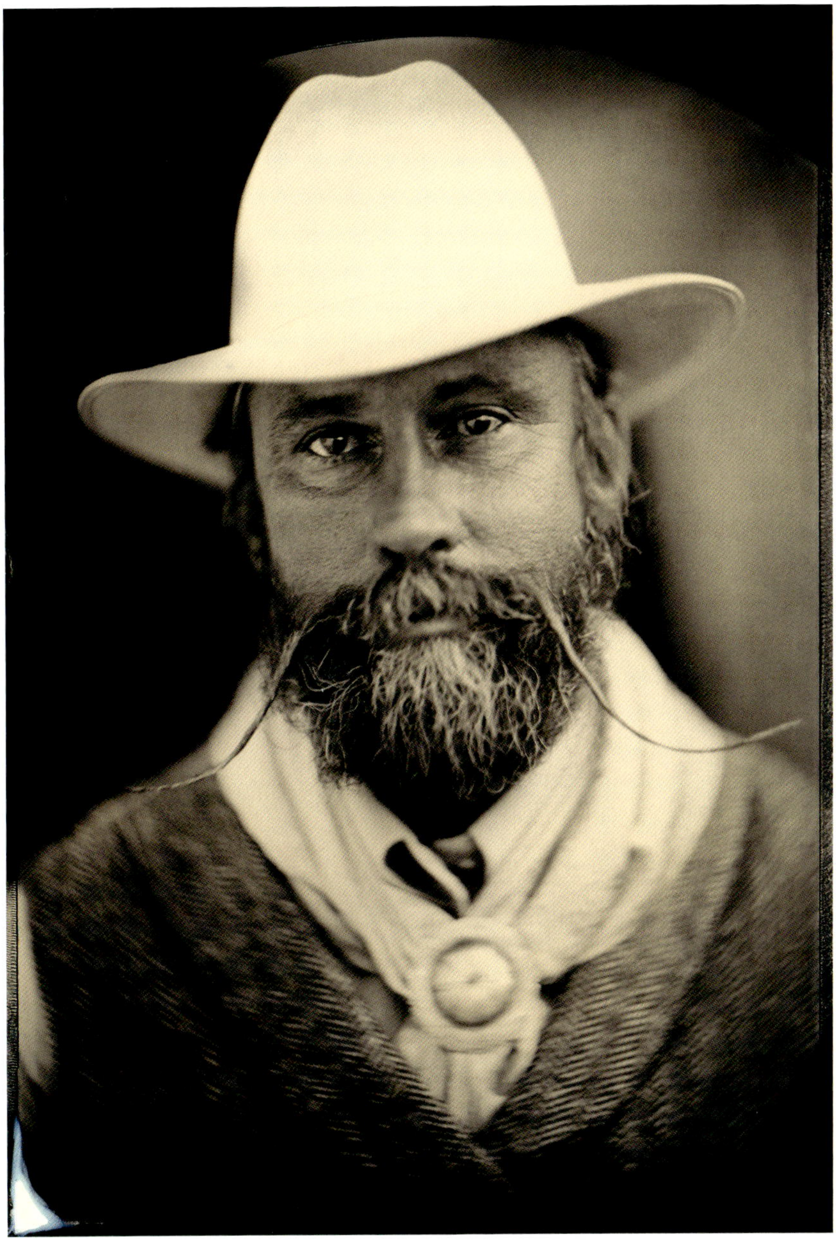

PLATE 35

Tim Bean

V BOX LAND & LIVESTOCK, OREGON

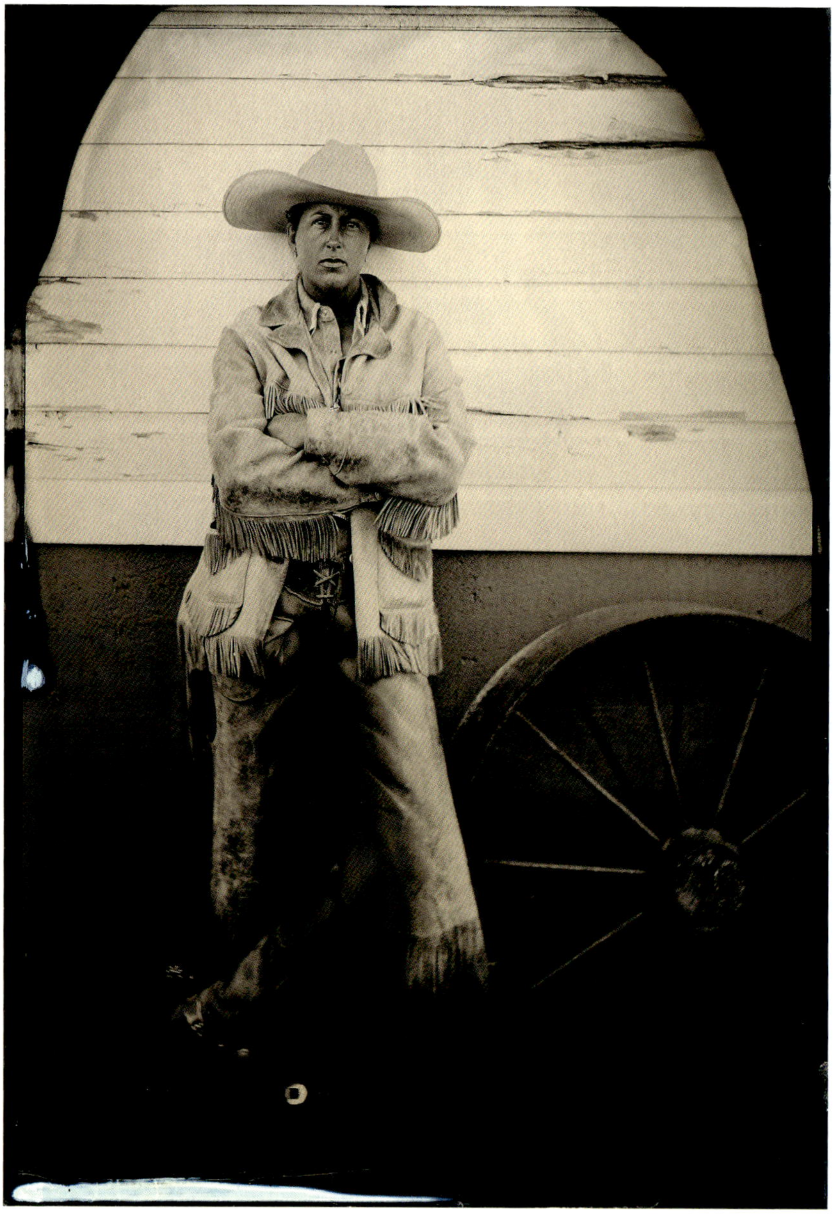

PLATE 36

Monique Miller

MILLER CATTLE COMPANY, MONTANA

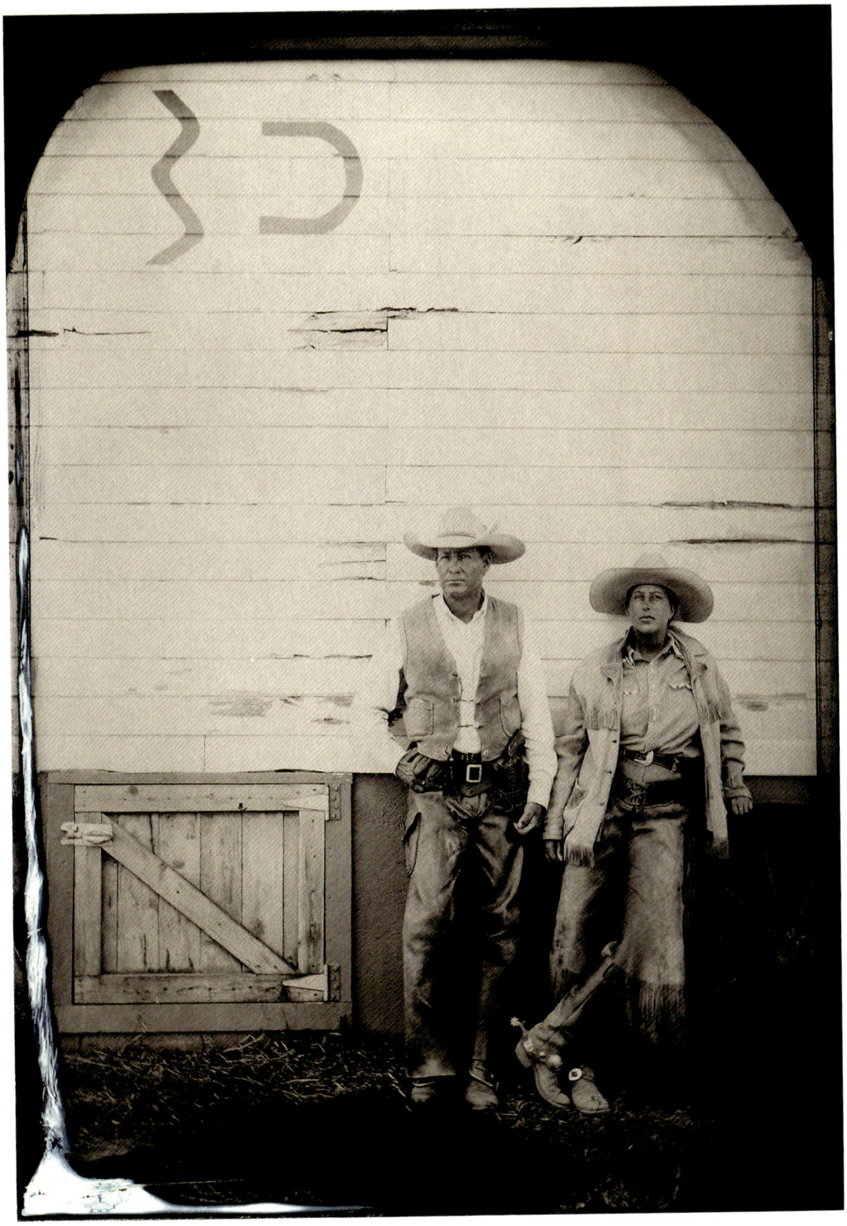

PLATE 37

David and Monique Miller

MILLER CATTLE COMPANY, MONTANA

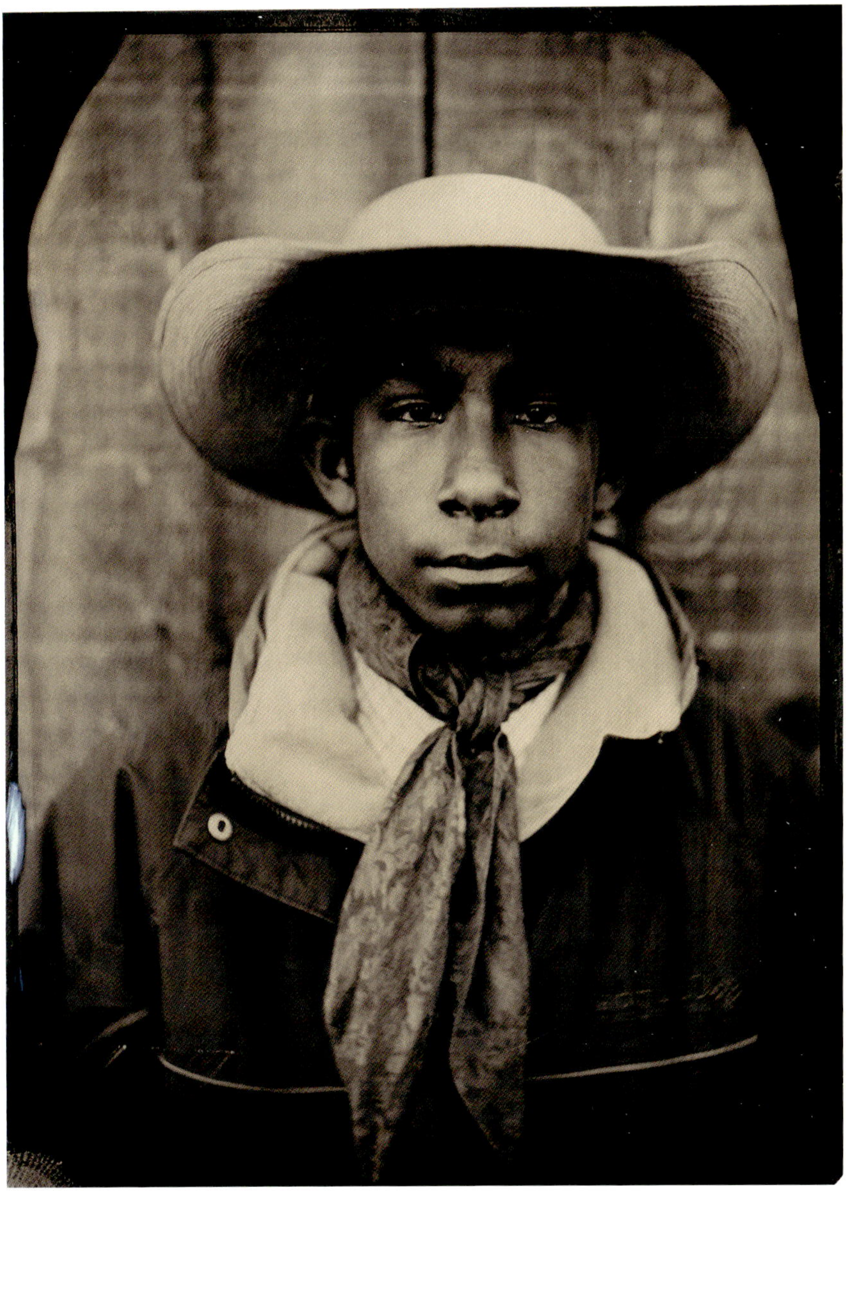

PLATE 38

Gordan García

DUCK VALLEY RESERVATION, NEVADA

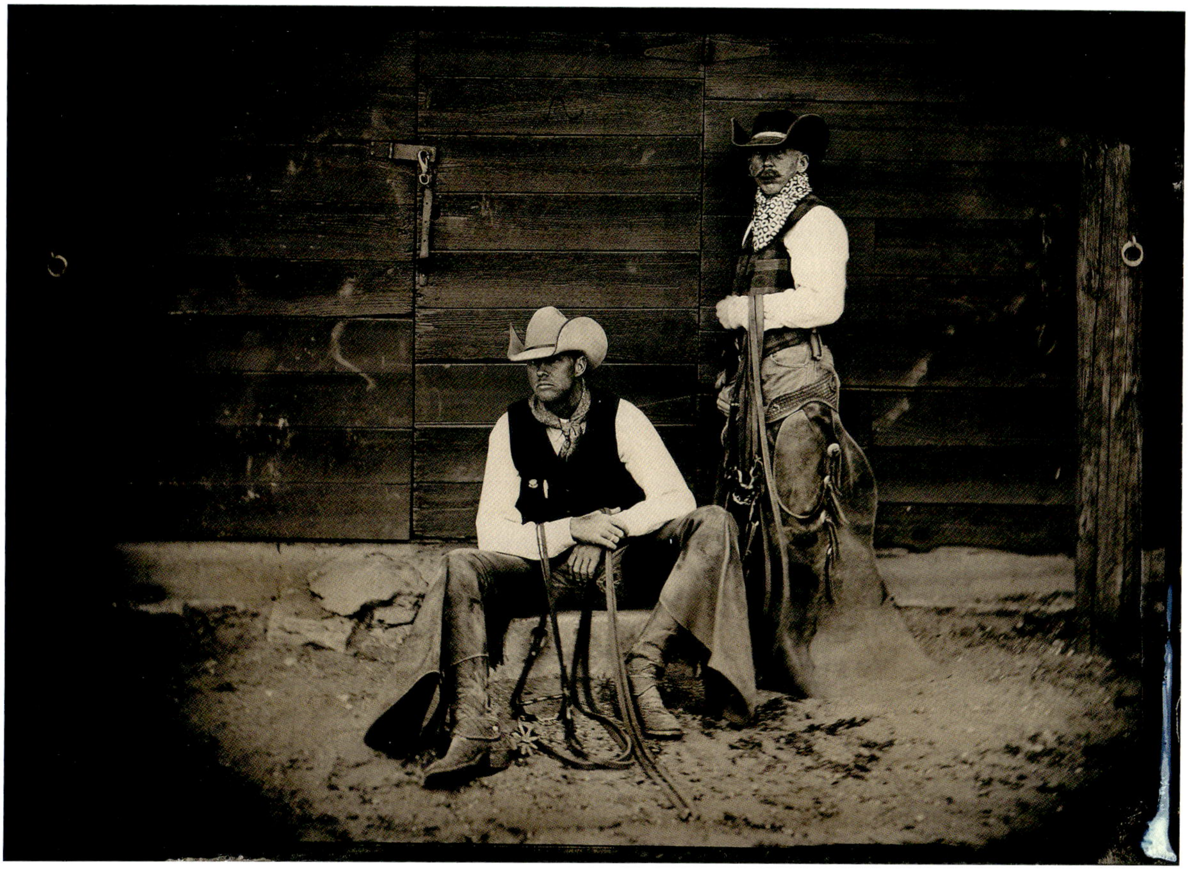

PLATE 39

Quentin Marburger, Cliff "Frosty" Foster

JA RANCH, TEXAS

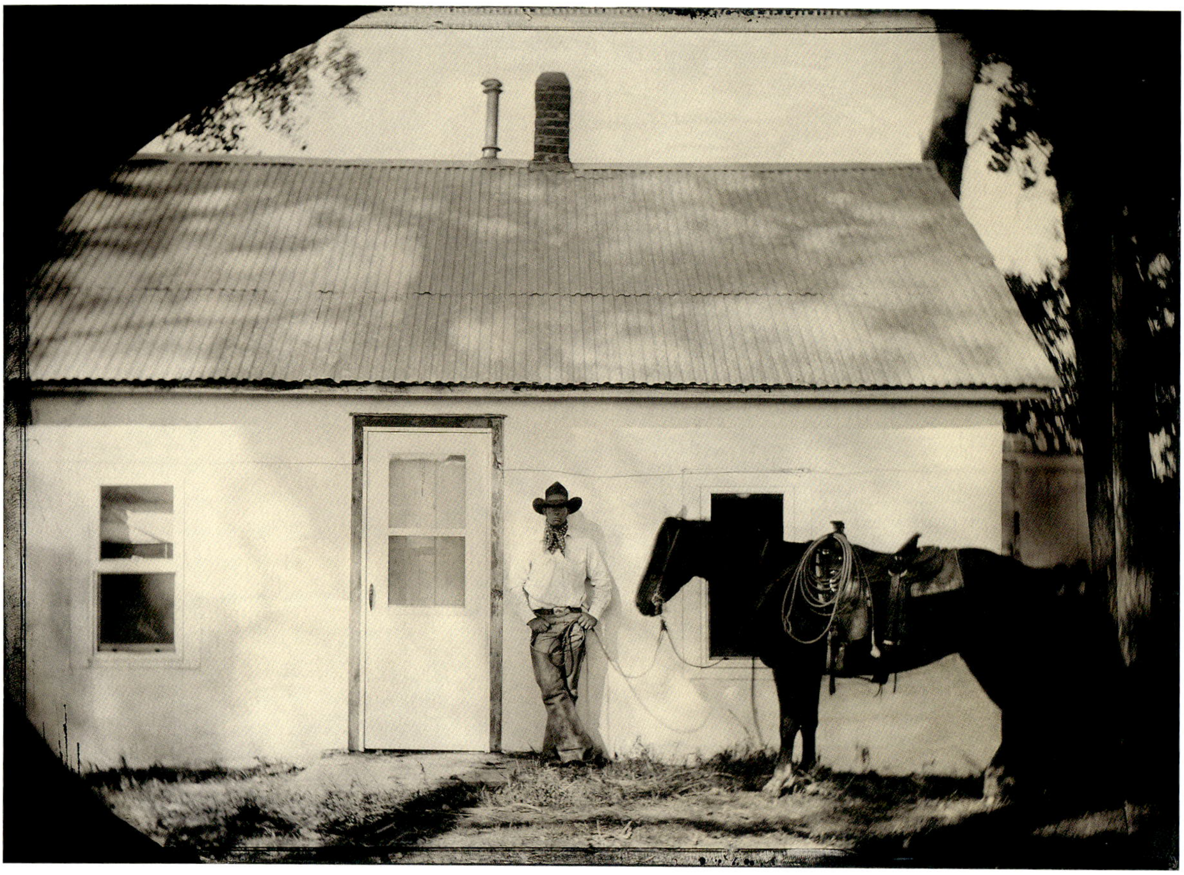

PLATE 40

Larry Hengstler

HAYTHORN LAND & CATTLE COMPANY, NEBRASKA

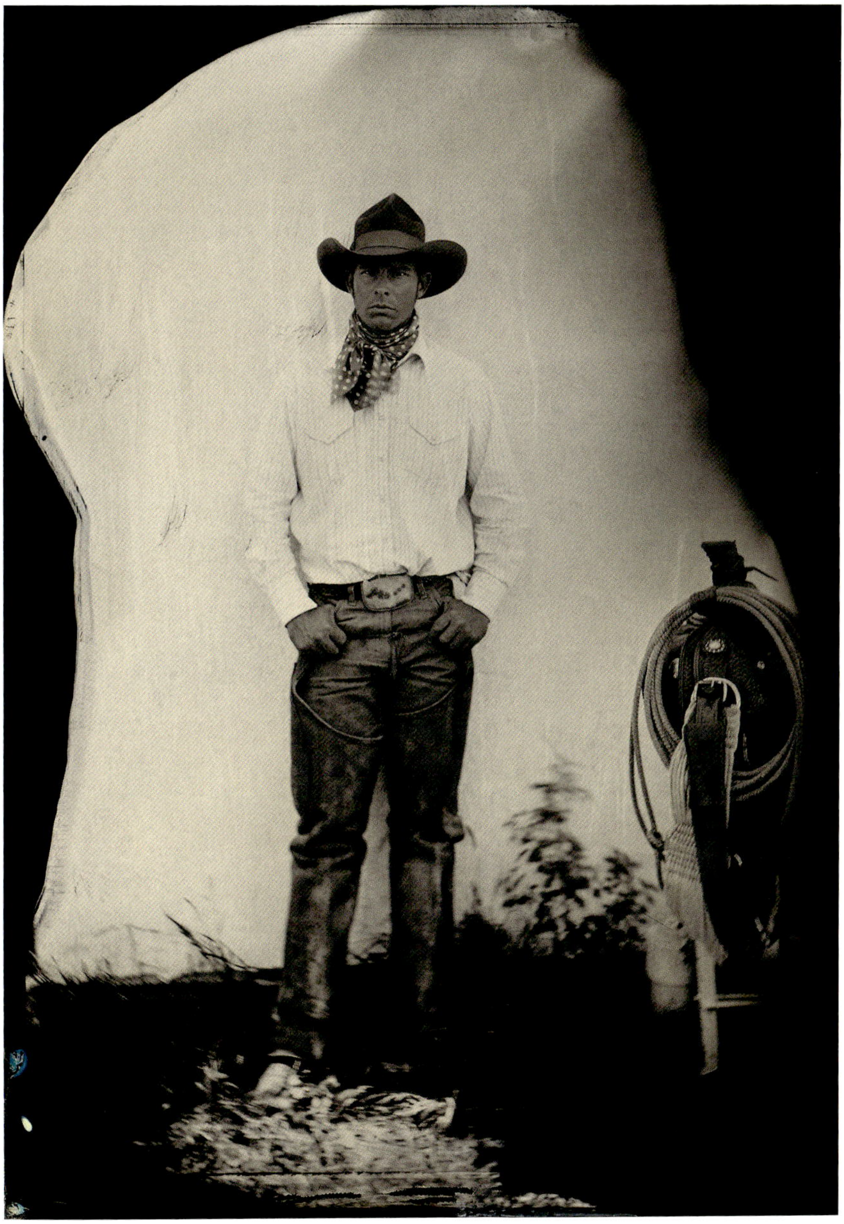

PLATE 41

Larry Hengstler

HAYTHORN LAND & CATTLE COMPANY, NEBRASKA

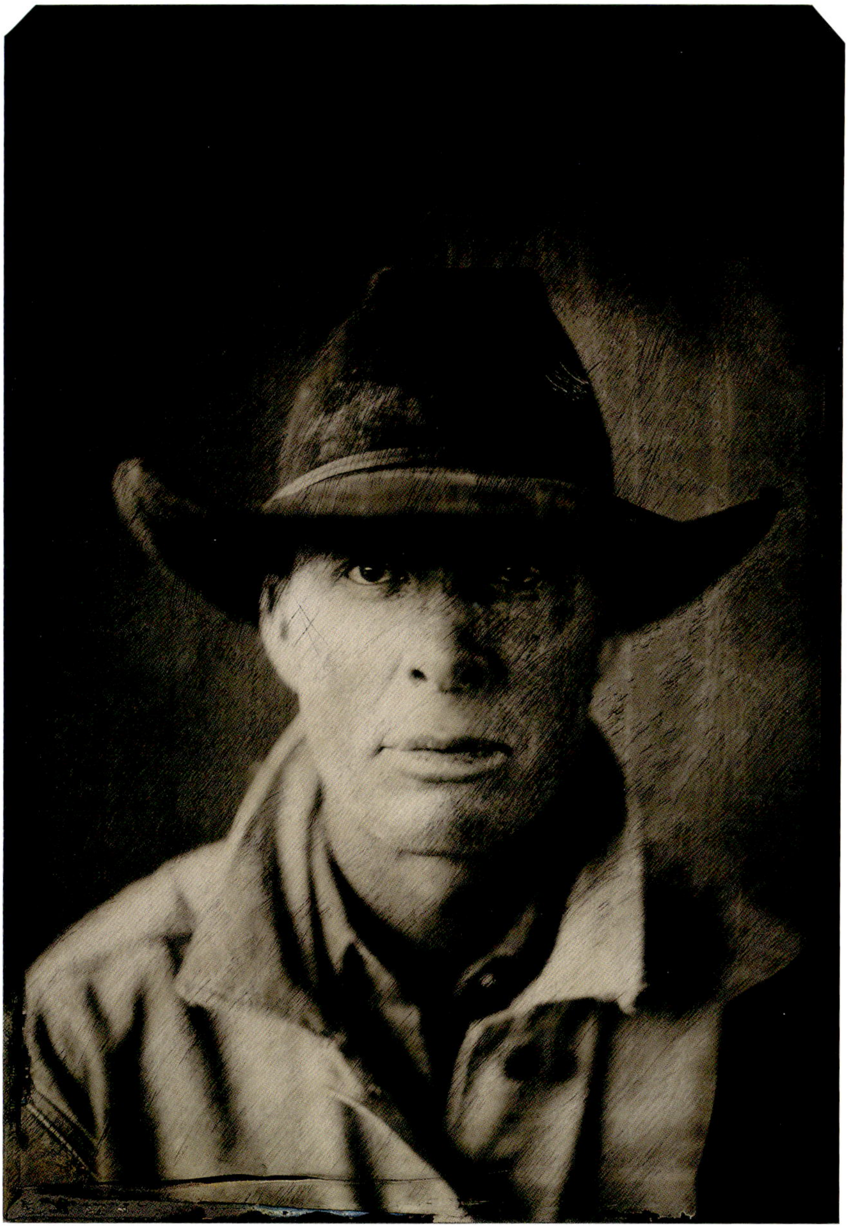

PLATE 42

Bryson Wright

TLW LIVESTOCK, SOUTH DAKOTA

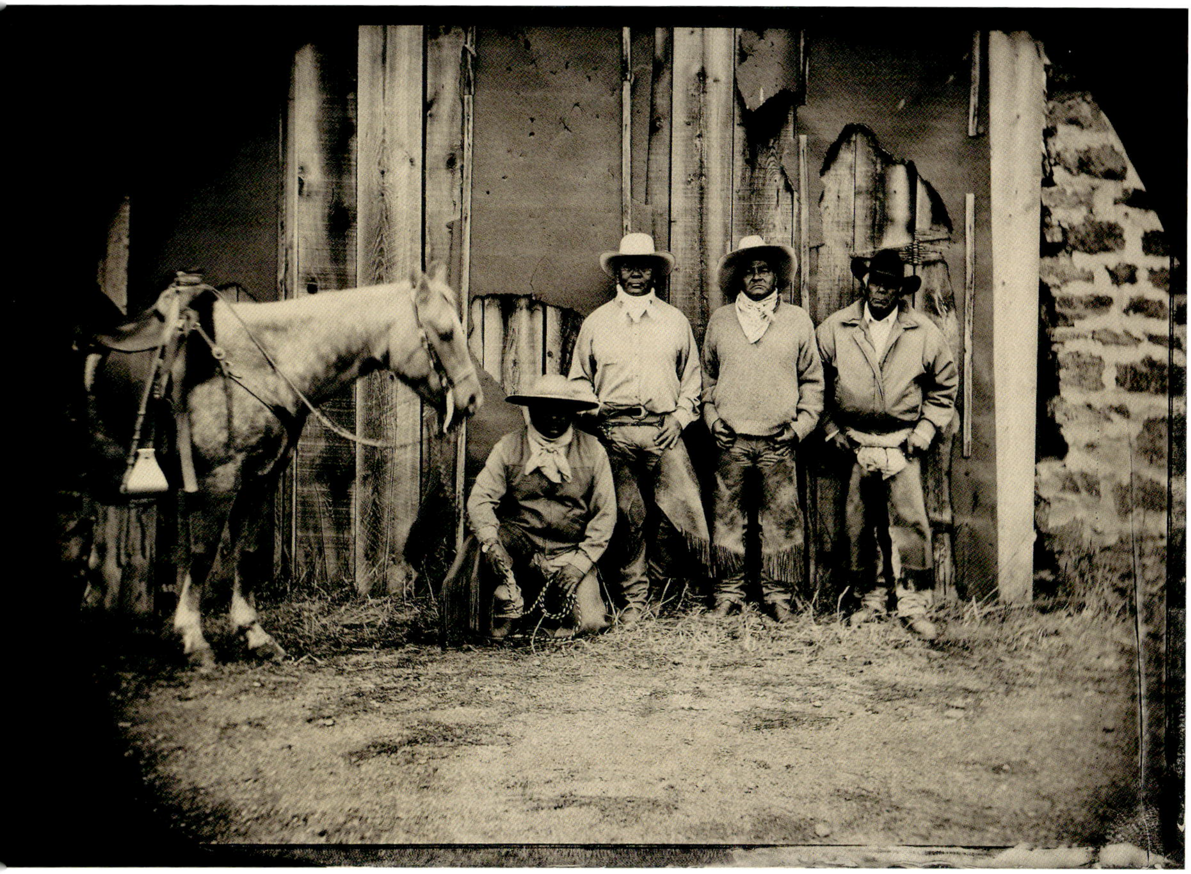

PLATE 43

Nathan Kelly, Sr., Jr. Knight, Reggie Sope, Delbert Jim

DUCK VALLEY RESERVATION, NEVADA

I grew up in the northern part of the Florida Panhandle. Worked for fifteen years in criminal justice for several civilian departments and one federal department and drove a truck for many years. Every time I crossed this state, Nebraska, this state just screamed to me. I got hijacked by Nebraska, and after I moved here, I started breeding horses. I breed quarters, paints, and Appaloosas.

Horses are my passion in my life. I think horses. You know, I eat, dream horses. Horses is a sickness. It is a disease. You can't like a horse; you either love them or you hate them. There's no in-between. And I have it bad. Horses are my life.

A horse would never, ever do anything willfully on purpose to hurt a human, unless another human give him a reason to get even. I don't thump on my horses. I raise them not to appreciate being thumped on. I treat my horses like I treat most people. I don't thump on people and I won't take a thumpin'.

The greatest high is to take a stud and a mare and put them together and eleven months, usually two weeks and three days later they put me a baby on the ground, and that baby is born so intelligent. Just to take something that don't know anything and teach it everything that I know and see it take it willingly. To take that baby from birth to being a seasoned adult and have a super good relationship with that animal to where that animal love to see you come, hate to see you go is the greatest high in the world. You can't get past that.

I wear my boots, my spurs, my chaps, and because I took an oath to uphold the Constitution to defend from any enemies domestic or foreign, I take it upon myself to own and bear arms, and I will always do this, you know. If we don't, it's gonna be taken away from us. I have a .44 Magnum on the right side, .357 on the left side, and 100 rounds on my gun belt.

I have—I had three children. I lost one in May of this year, my oldest, my daughter. I have a son in California. I have a daughter in Kansas. My family, for as far as I can remember, has been herdsmen. My grandfather, my great-grandfather, my father, and now me. When I leave and cross the river there won't be any more from my family doin' what I do. It was surprising to me to learn that that many of my relatives was in the business that I'm in, and I am proud to be associated with a business, a career, that runs so deep into my country's history.

I have a deep, deep passion for this country, mother earth, and livestock.

JIM MYRICK
BROKEN ARROW EQUESTRIAN, NEBRASKA

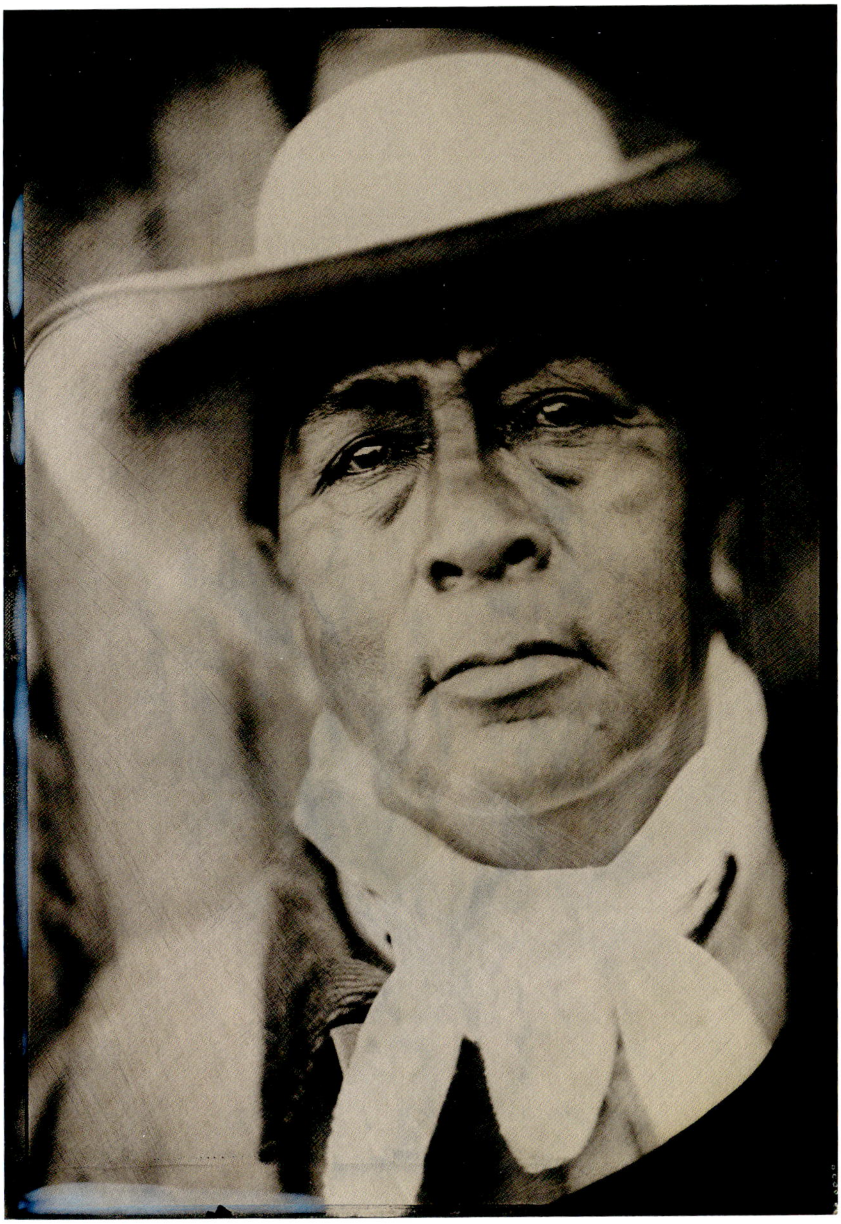

PLATE 44

Jr. Knight

DUCK VALLEY RESERVATION, NEVADA

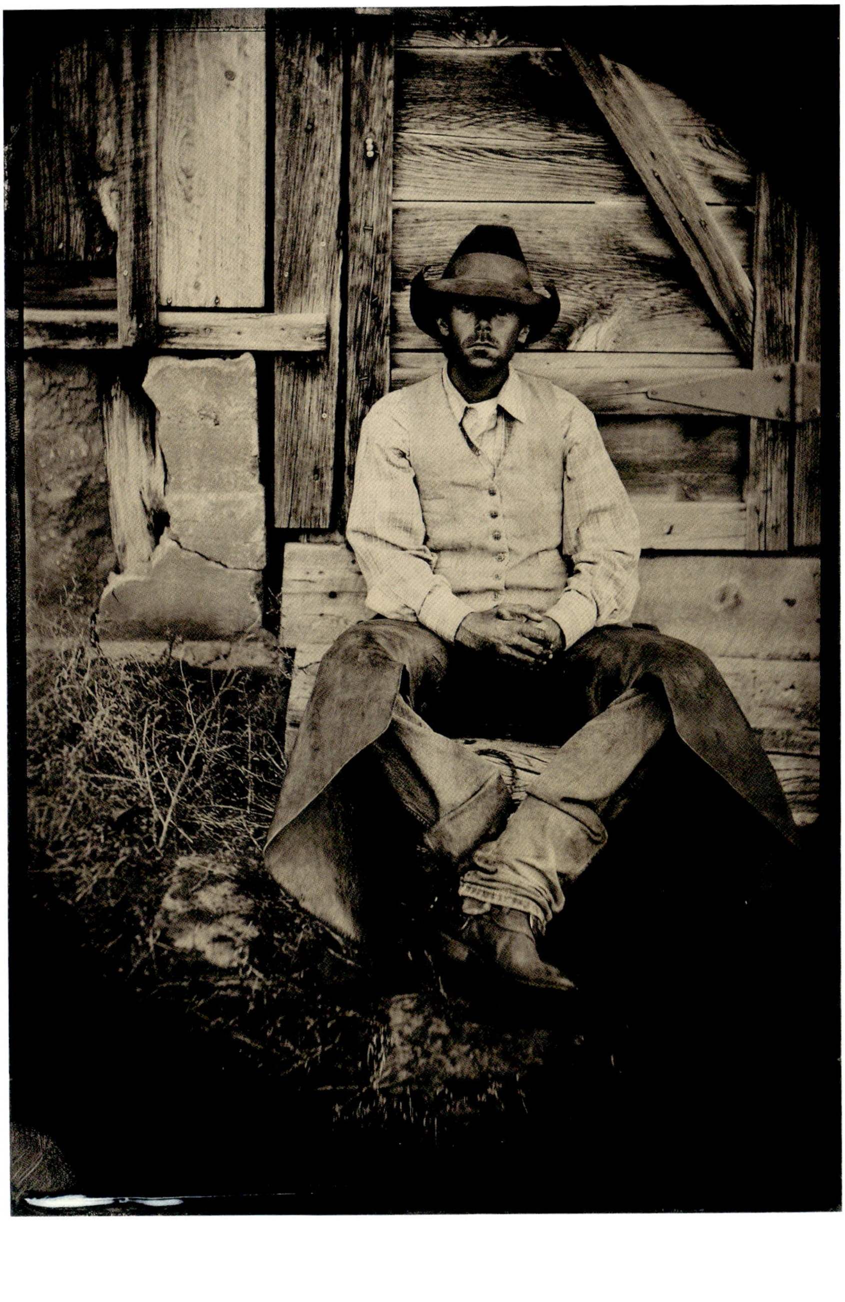

PLATE 45

Heath DeNell

DIAMOND A RANCH, ARIZONA

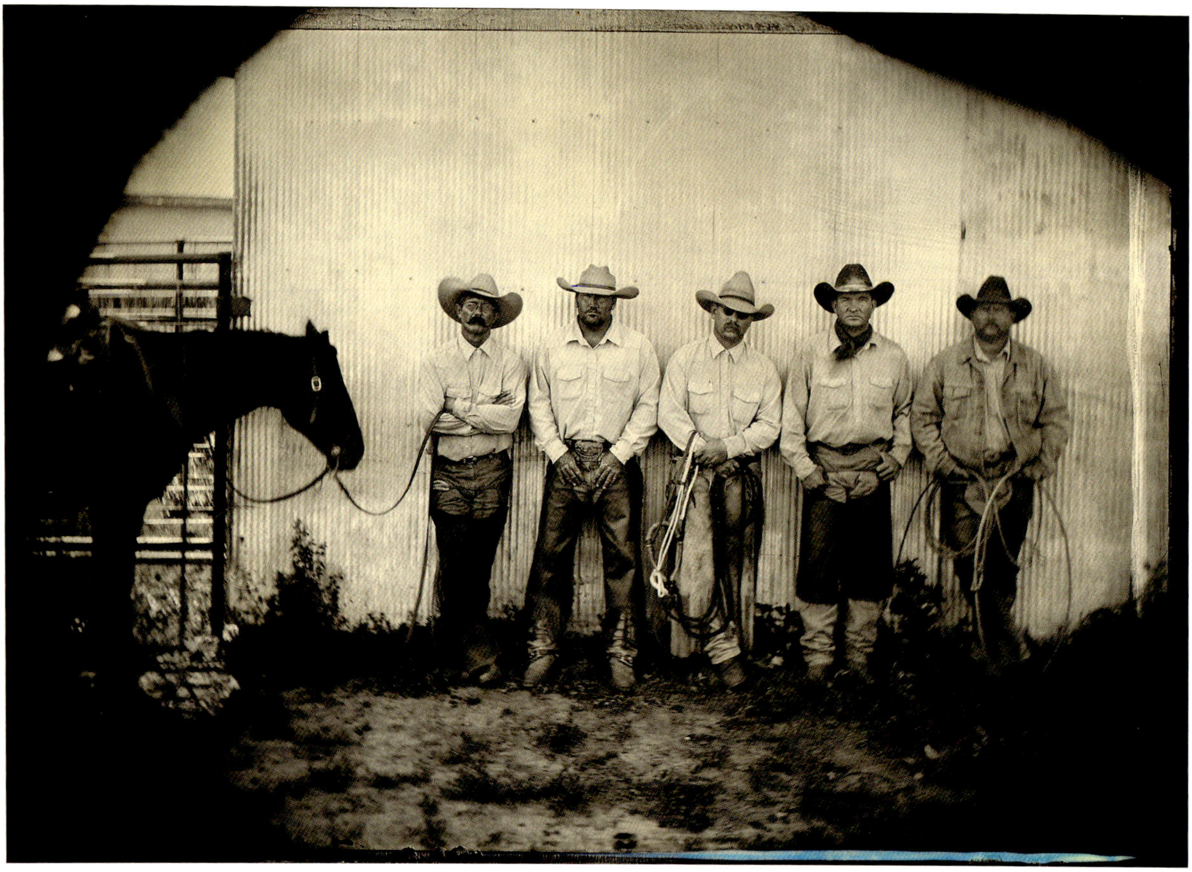

PLATE 46

Marlin Waldrop, Jimmy Dixon, Will Campbell, Rodney Barby, Shawn Campbell

BAR B RANCH, OKLAHOMA

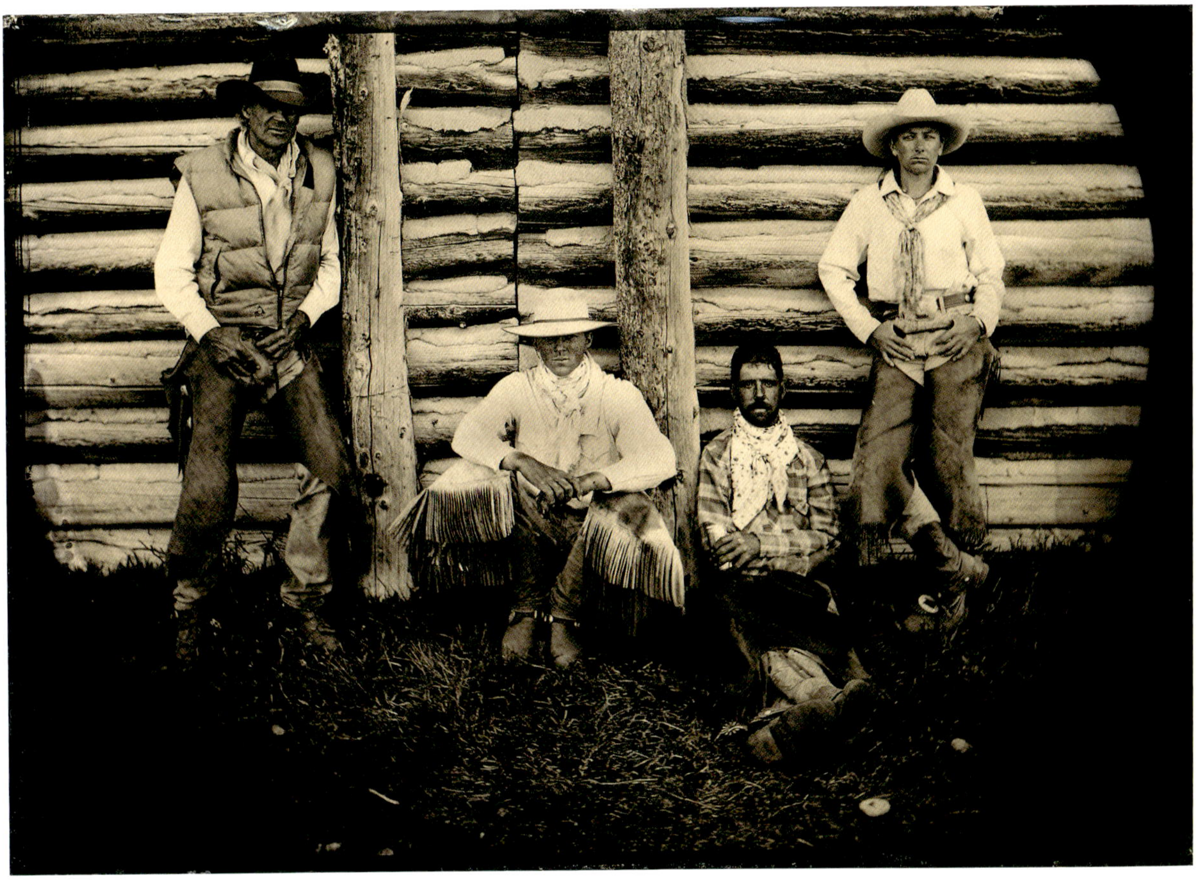

PLATE 47

Art Robinson, Eric Johnson, Wes Miner, Jodi Miner

SNOWLINE RANCH, MONTANA

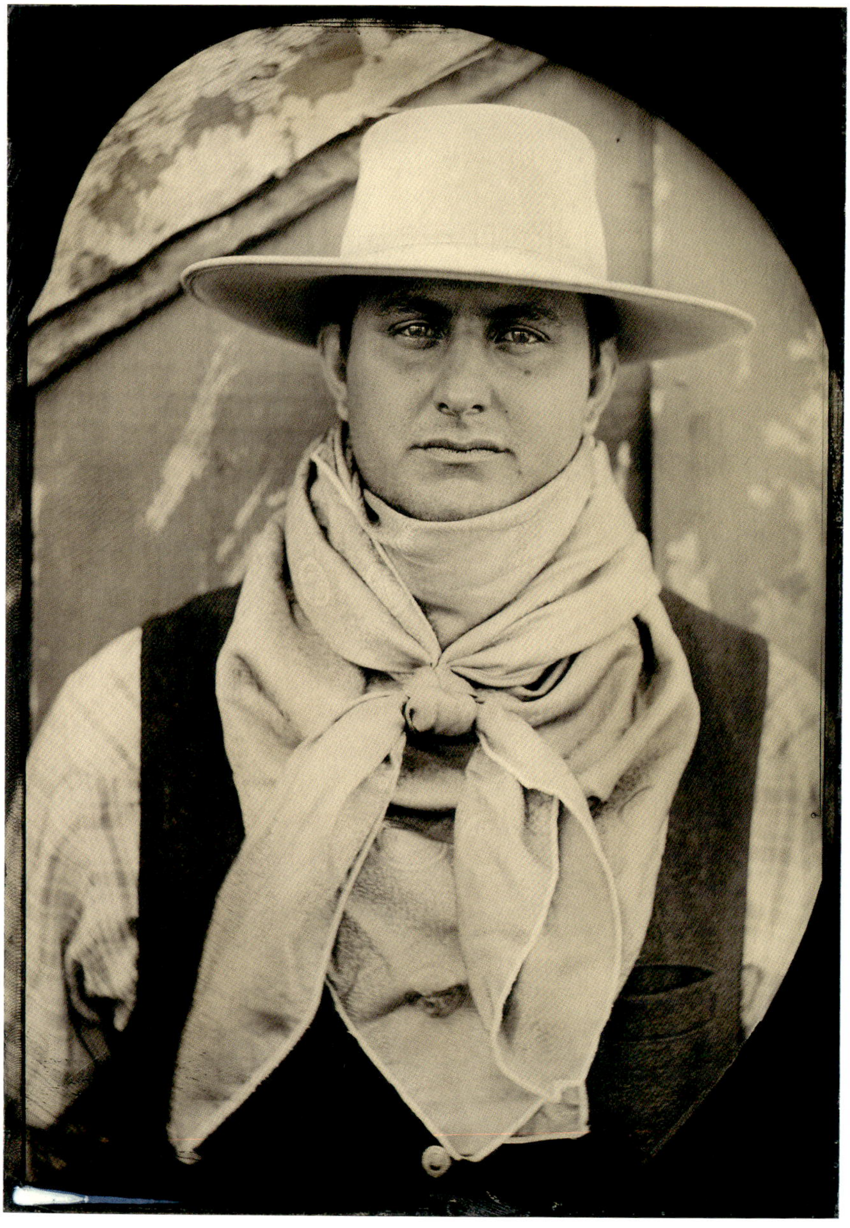

PLATE 50

Jimmy vanBelle

ZX RANCH, OREGON

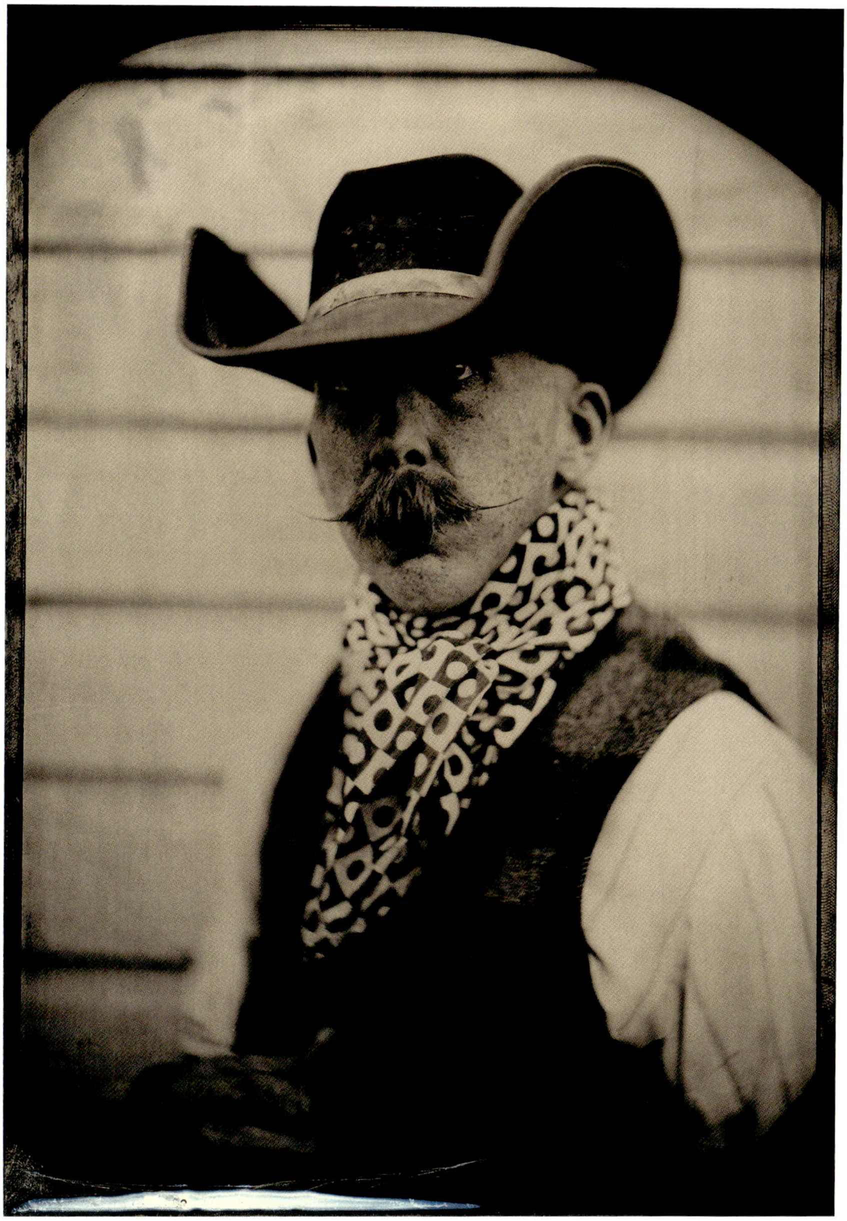

PLATE 51

Cliff "Frosty" Foster

JA RANCH, TEXAS

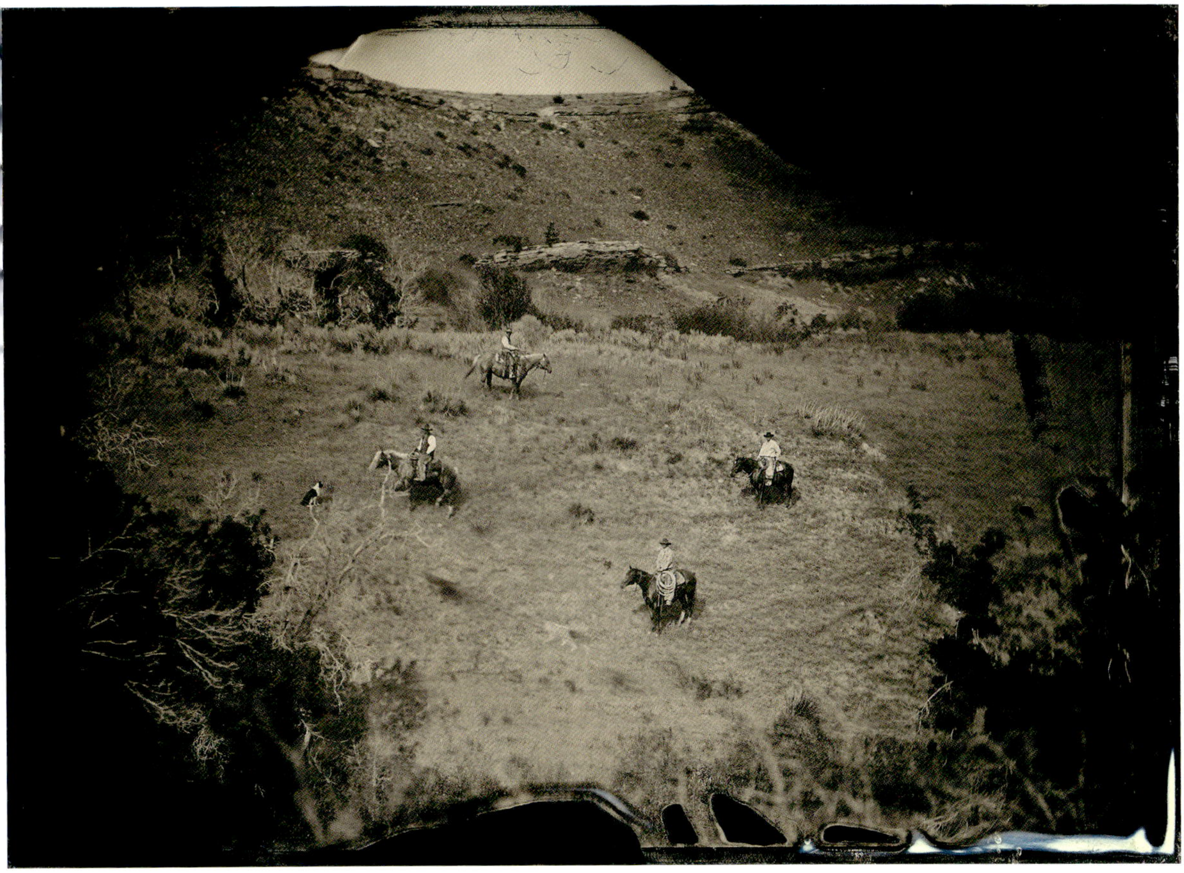

PLATE 52

Martin Anseth, Skeeter Redding, Silas Ivory, Scott Arnold

EZ RANCH, MONTANA

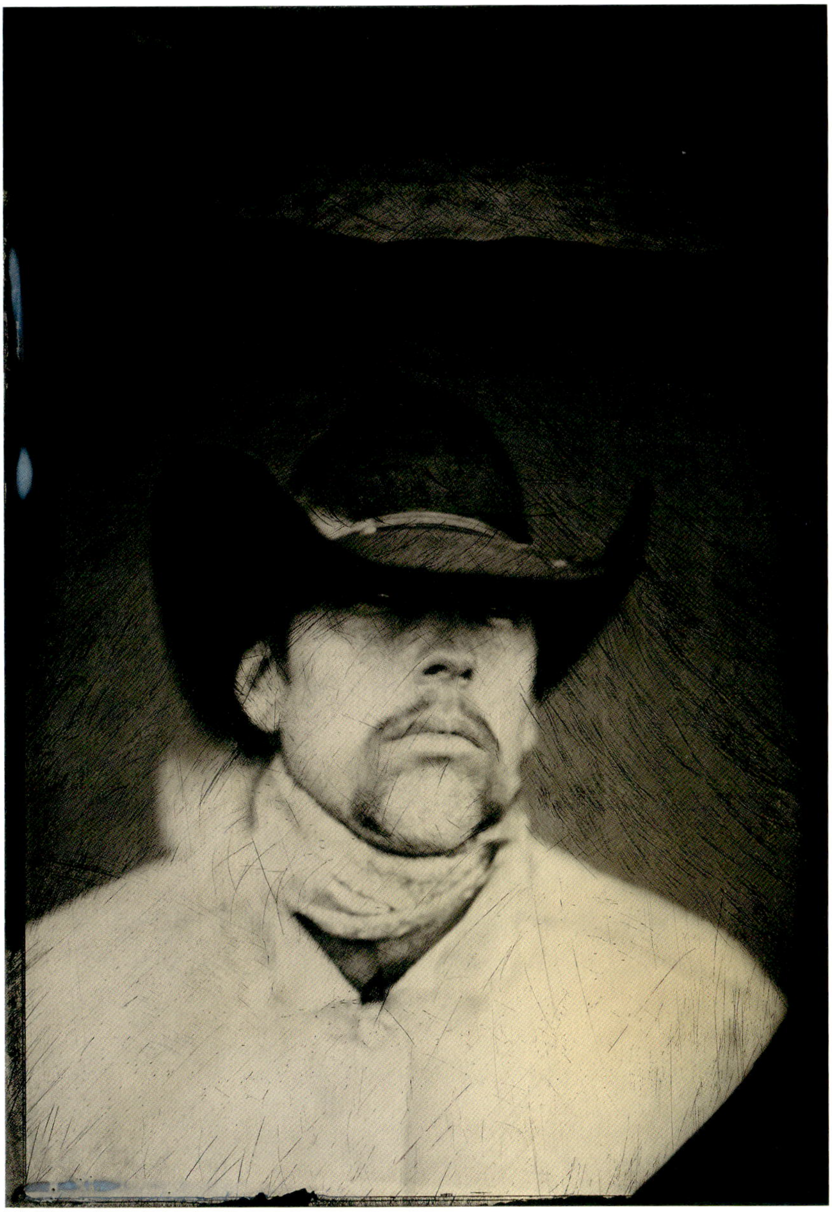

PLATE 53

Cody Taylor

PITCHFORK RANCH, TEXAS

I was born in Idaho and moved to Oklahoma and just kinda come back up here. Just cowboy'd around a little, you know, worked in several big feedyards and outfits all over. I just like to aggravate cows, you know. I eat beef to get even, so it's kind of a good job. But I like this northern country quite a bit. I've been down to Texas and over to Kansas and Nebraska and all that and this is just kinda where I like to go. I always end up back here in Wyoming. Nice piece of country.

I've never really had any other job. I grew up on a pretty small outfit. Dad raised some cows, plenty of colts and shit around for me to do, and I just kinda never grew up and just kept going. I rodeo'd a little bit through high school, and well, I needed something that paid everyday and this works . . . works for me. Just the lifestyle. It's quiet, you know. You don't get too excited, you know, I don't have to see a lot of people and I'm out away from everything. I just wanna aggravate, you know, some cows and just kick a dog every now and then; stay happy, you know. If you're not happy, you're wasting time. I think every now and then, you know, a feller wants to rope something just to hear it beller, and you can't do that in town.

JUSTIN ROGERS
PADLOCK RANCH, WYOMING

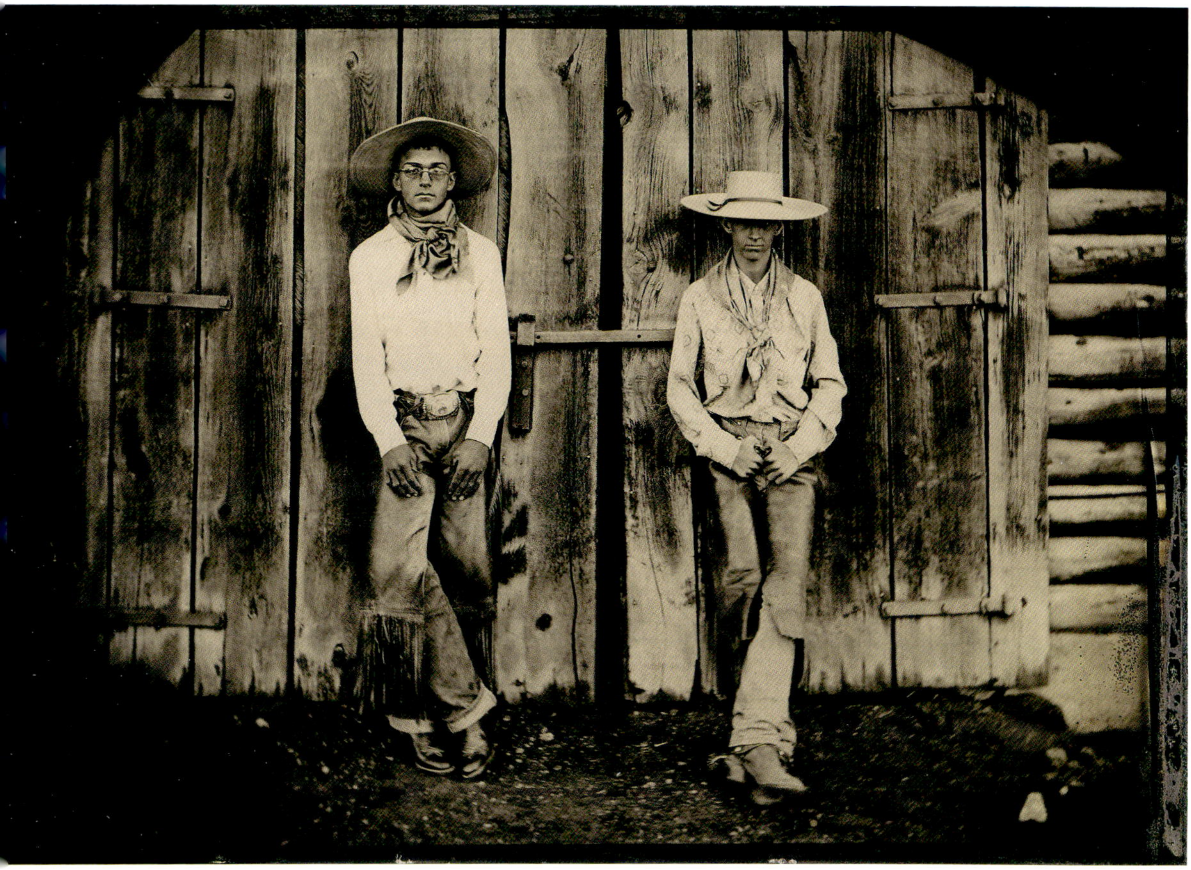

PLATE 54

Chase Sligar, YP RANCH, *and Clay Sligar,* SPANISH RANCH
NEVADA

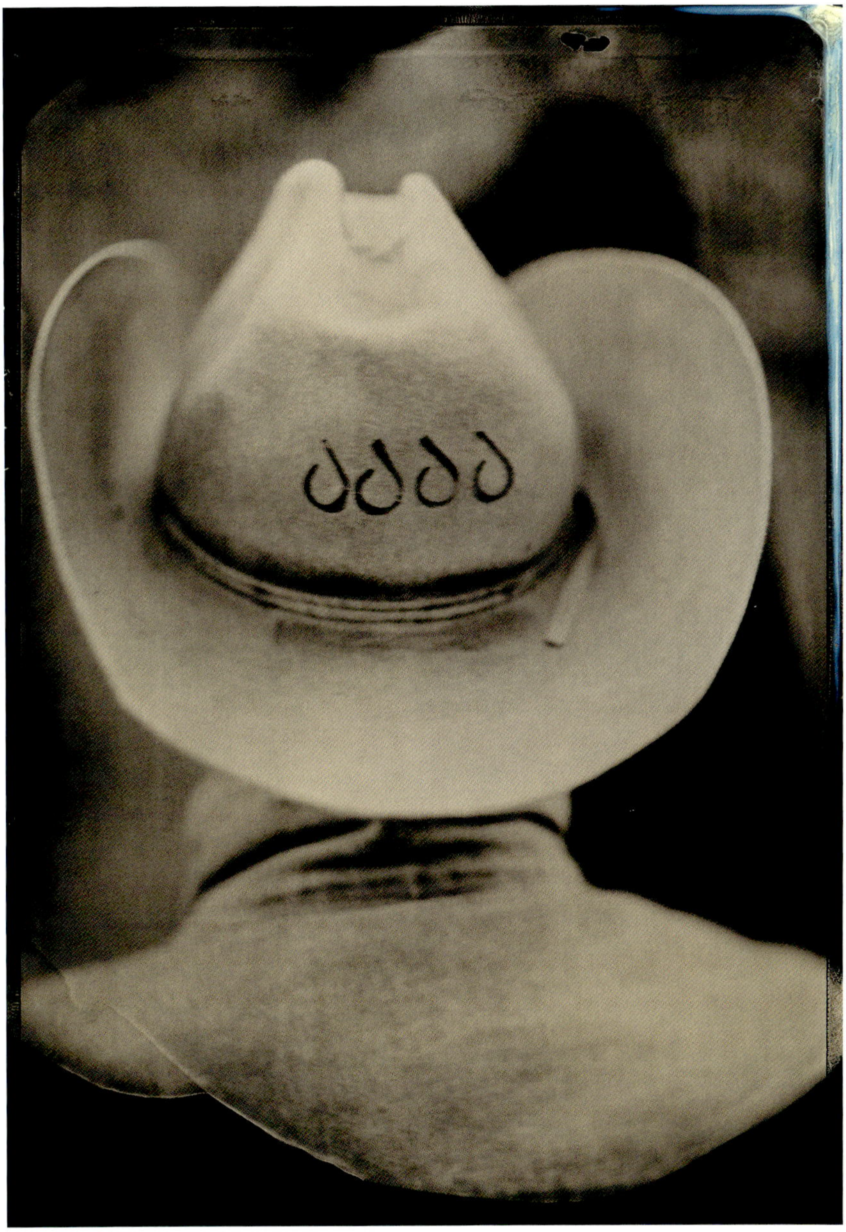

PLATE 55

Cody Bell

6666 RANCH, TEXAS

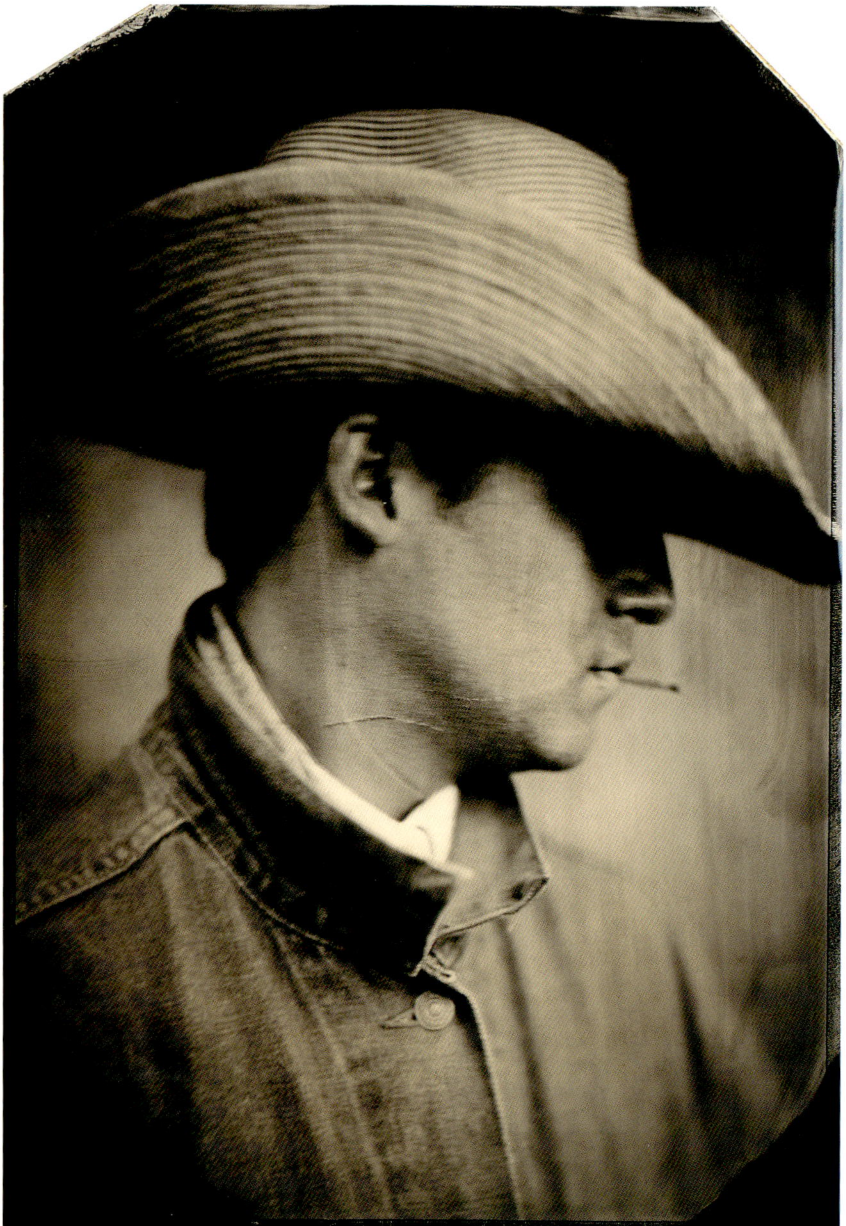

PLATE 56

Dustin Haney

PITCHFORK RANCH, TEXAS

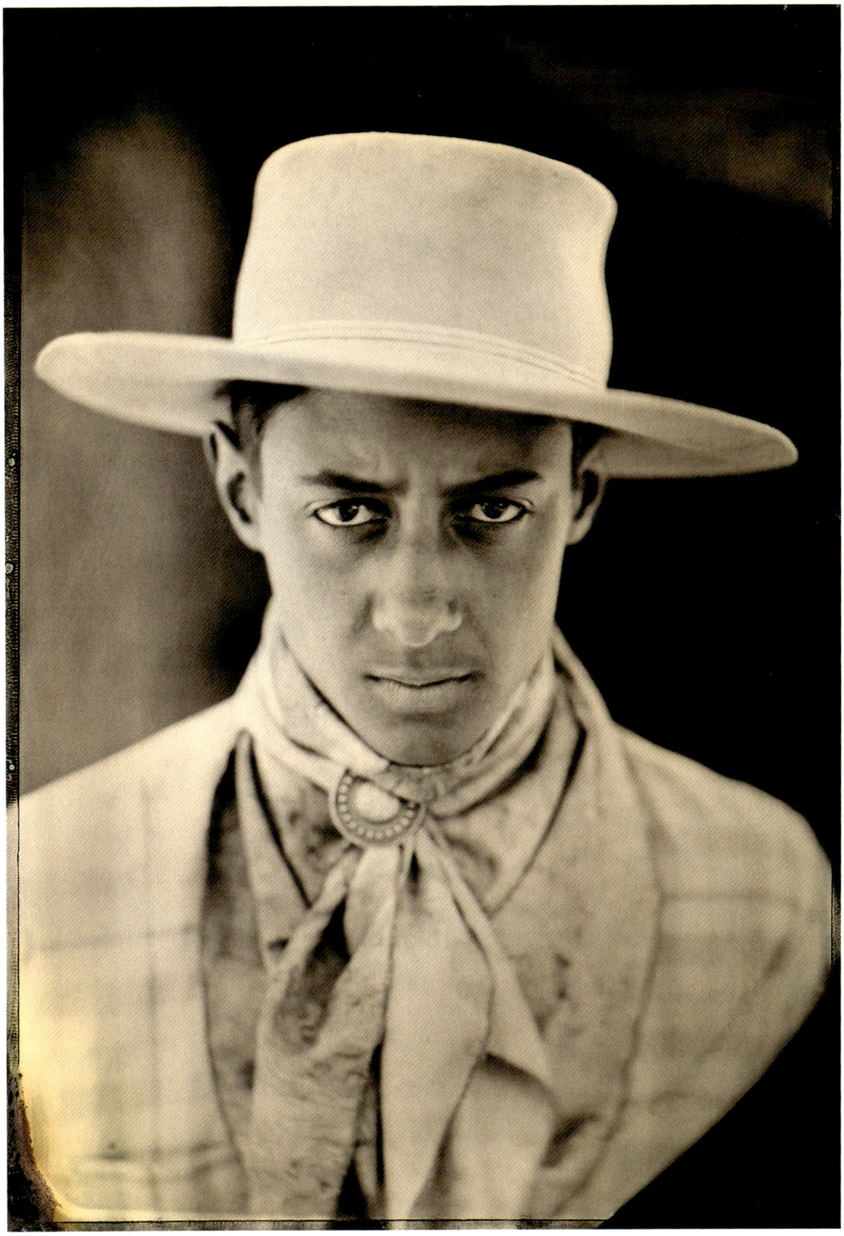

PLATE 57

Casey DePaolo

BUTTE CREEK RANCH, OREGON

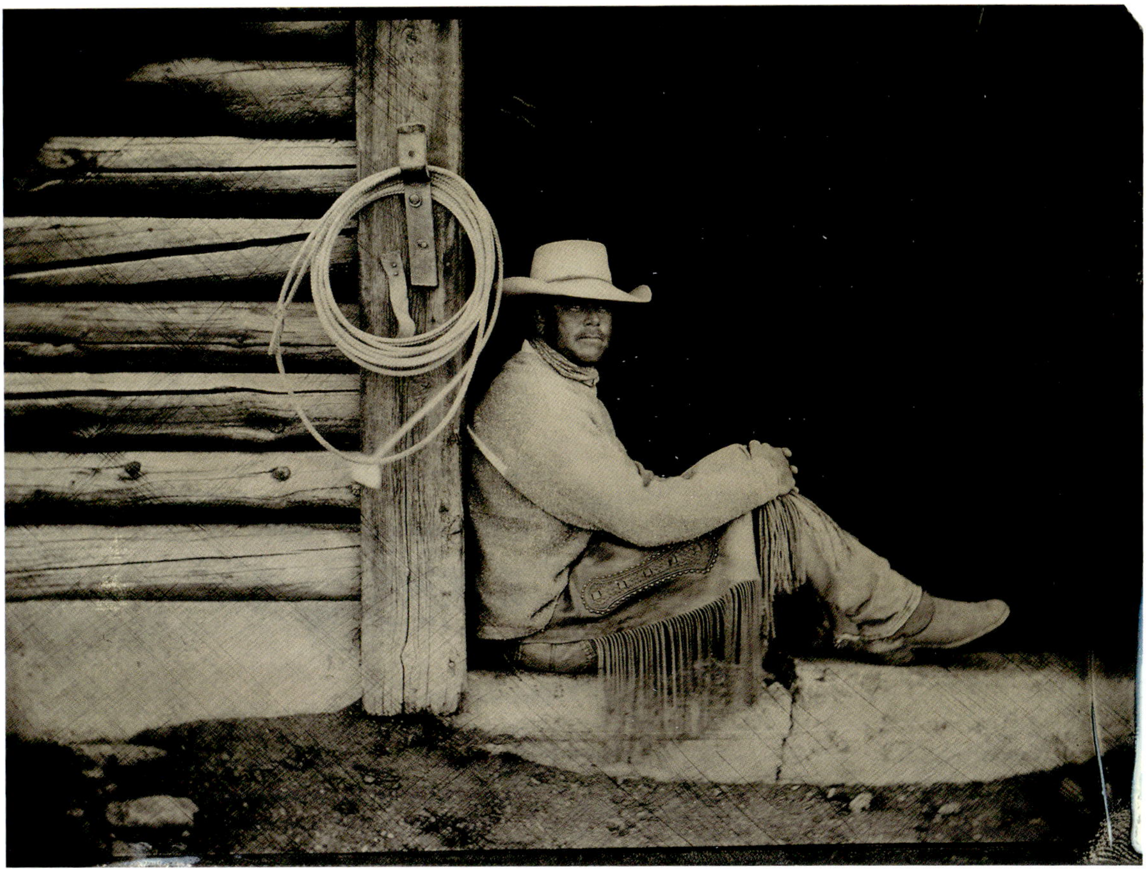

PLATE 58

Dan Lock

VAN NORMAN RANCH, NEVADA

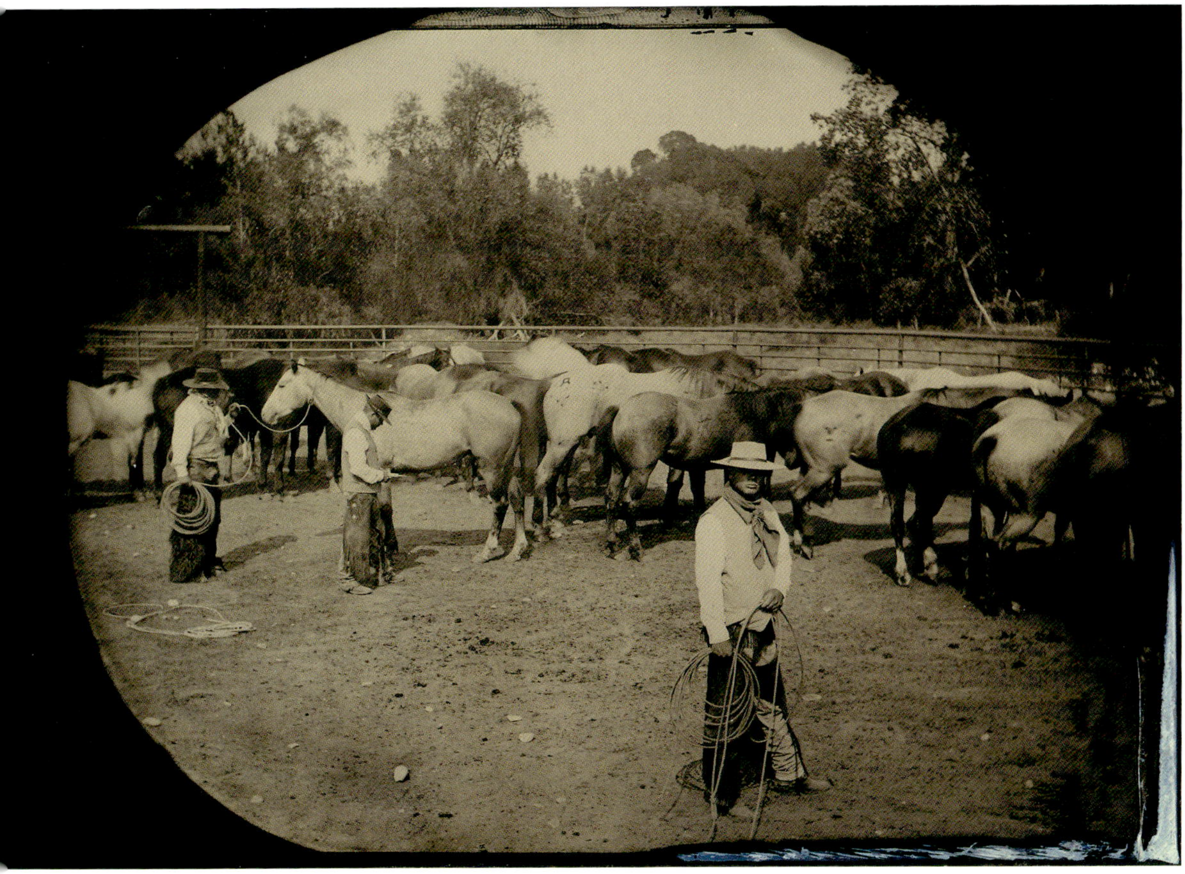

PLATE 59

Kirk Lohof, Blake Rainsdon, Corey Northup (front)

SUNLIGHT RANCH, MONTANA

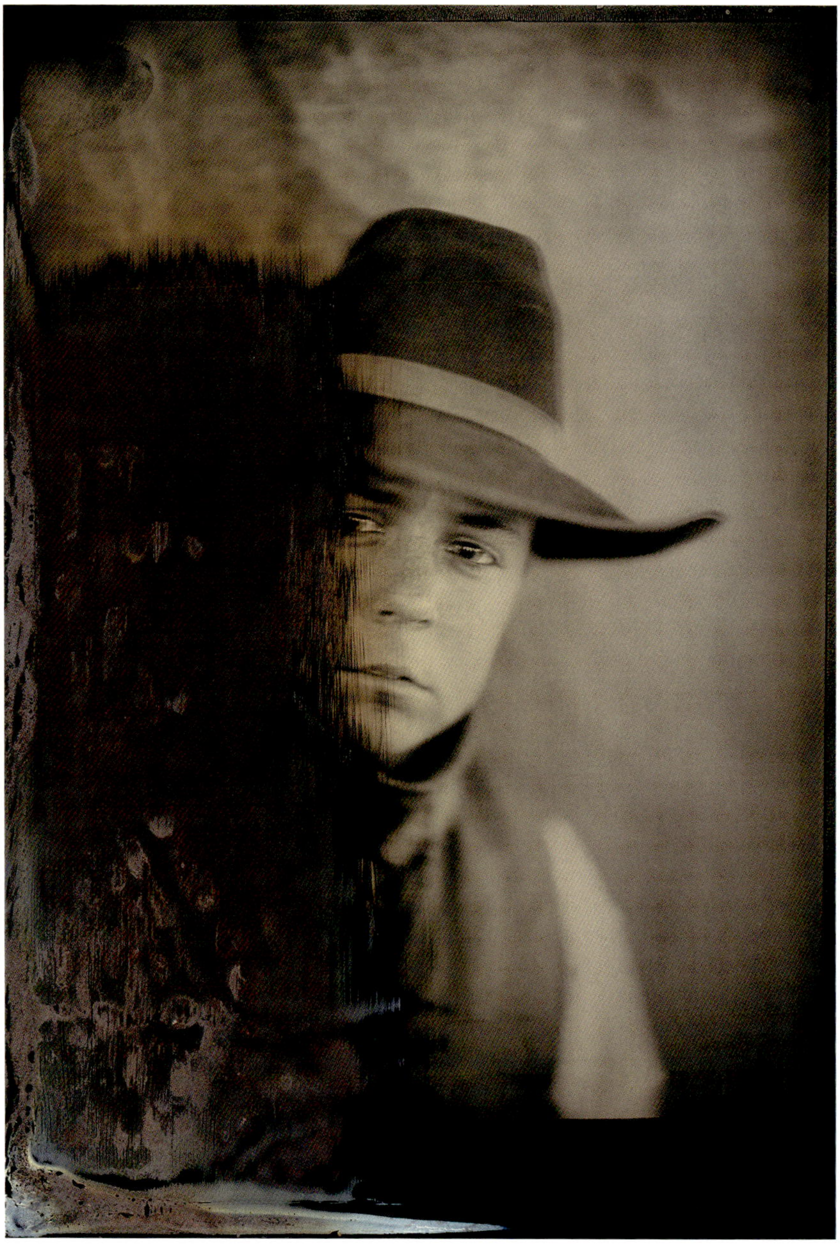

PLATE 60

Brandon "Bear" Ryan

LACEY LIVESTOCK, CALIFORNIA

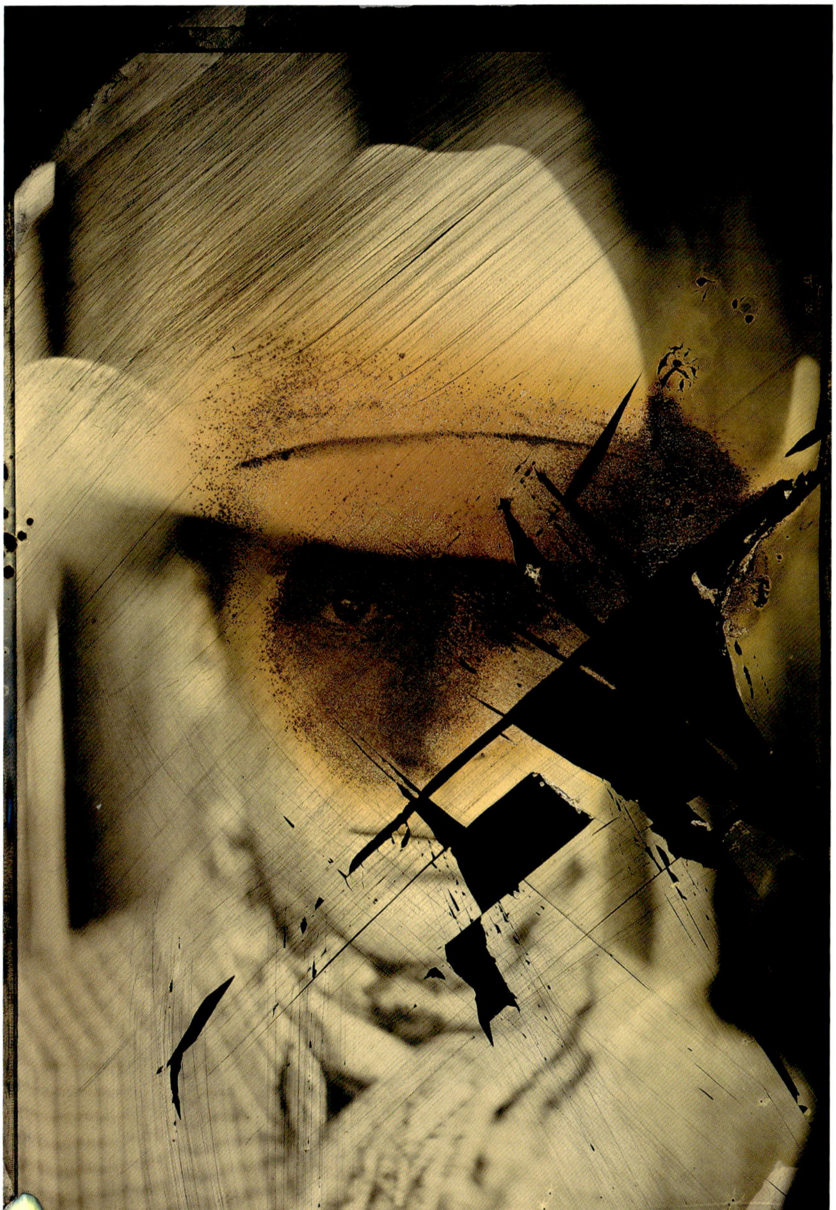

PLATE 61

Jake Wagner

RA BROWN RANCH, TEXAS

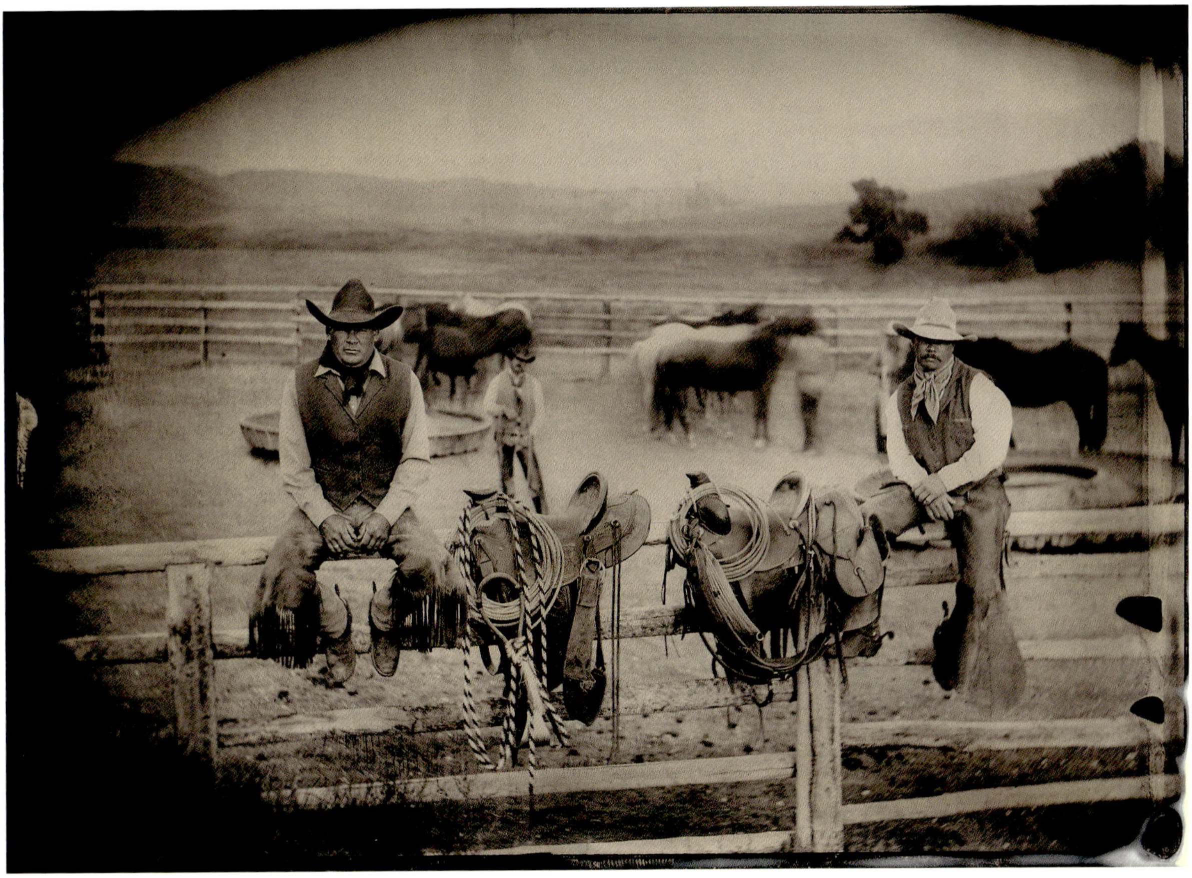

PLATE 63

Chad Milius and Pat Crisswell (on fence), Brandon Ellison, Barry Simpson (in corral)

PADLOCK RANCH, WYOMING

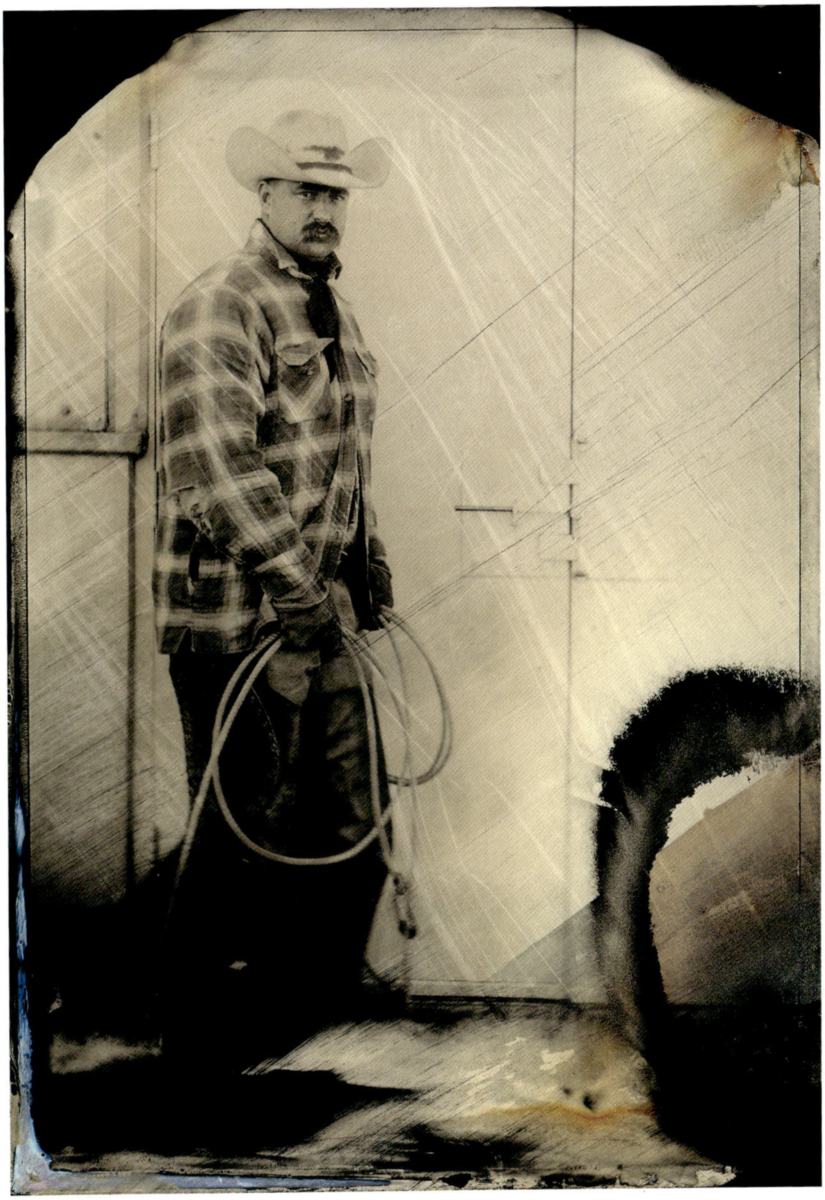

PLATE 65

Brent Brownlee

TRIANGLE RANCH, TEXAS

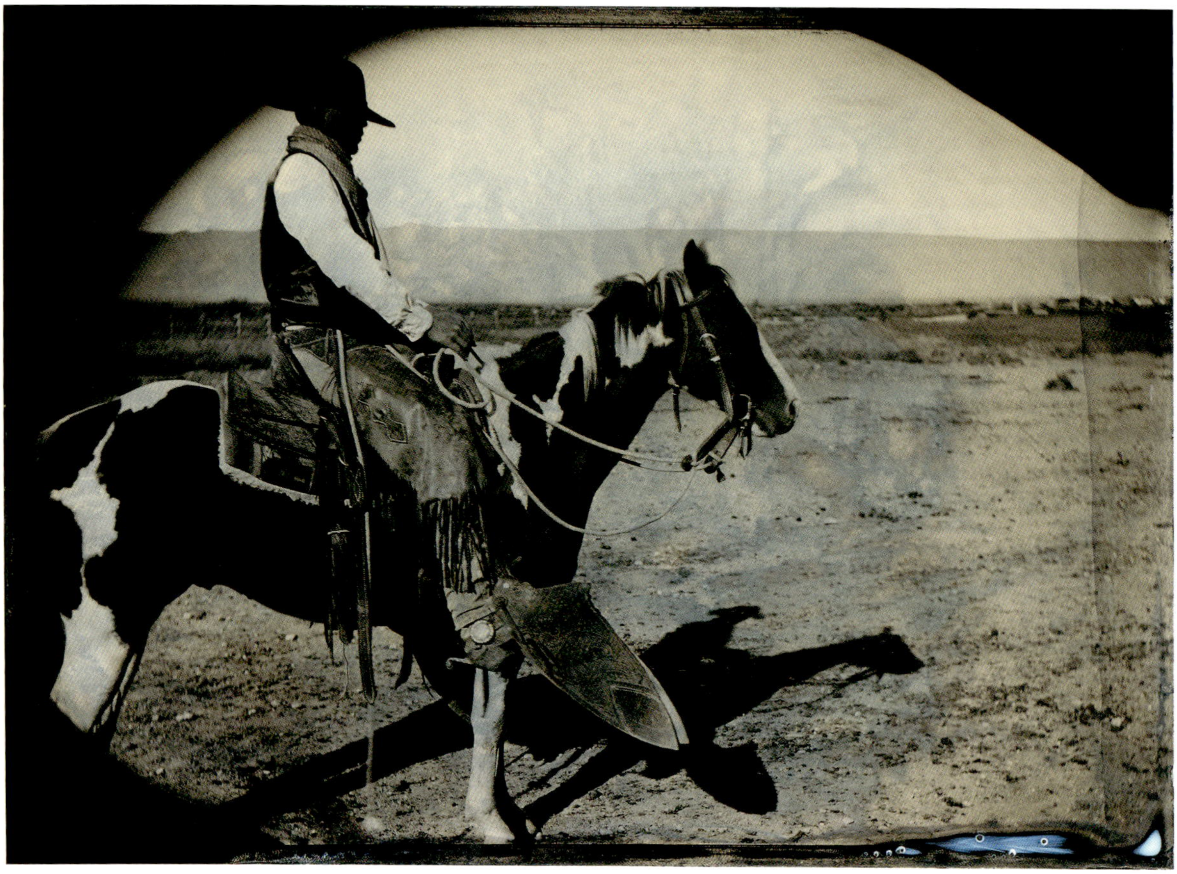

PLATE 66

Clint Damewood

ZX RANCH, OREGON

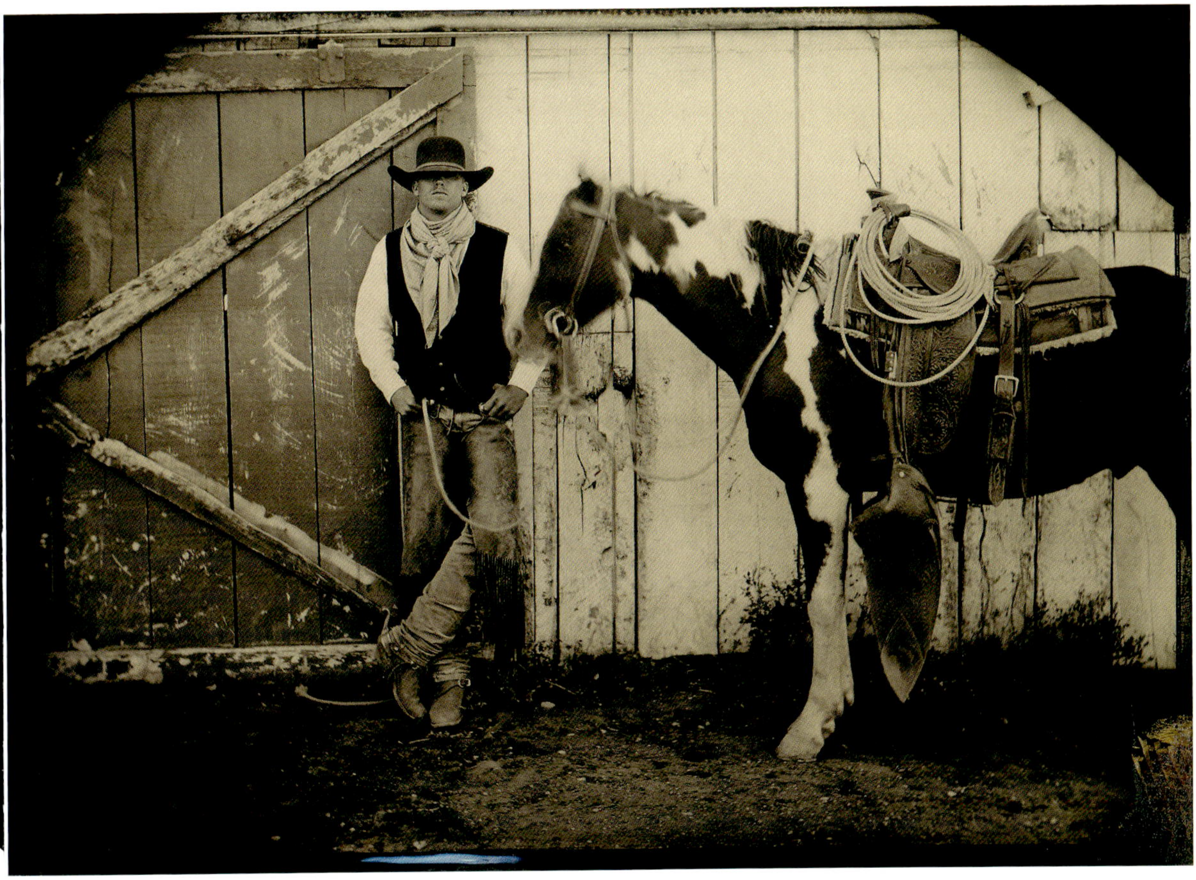

PLATE 67

Clint Damewood

ZX RANCH, OREGON

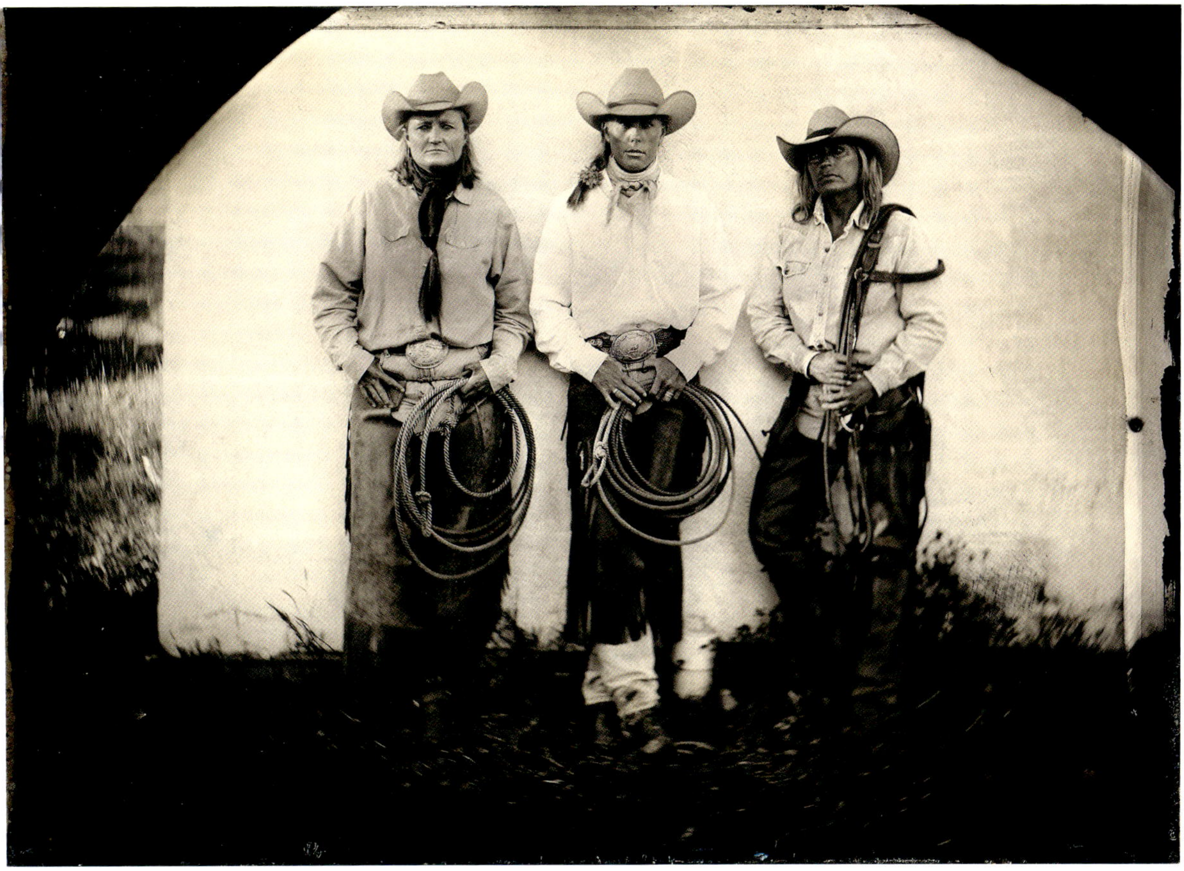

PLATE 70

Kelly Sullivan, Mitzi Goodman, Loriann Lindner

HAYTHORN LAND & CATTLE CO., NEBRASKA

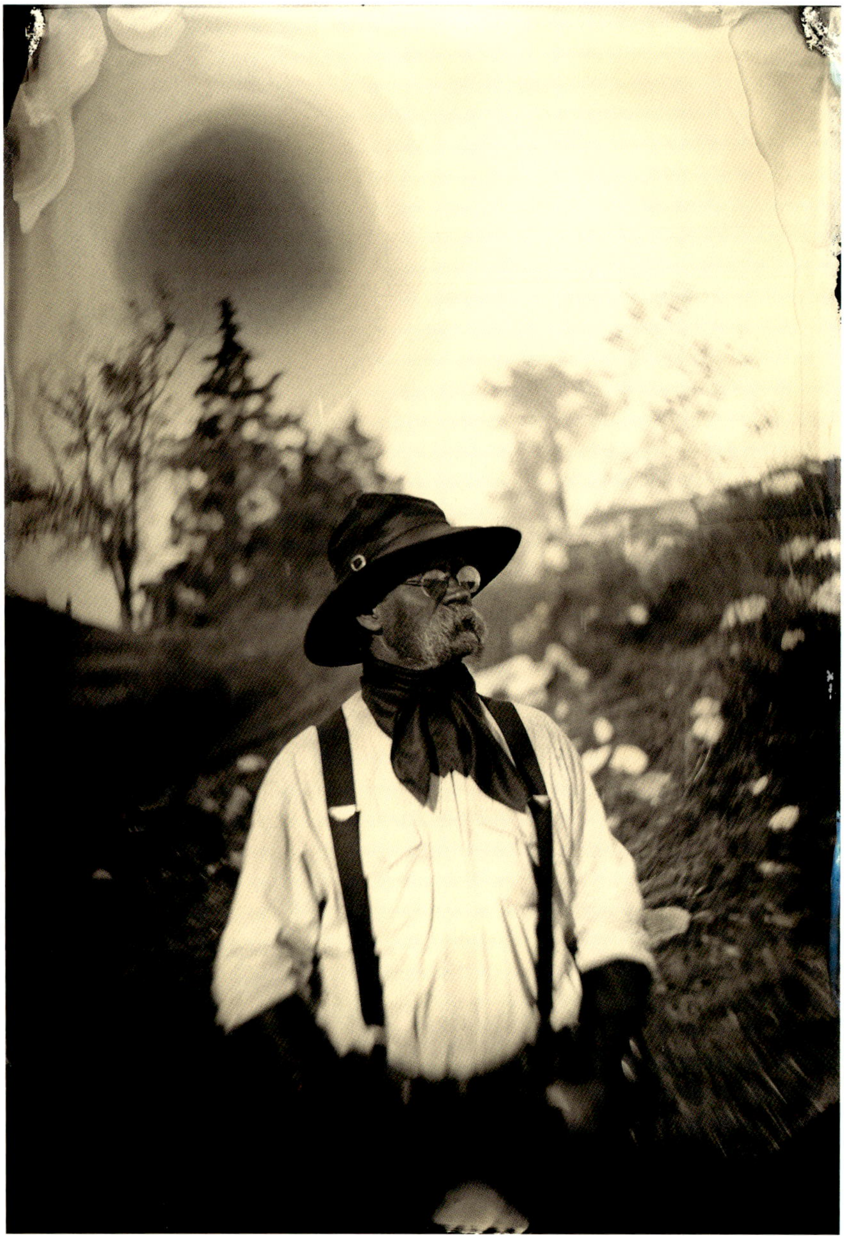

PLATE 71

David Ross

PITCHFORK RANCH, TEXAS

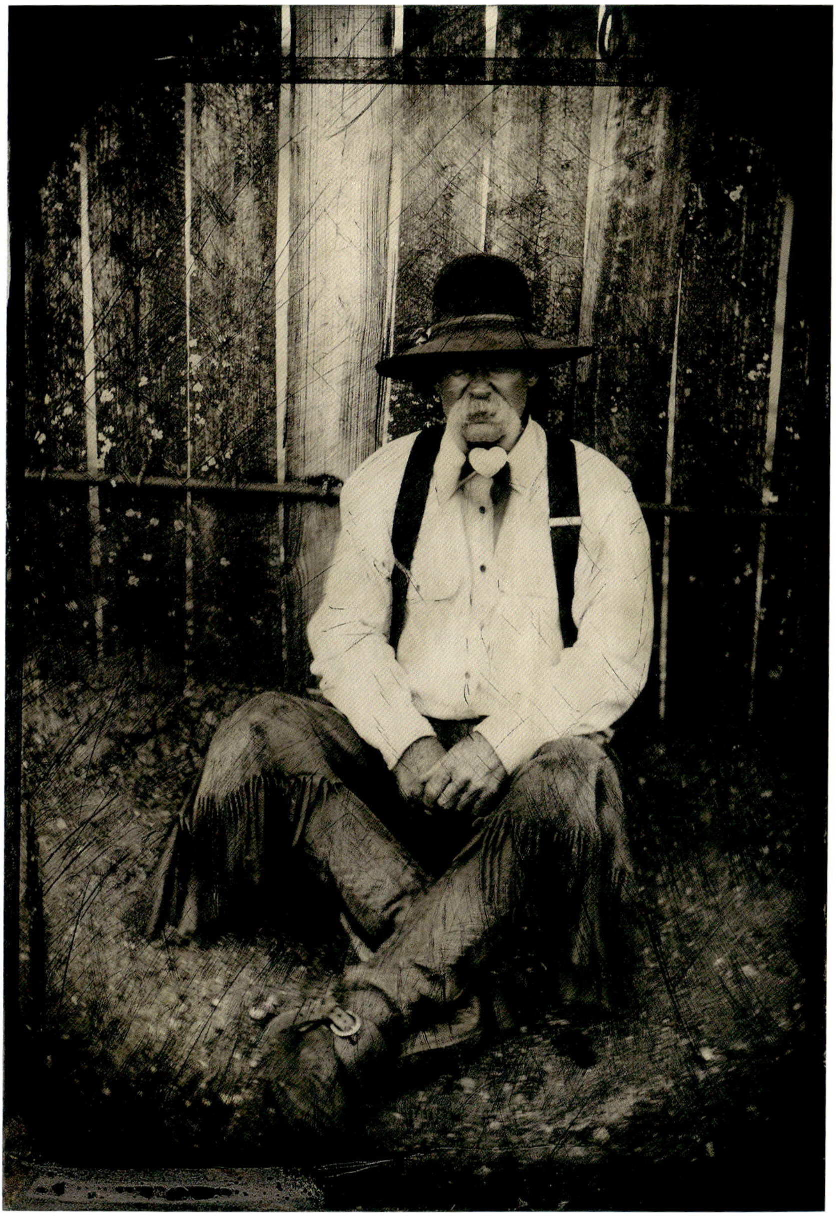

PLATE 72

David Ross

PITCHFORK RANCH, TEXAS

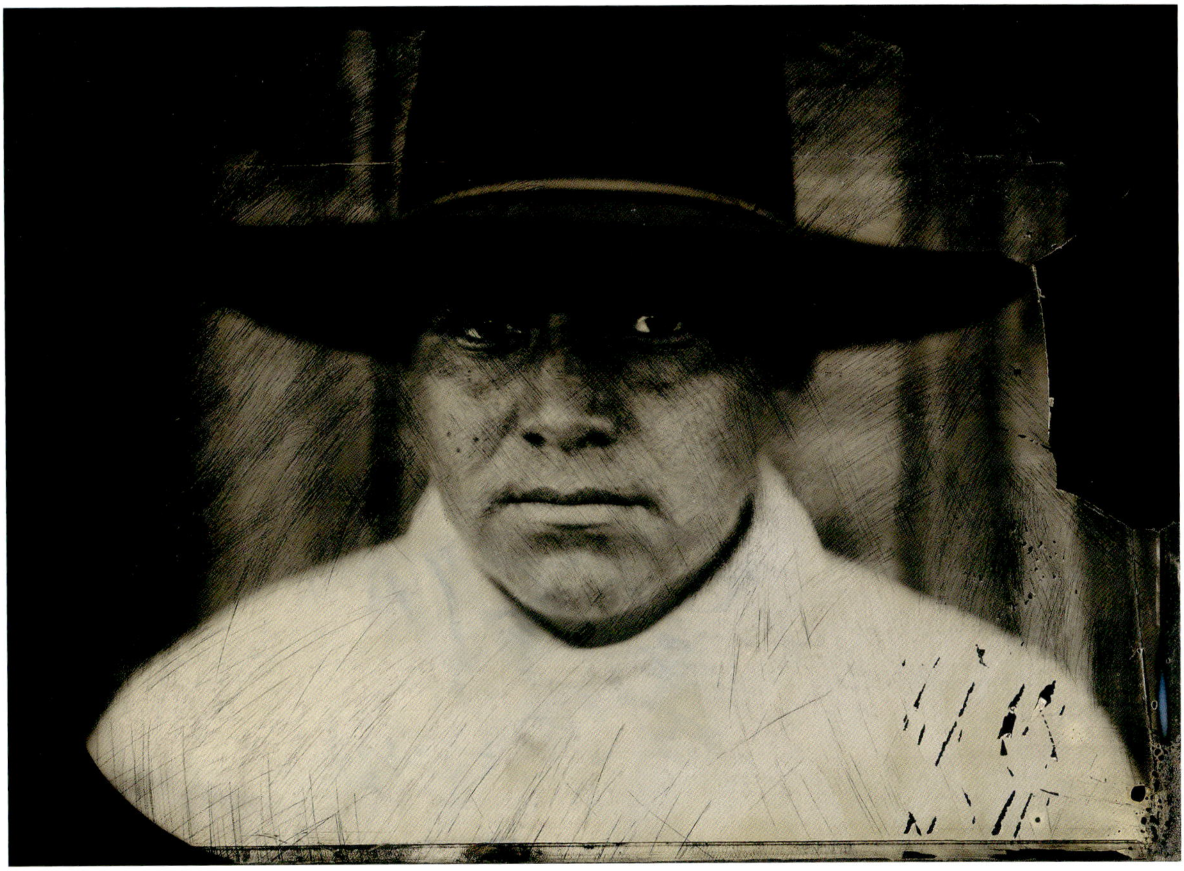

PLATE 73

Nathan Kelly, Jr.

DUCK VALLEY RESERVATION, NEVADA

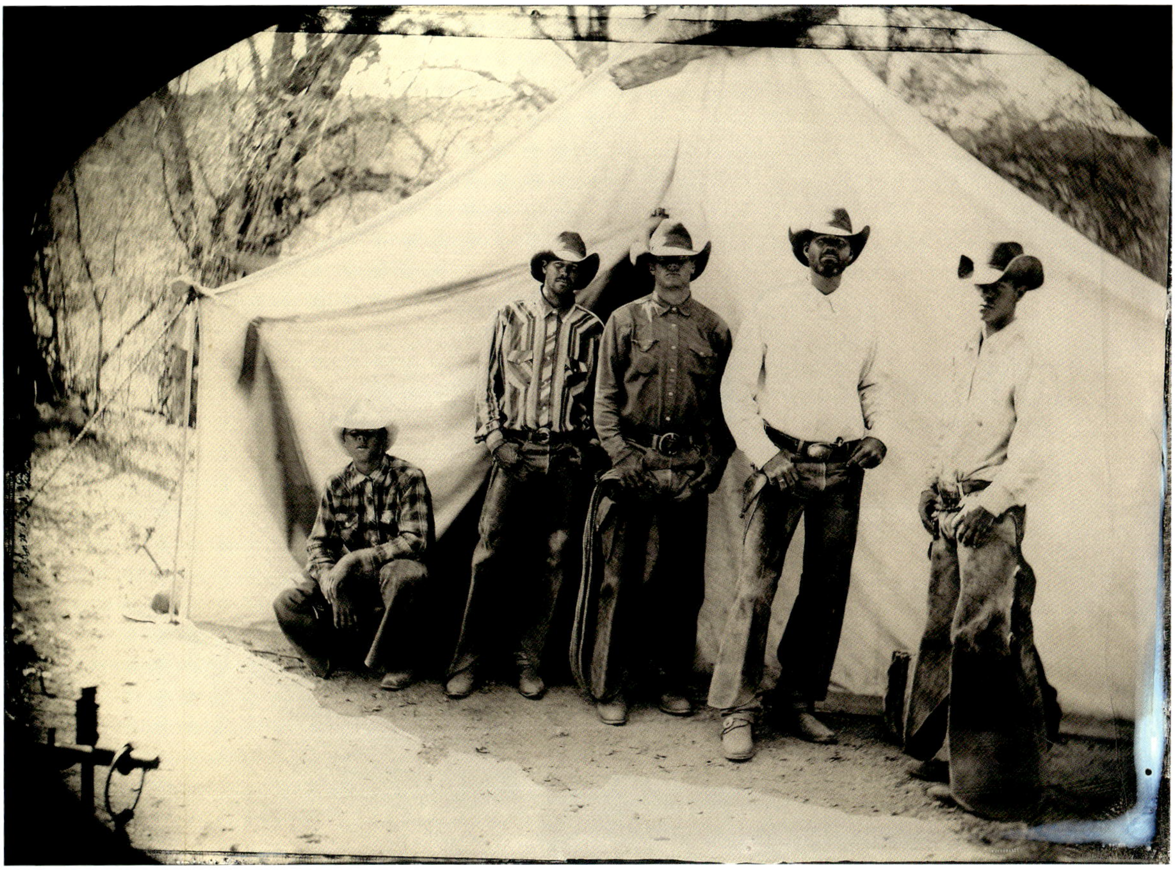

PLATE 74

Jake Prince, Toby Foote, Tim Mertzweiller, Wes Foote, Kyle Stone

ORO RANCH, ARIZONA

I never start as cowboy. My dad he work in paper mills in Quebec. My uncle had little farm, maybe fifty head, and I always been at his place and pass all summer there, work for him. That give me taste, I guess, and after that I always been in bush days off when I was in high school just hunting, fishing, or riding in bush. I been college for learning how to make farm, bookkeeping, and one my friends he work here. Every month he just call me, tell me all the story about place here. He was riding horse and push horses and was look nice and just kinda piss me off every time he call me. I say want to go there, and one winter he just came back and said, "Come with me; let's go," and I said, "I don't know, Pete." My girlfriend's here and she just look at me and said, "Yeah, if you want to go, go ahead." I just turned around and said, "Pete, call your boss, I'm going." I say good-bye my girlfriend. I was supposed to just come here for a few months, six months, maybe a year, cause go back my girlfriend, but I guess 5,000 clicks, long way for relationship and that never work out and so I'm stay here now three years and a half, just about four years now.

I like country here better. For the winter I'm just watch, take care, what, 800 cow and I just by myself. It's two months straight. I got days off for Christmas, but I don't come out every week. I pass by myself two months straight there and take care of them cow, and I like that. Sure it's not always funny you go ride at minus 20 and the wind blow. But I shoot stuff around like wolf. Last year, wolf try and kill a calf and cow and I scared them but two face me up but I saw fourteen that day, and day after I try to go back there and shoot them and they were all there fourteen again. We got lots of trouble with wolf.

If I go back home, I got nothing to do. It will be boring. Back home again you got horse to do some trail ride, some rodeo, but you don't push cow with them. It's way different—everything. I go back home for my holiday and I just go shopping with my dad in store and I just look like alien. Everybody just turn around and just look at me, and my daddy just laugh and laugh. Back home don't have flat hat like mine. It's buckaroo style; it looks like I'm all Western and I like the way it is.

MAXIME GAUTHIER
GANG RANCH, BRITISH COLUMBIA, CANADA

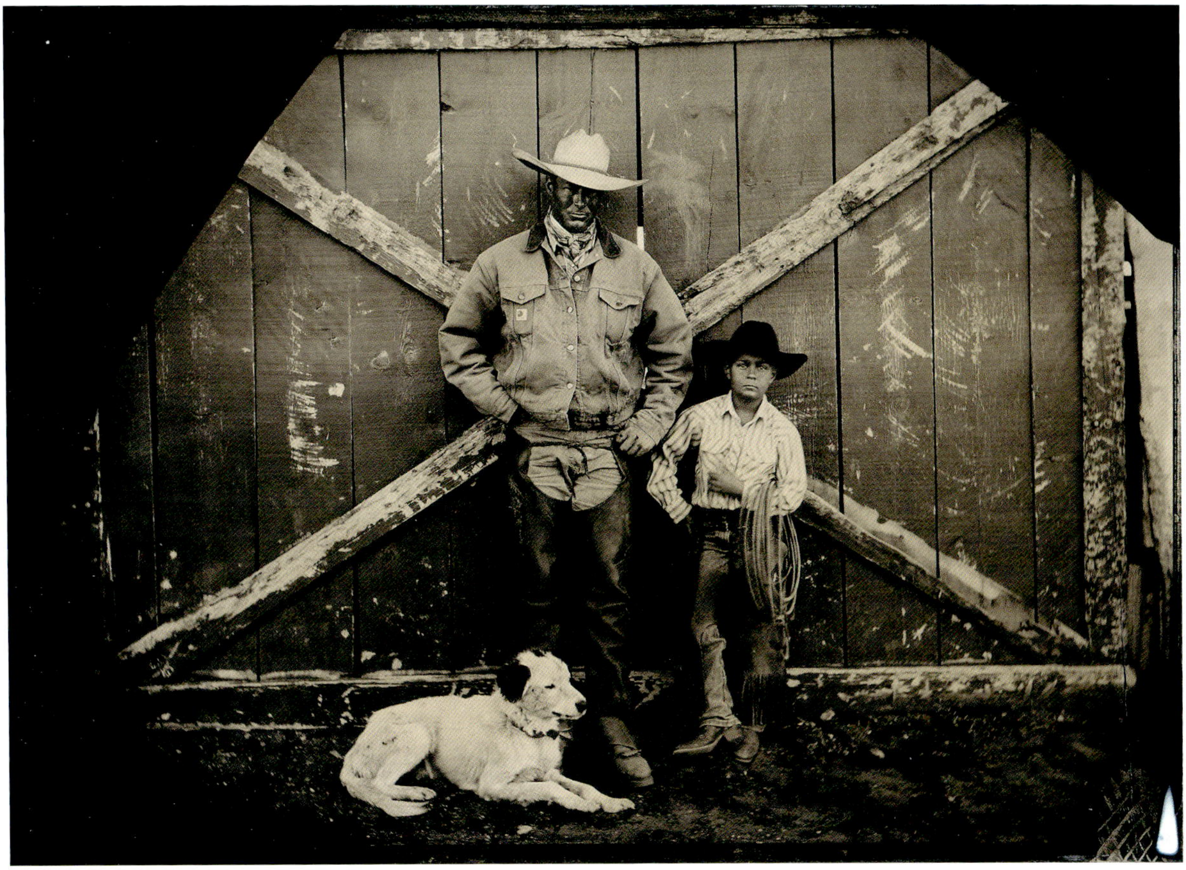

PLATE 75

Cleve and Quentin Anseth, with Gus

ZX RANCH, OREGON

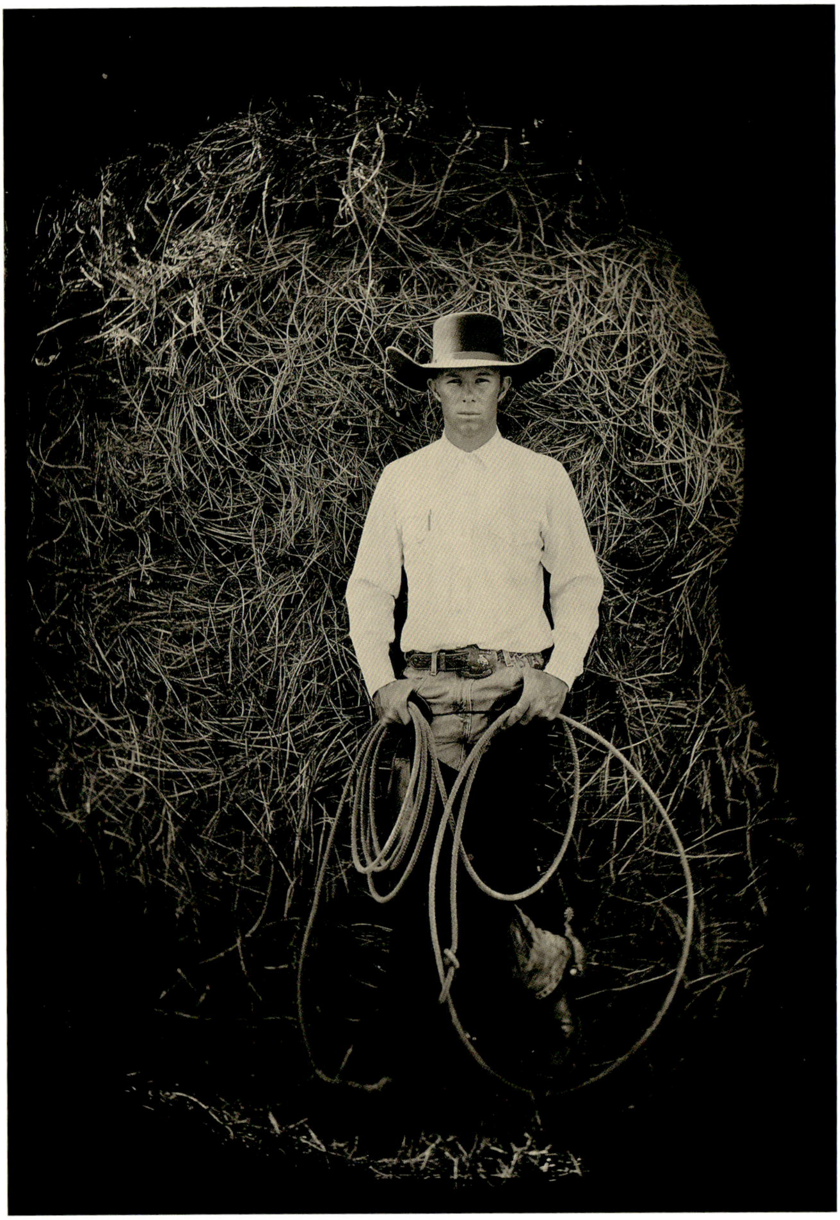

PLATE 76

Jessie Hefner

HAYTHORN LAND & CATTLE CO., NEBRASKA

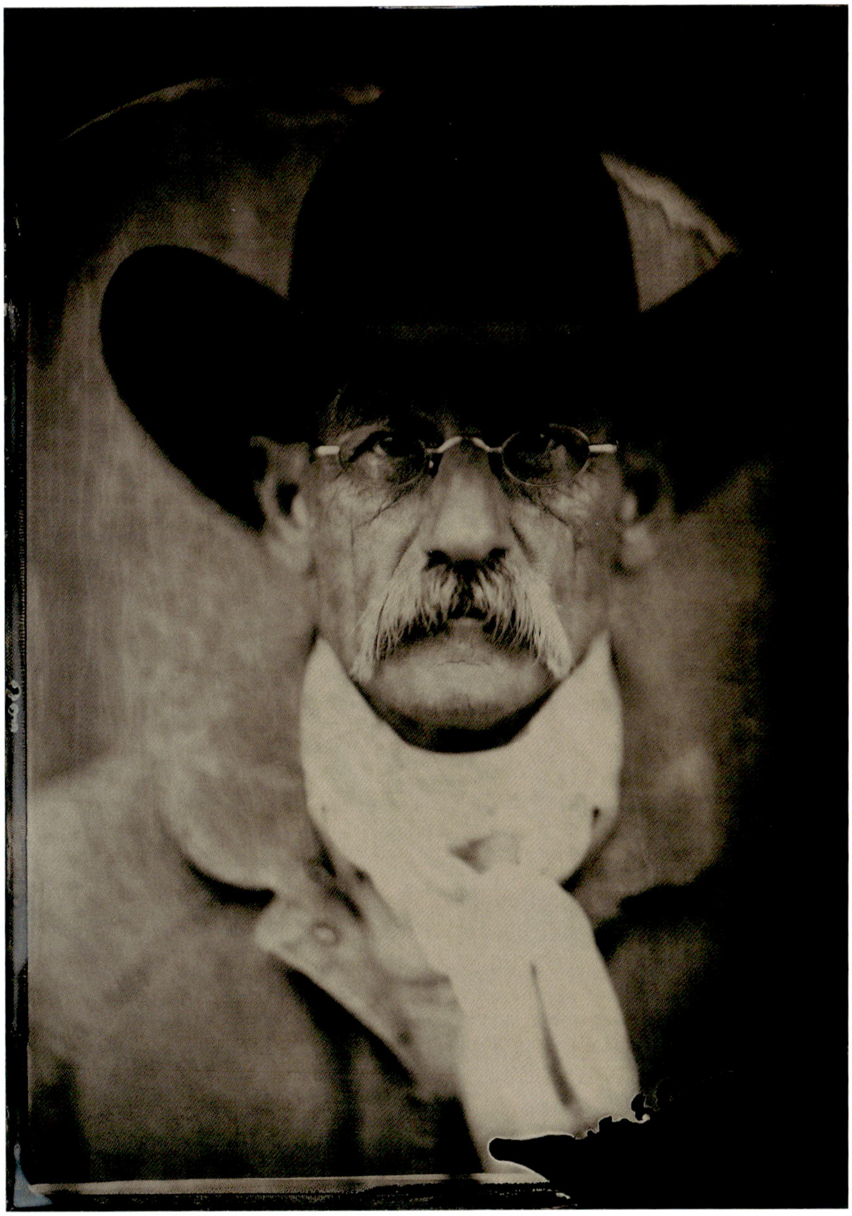

PLATE 77

Gary Loveland

V4 LAND & CATTLE CO., NEW MEXICO

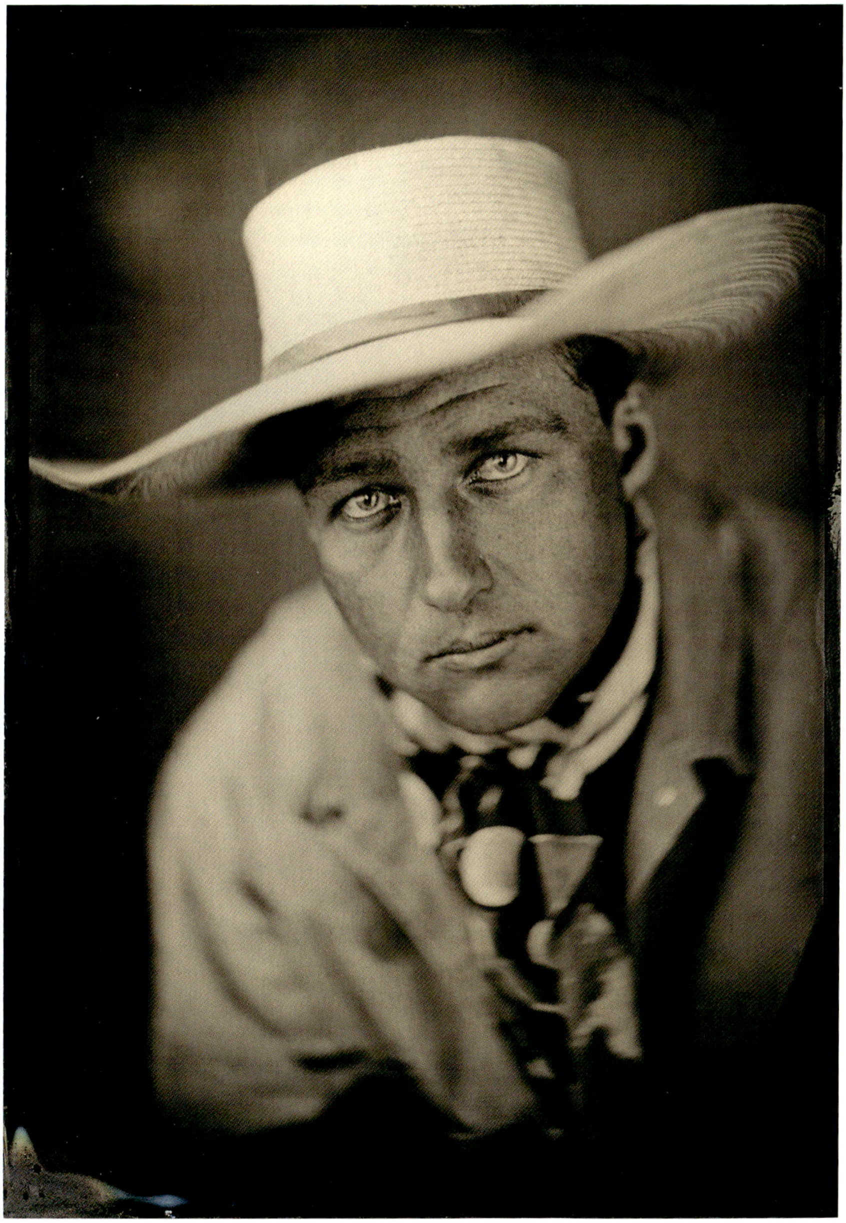

PLATE 81

Jim Young

SPANISH RANCH, NEVADA

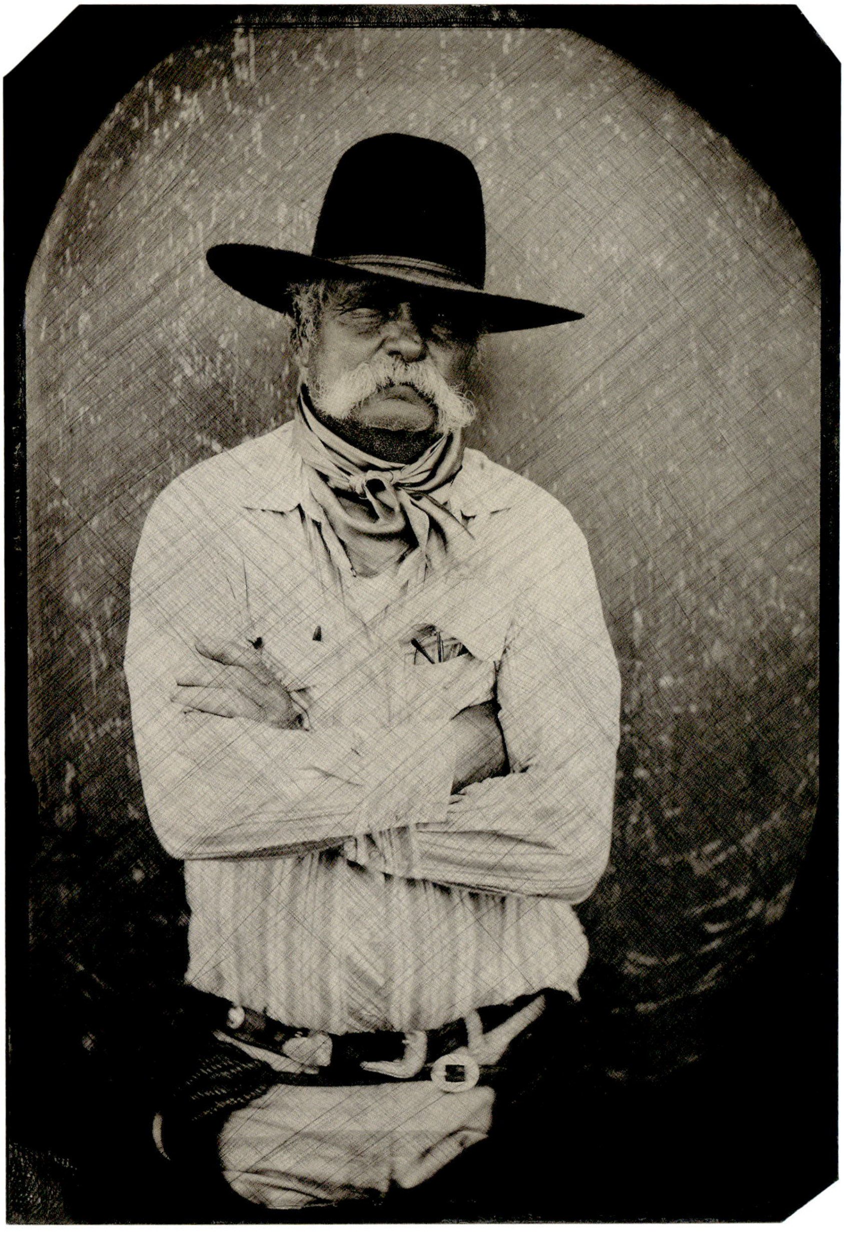

PLATE 82

Monk Maxwell

HOOFS & HORNS LIVESTOCK, ARIZONA

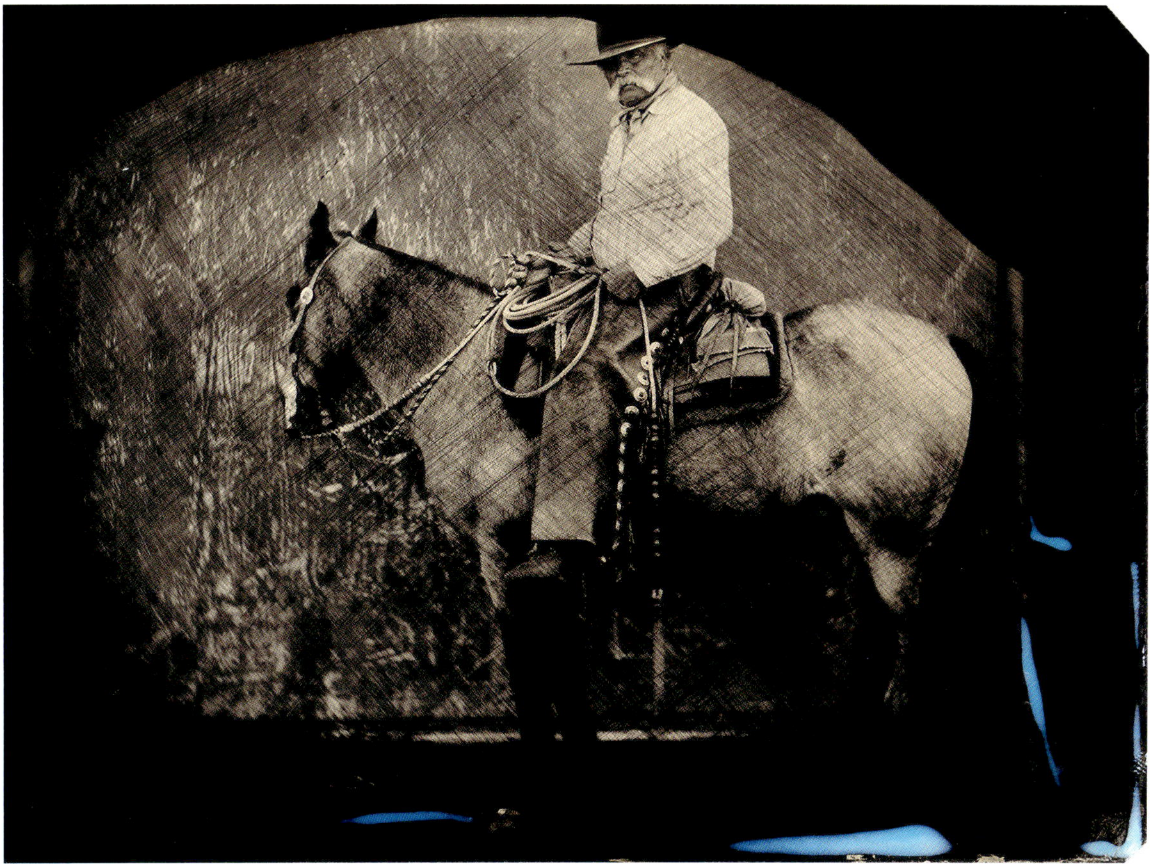

PLATE 83

Monk Maxwell

HOOFS & HORNS LIVESTOCK, ARIZONA

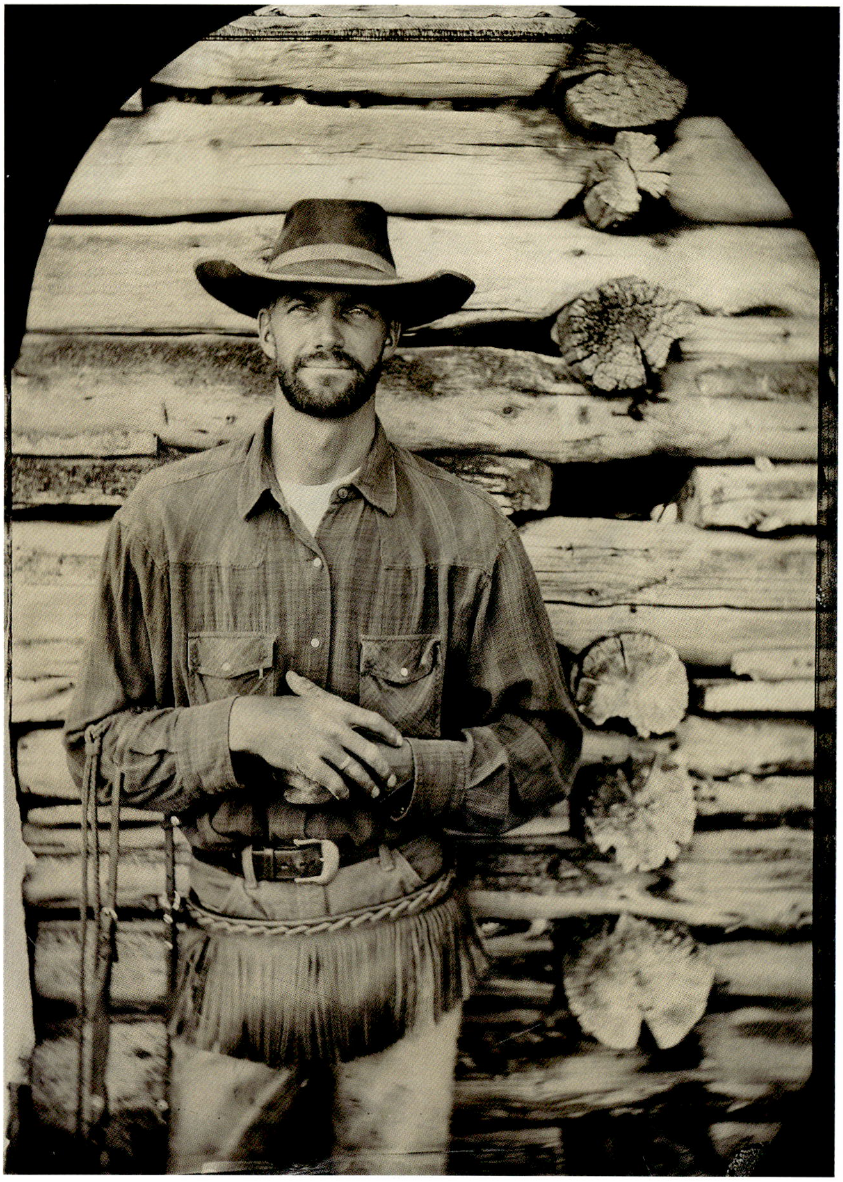

PLATE 84

Ira Wines

SPANISH RANCH, NEVADA

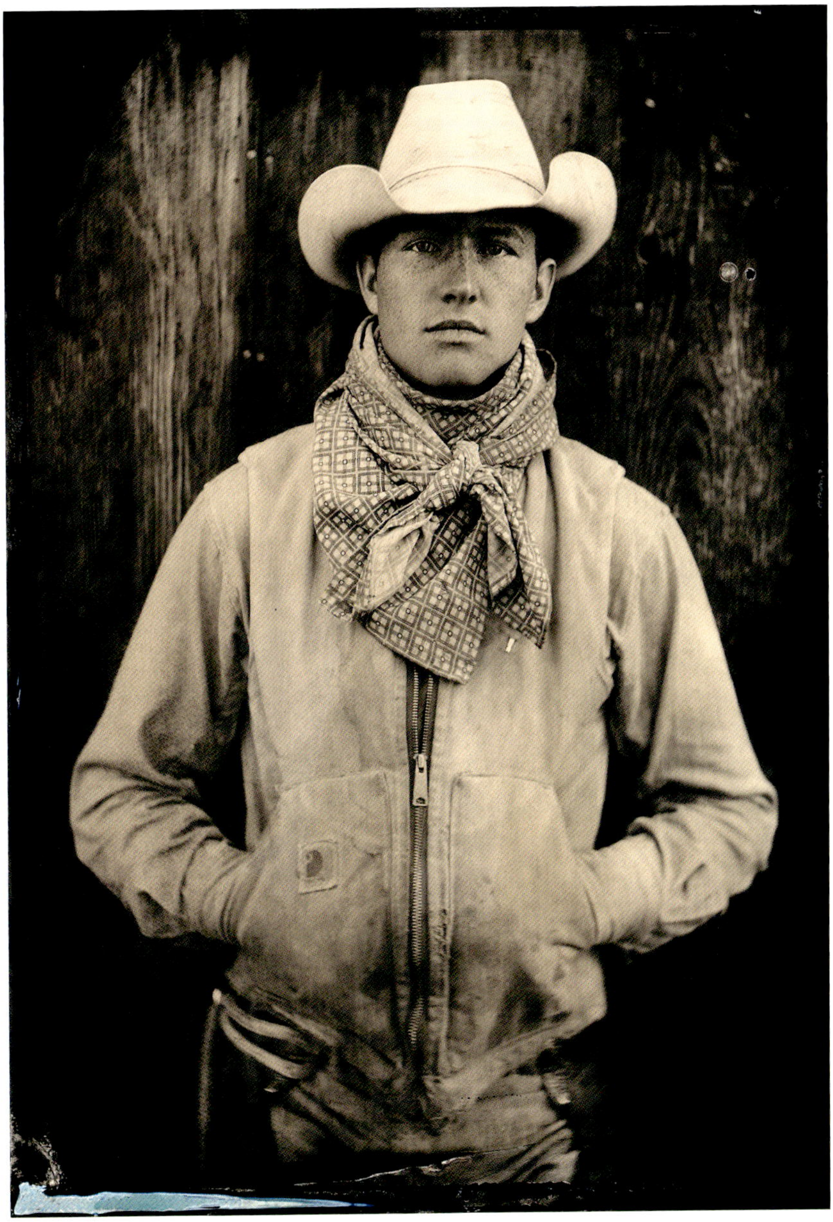

PLATE 85

Cameron Jacobs

DOUGLAS LAKE RANCH, BRITISH COLUMBIA, CANADA

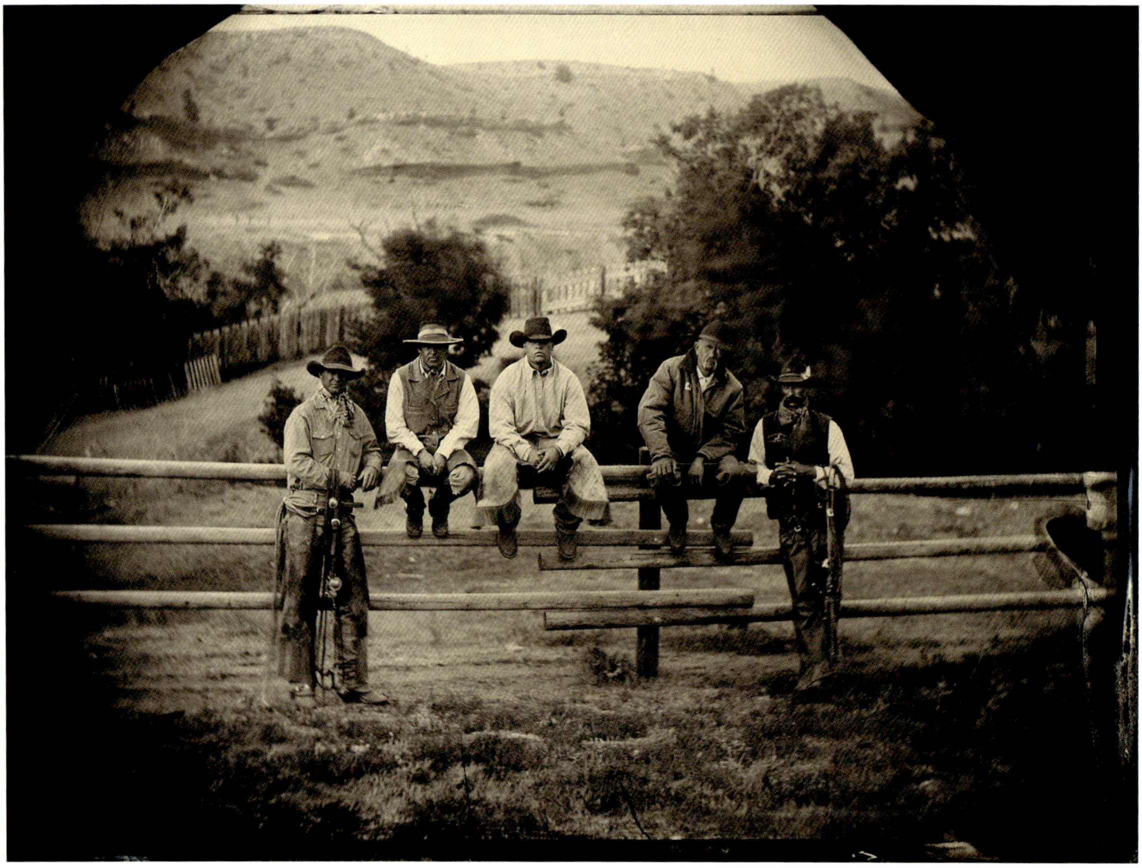

PLATE 86

Scott Arnold, Skeeter Redding, Silas Ivory, Royce Hanson, Martin Anseth
EZ RANCH, MONTANA

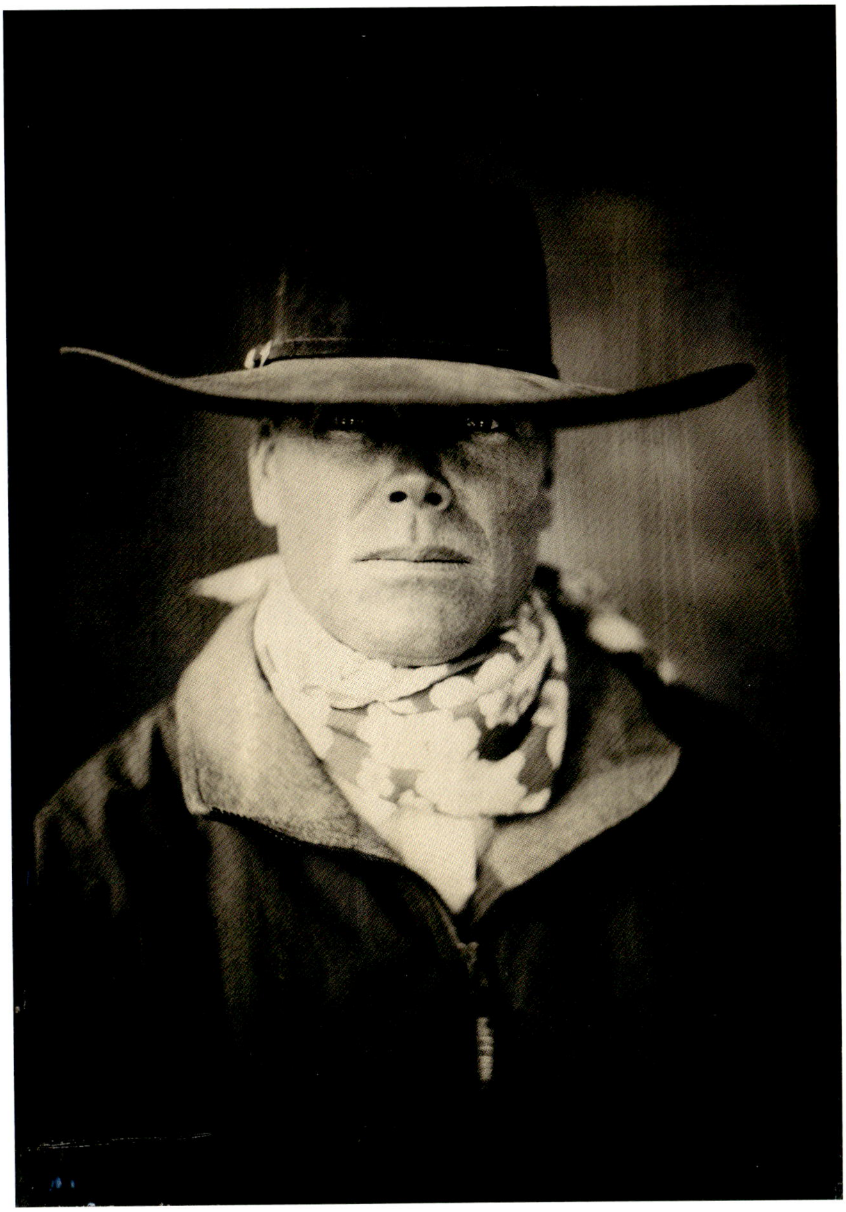

PLATE 87

B. J. Wachob

WACHOB RANCH, NEBRASKA

My mother, when I was a little boy, she didn't think I was gonna talk, and most kids say "mommy" and "daddy" at least by the time they're two, but I wasn't sayin' nothin' and my mother was really worried. But one day they was drivin' a bunch of cows and horses down the road, you know, and I see these horses goin' by, and I said, "Mommy, a horse!" So she knew that there wasn't anything wrong with me. But all the little she knew, there was a lot wrong with me, cause anyway the horses have been in my mind ever since, and I'm goin' on seventy years old. My dad told me one time when I was about nine, he said, "Well, why don't you just chop your damn head open; it'll be full of horses." I haven't changed too much. My world has always consisted of horses and cows and cows and horses.

I got a diploma in the school of hard knocks and I'm very proud of it. I don't read and write very good, but I enjoy the life that most people just dream about. I've been a buckaroo and I'm very proud of it. There's cowboys and gauchos and punchers and everything, but a buckaroo, in my opinion, is king. He takes pride in all that he does. Not only the way he dresses, the way he handles himself. He takes pride in his horse. I never leave the barn without a moustache knot tied in my horse's tail. A lot of people ride the horses, their tail a-draggin' like some old wild mare. Gee, don't they care anything about 'em?

Buckaroos have nice long reatas; they have horsehair McCartys [reins]; they have silver-mounted spurs and silver-mounted bridles, you know. And a lot of people from the south, they don't take that kind of pride in their stuff; though they do a good job, they just don't have no pride. An old guy told me one time when I was a kid, he said you look at a man's outfit and you can tell where he come from and you can tell what kind of a cowboy he is. It's true; it's true.

One time back in the '60s I shaved my moustache off and my oldest daughter, I scared her. She didn't know who I was, so I swore if I ever put it back on, I'm gonna take it to the grave and I'm not shavin' it off. I'm not shavin' it off. It's been a lot longer than it is now, and I get off to open a gate and some gates have a wire around the post to shut the gate, and you get your 'stache hooked in there and you turn around and take off but it jerks you right back there really fast. So it's not always where it's supposed to be.

Being a buckaroo means great freedom. It's no man owns you, you know, no man owns you. No words can describe it. I worked in a sawmill one time. It lasted one day. I worked on a railroad one time. That only lasted one day. And the rest of the time, I spent my time on horseback. The smell is just—it's like heaven. One time when I was at the YP before I got all crippled up, I was out

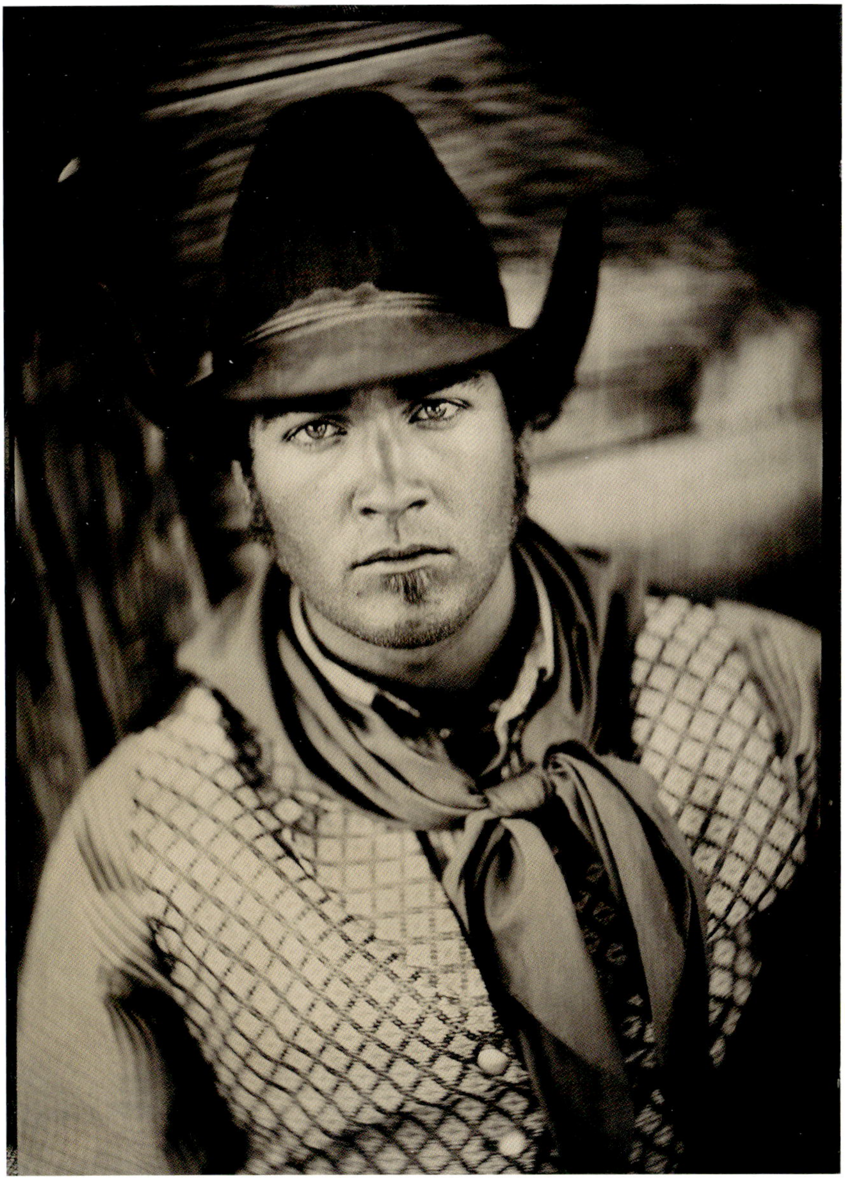

PLATE 88

J. B. Kessler

DIAMOND A RANCH, ARIZONA

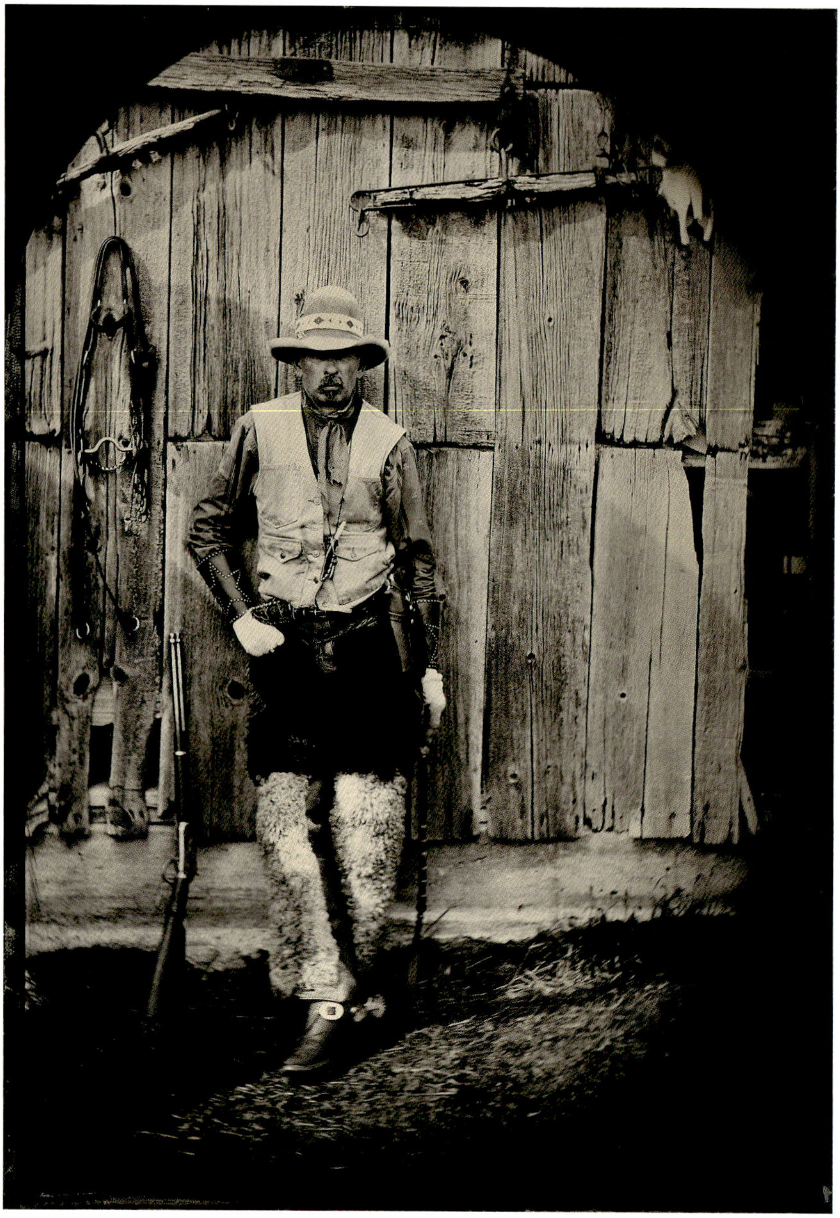

PLATE 89

Tom Kelly

THE COCKLEBUR, NEBRASKA

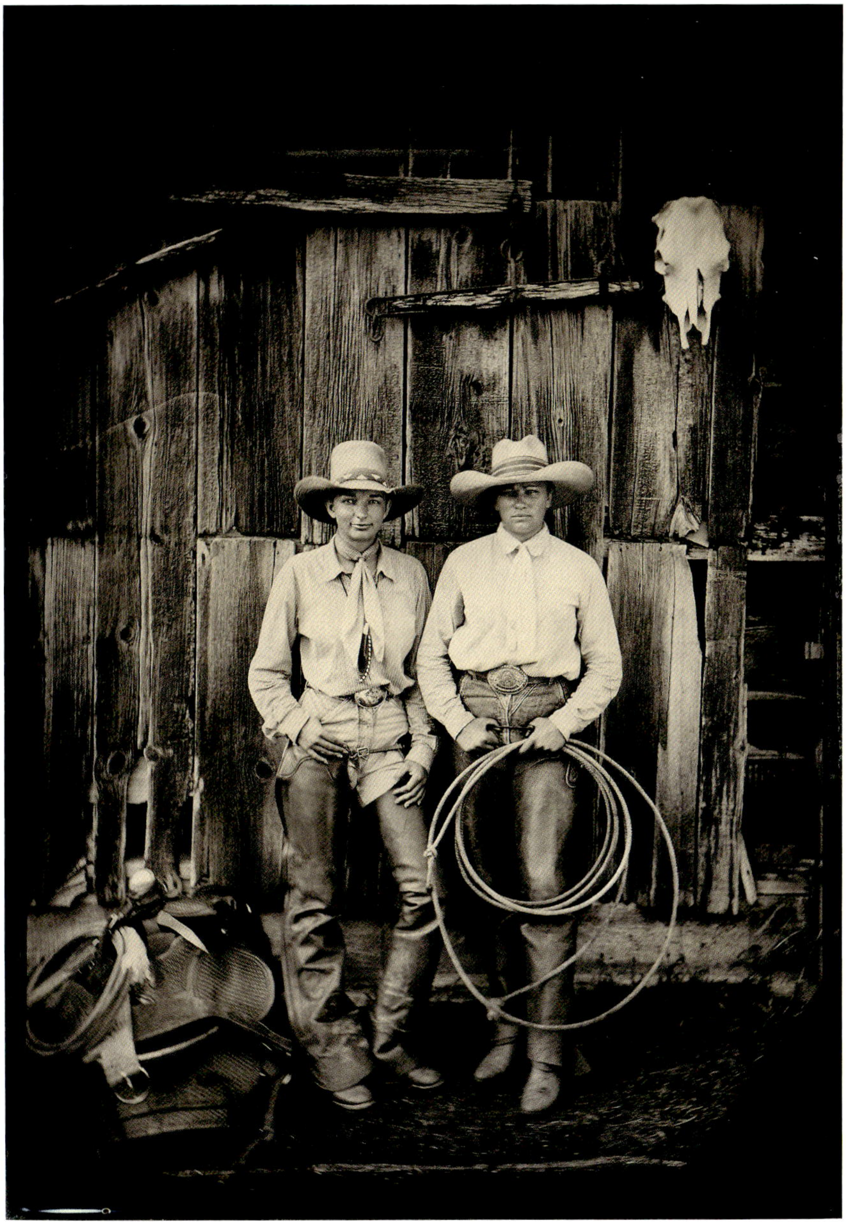

PLATE 90

Mary Ann and Katherine Kelly

THE COCKLEBUR, NEBRASKA

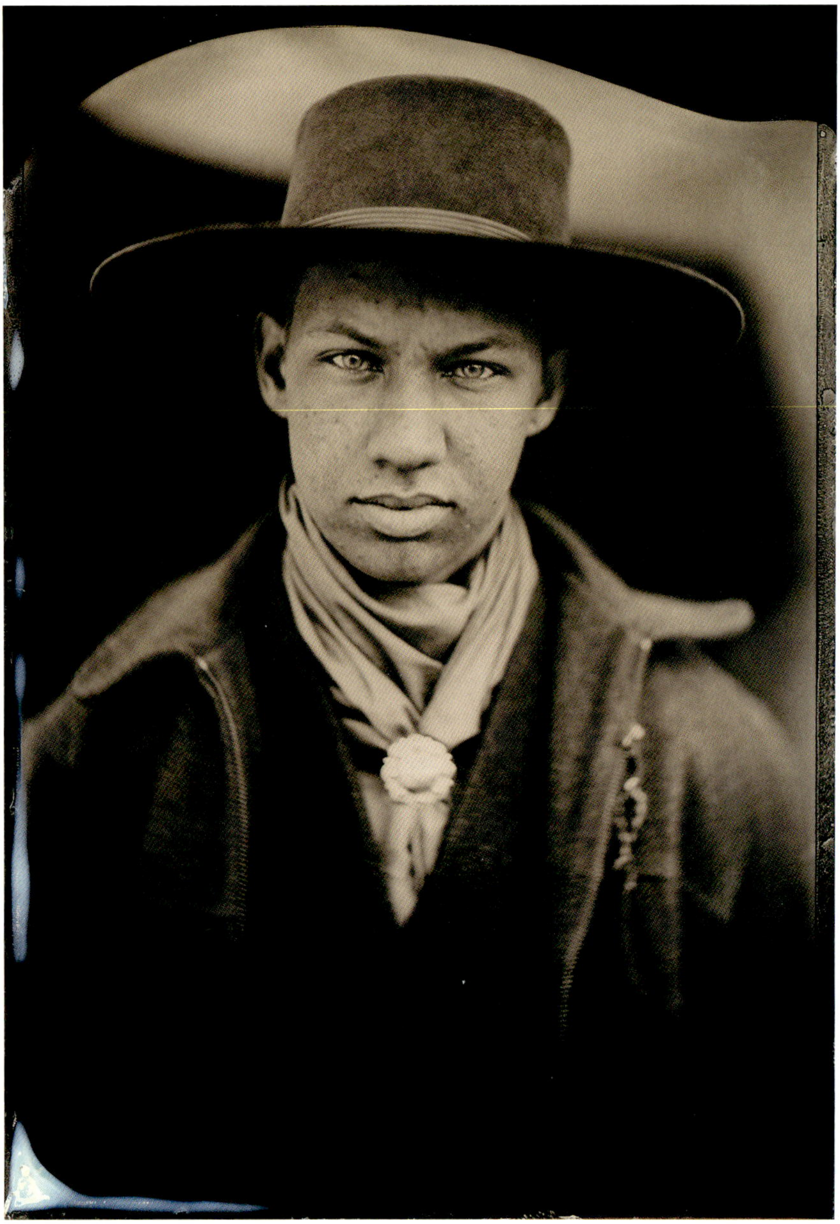

PLATE 91

Jason Rebitzke

BUTTE CREEK RANCH, OREGON

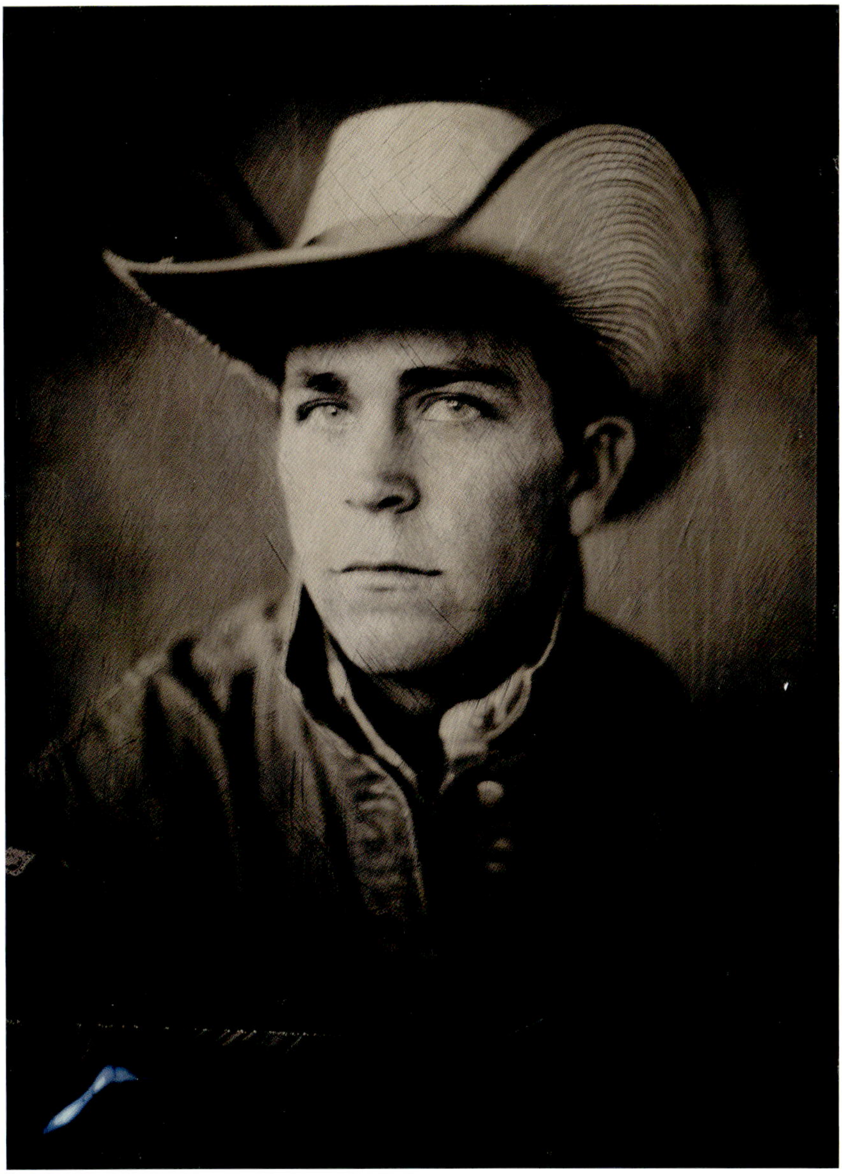

PLATE 92

Justin Gibbs

SPRIGGS STABLES, NEW MEXICO

there, fifty miles from the ranch headquarters and had about 200 head of cows and some calves and was comin' up this Trail of Tears and I got up on top and the cows, I let them stop, and there was some little calves suckin' and then layin' down. I just sat on my horse and I looked down. Gosh, I was right in the middle of God's flower garden. The wildflowers were just everywhere. The smell was so great. And I couldn't help but say, "Thank you, Lord; thank you, Lord, for just lettin' me be out there."

[After his horse fell on him] they told me I could never buckaroo again, you know. The doctor come in and told me I'd never ride horse again. I said, "Just cut off my head. I don't want to live. Bye." They said we're not gonna cut off your head, so I went on there. After I got hurt, the first three years I really didn't want to live. If I couldn't be a-horseback and buckaroo, what else could I do? Thank God I learned to braid a little rawhide. I've always made rawhide reatas in the wintertime, you know. Always liked to have rawhide reatas to pack on my saddle; I like to break in a brand new rawhide reata and when it's good and broke in and then you go out with the wagon and brand cows in June. I liked horsehair McCartys too, so I learned to make them.

There's a style of bein' a real buckaroo, a cowman, you know, knowin' his livestock, and the people don't do that today. They have ear tags in their ears, of all things, to know which cow's which. "Oh, that's #71, that's #44." They don't know one cow from another. It's terrible. It's terrible.

A good friend of mine, Ron Moore, said they'll never make a machine as tough as a buckaroo. Take the punishment, the cold, and the abuse. You know, a buckaroo, he rides on bad horses and gets crippled up and he's out in the cold, you know. I've been out when it's fifty below zero, you know, and spent my whole day out there. I've had my ears froze. My right ear—it's just by the grace of God I have a right ear.

I'm a very godly man, but I don't like to go to church cause I don't—those people don't wear hats. They don't wear hats. They don't love their God any more than I love my God. But they dress different, and I just don't want to be around 'em. I like to be around my kind.

MERLIN RUPP
OREGON

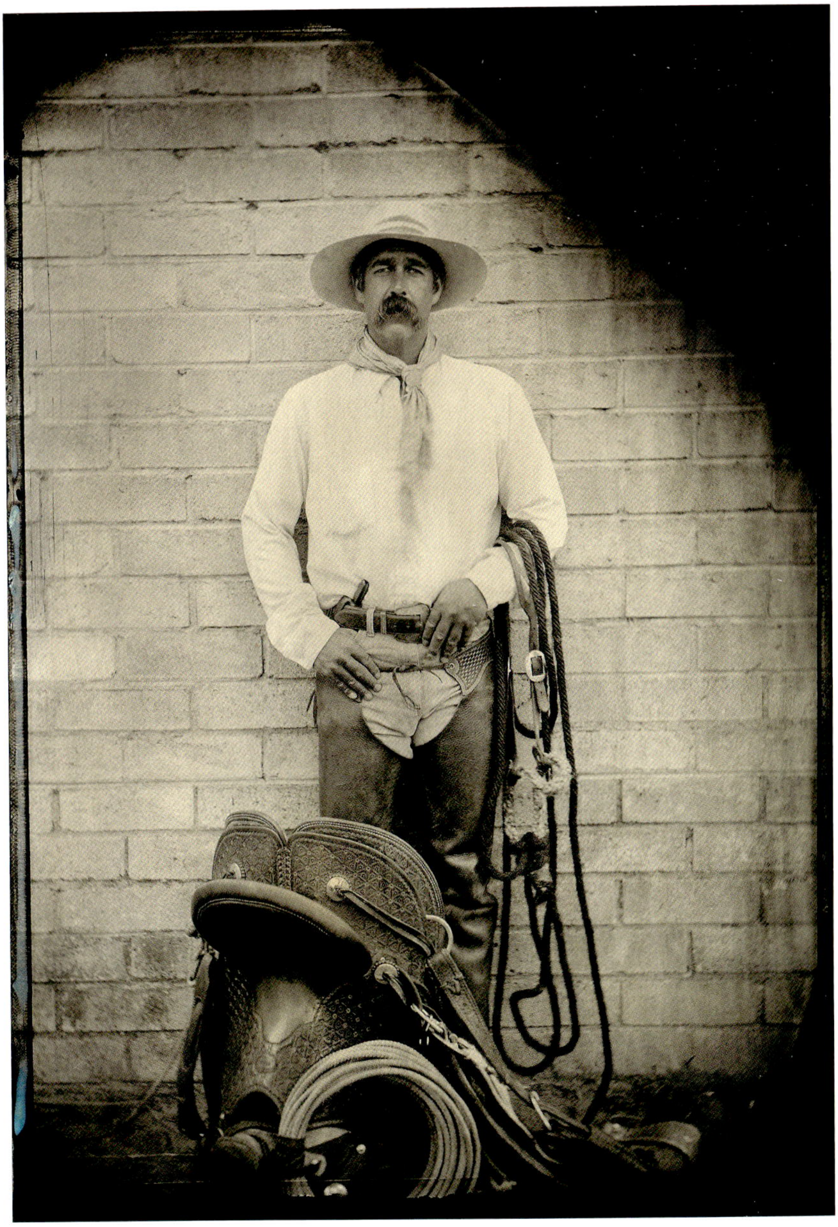

PLATE 93

Justin Bradley

RHOADES LAND & CATTLE CO., NEBRASKA

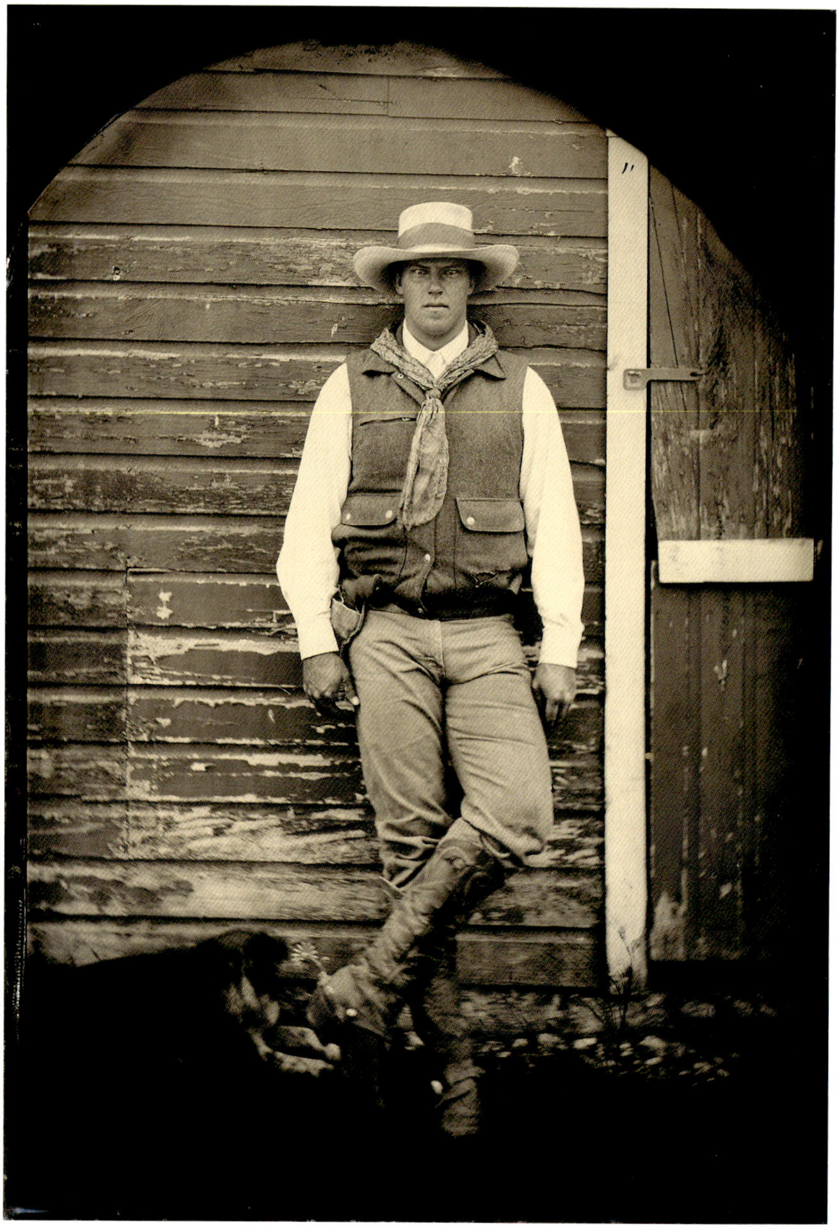

PLATE 94

Sam States

PADLOCK RANCH, WYOMING

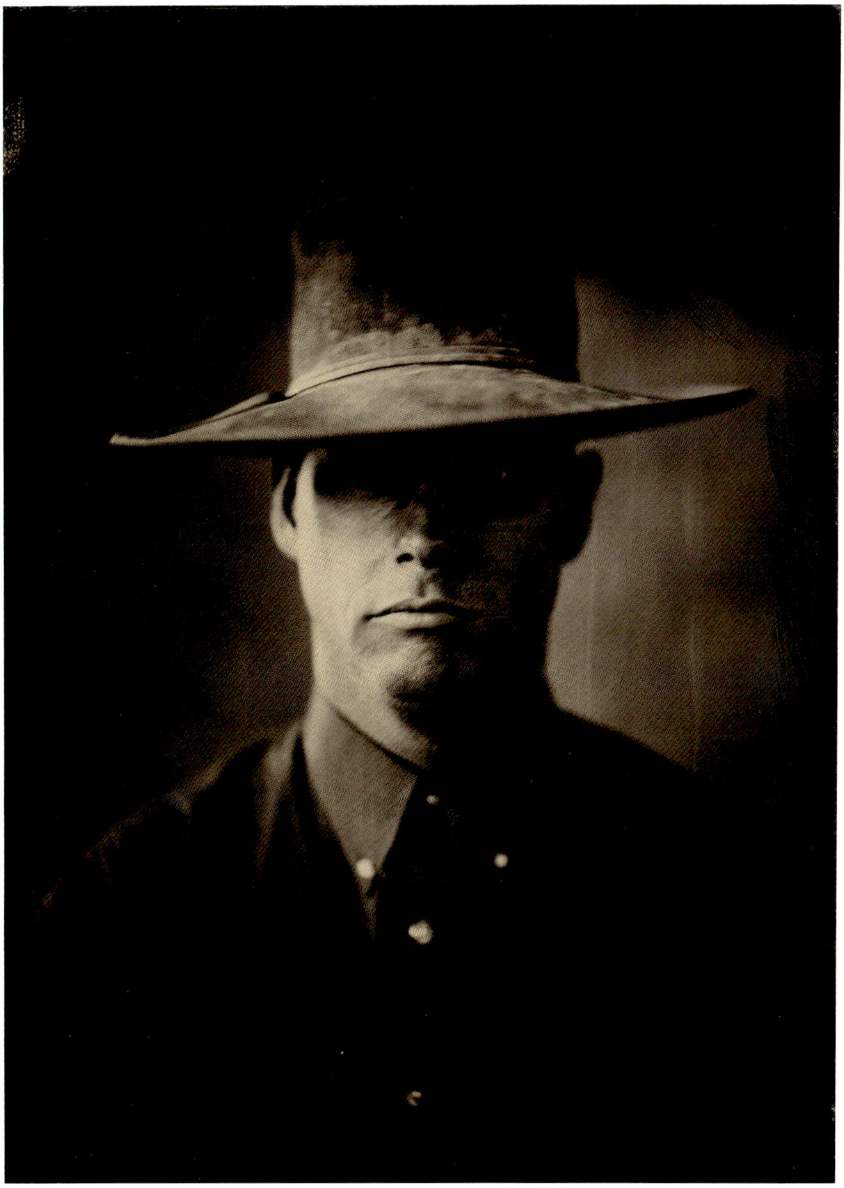

PLATE 95

D. W. Fowler

FLYING M RANCH, NEVADA

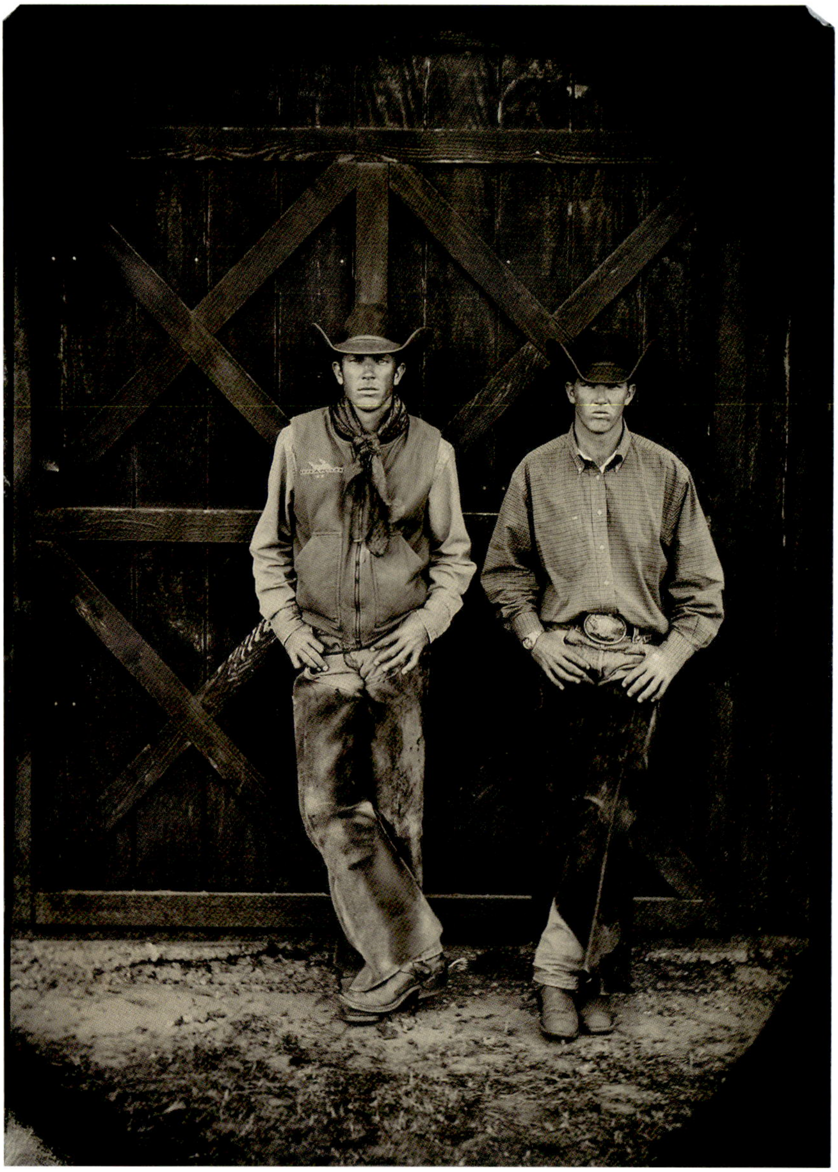

PLATE 96

Hunter Meinzer, Pate Meinzer

TONGUE RIVER RANCH, TEXAS

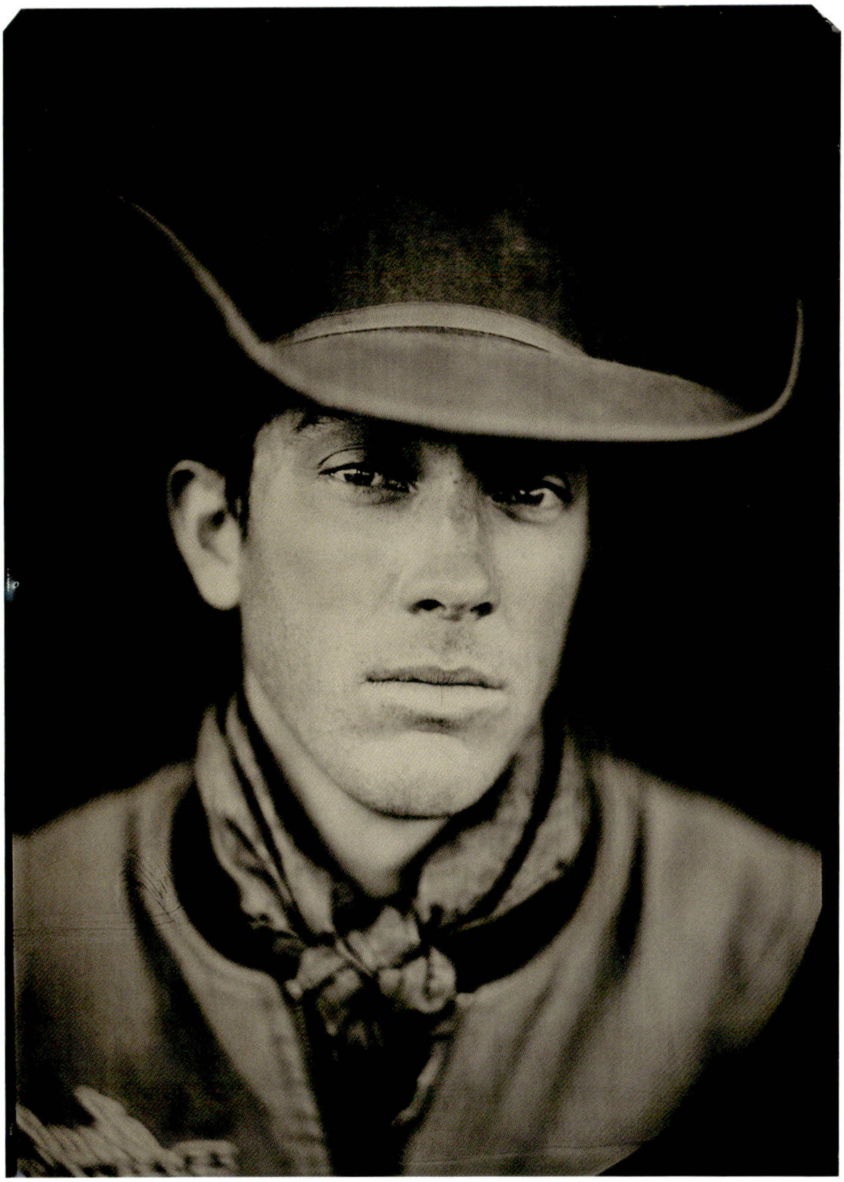

PLATE 97

Hunter Meinzer

TONGUE RIVER RANCH, TEXAS

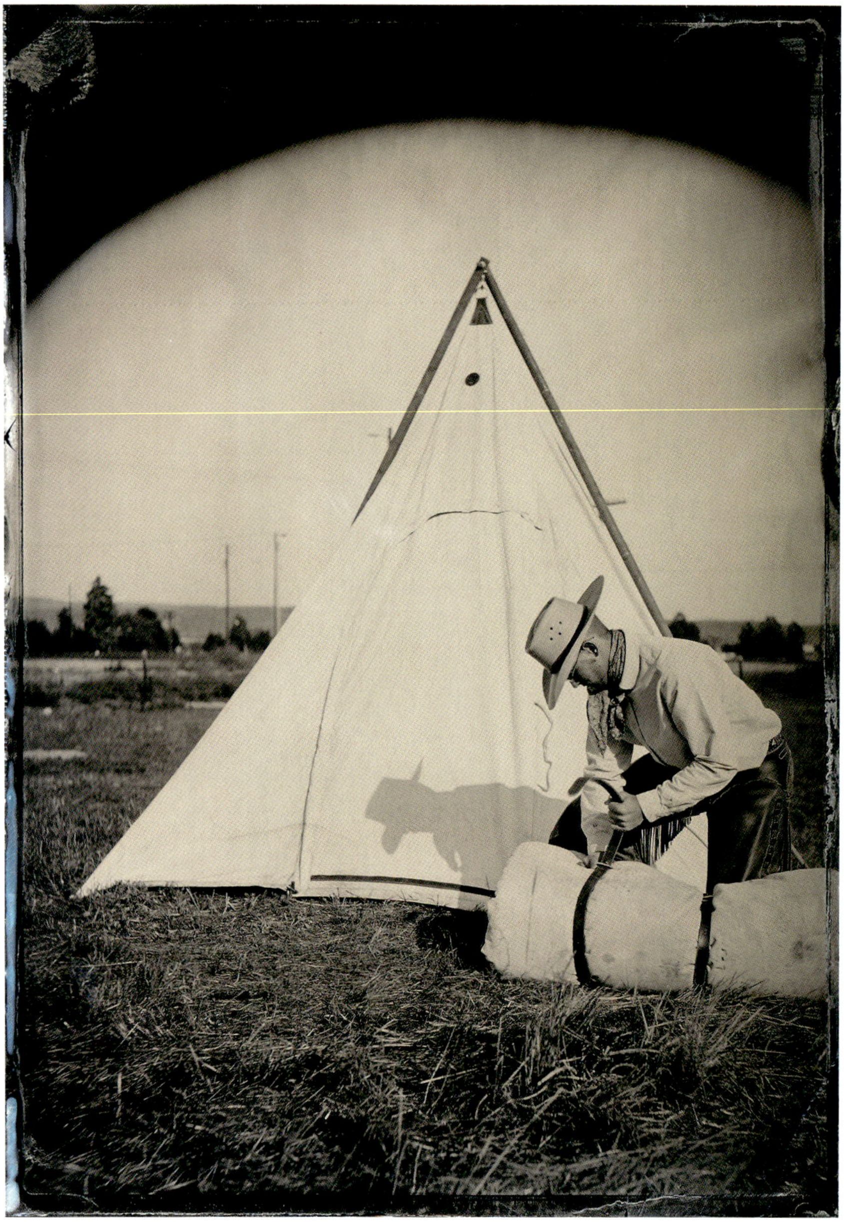

PLATE 98

John Wright

NEVADA

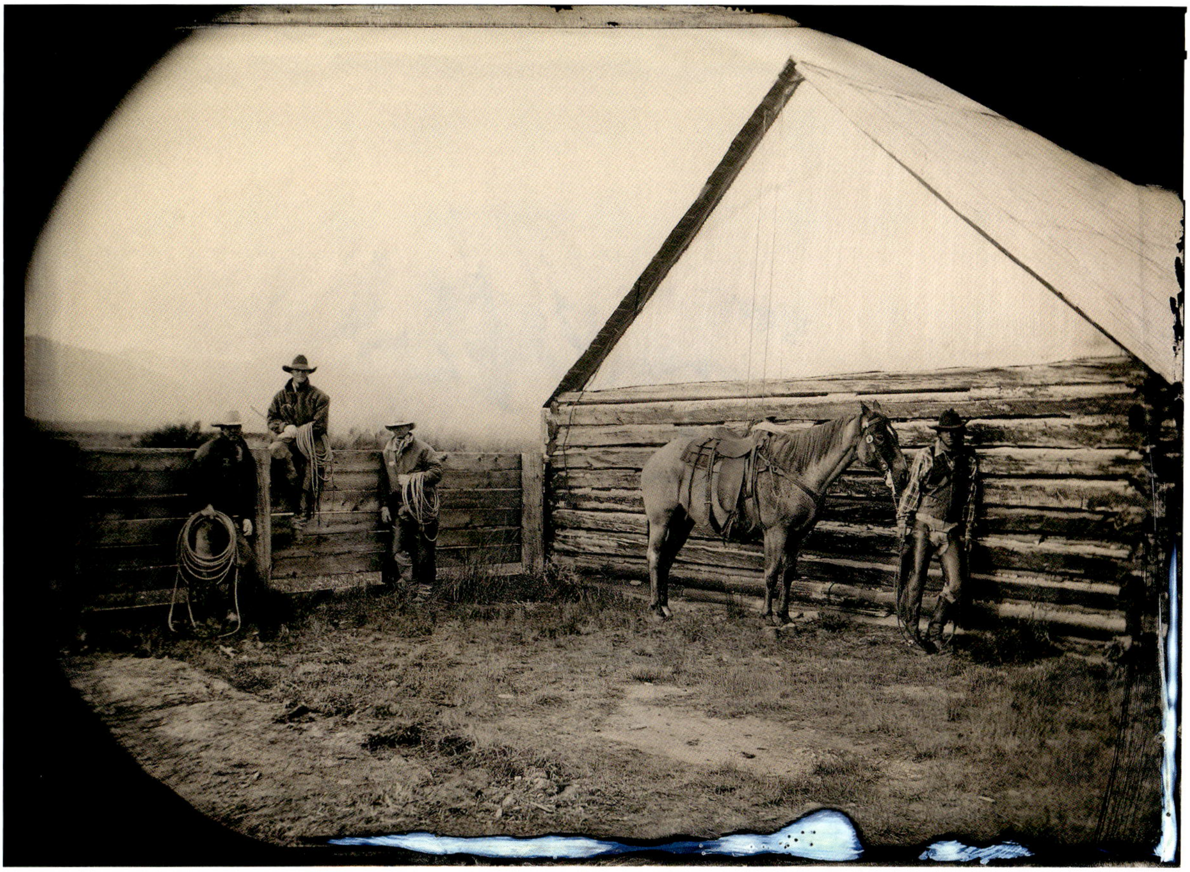

PLATE 99

Don Marxer, Jason Ward, Nate Smith, Luke Peters

DRAGGIN Y RANCH, MONTANA

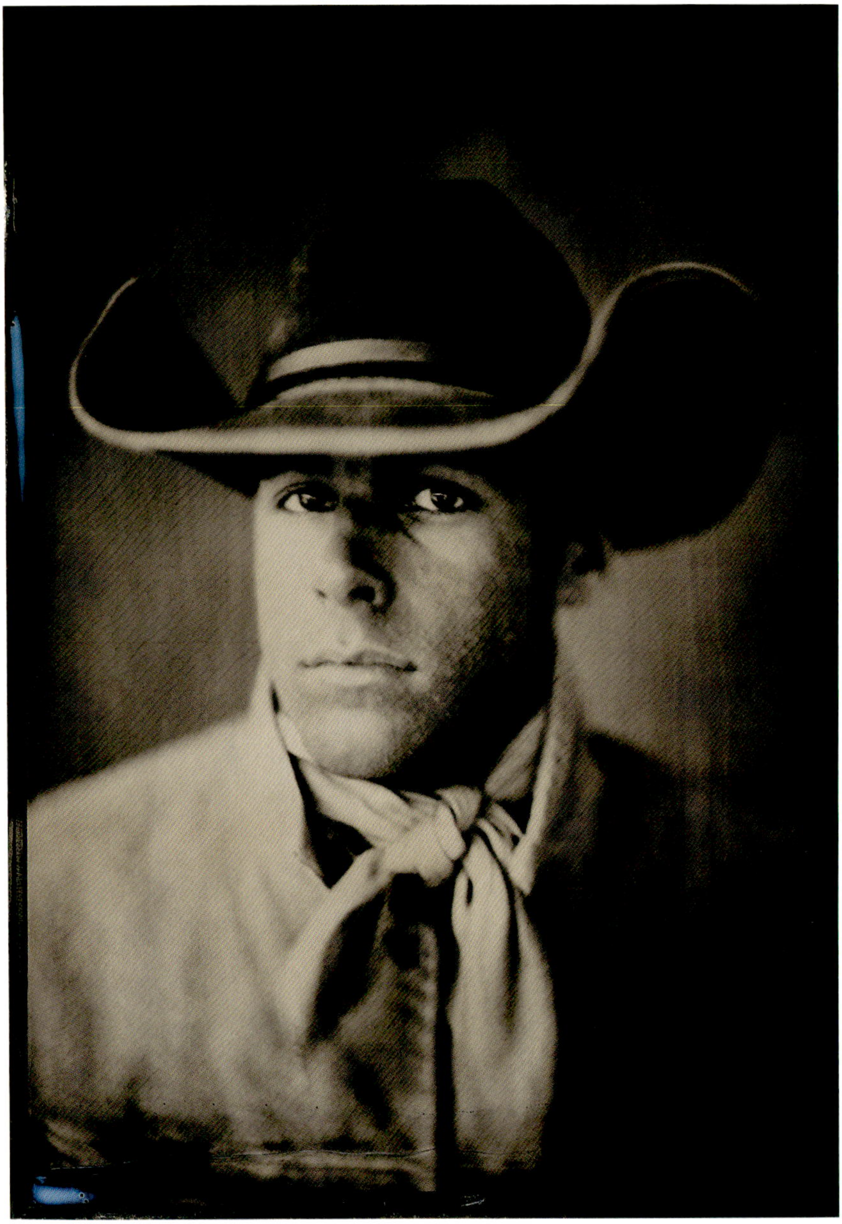

PLATE 100

Orren Koontz

TIMBERLAKE RANCH, COLORADO

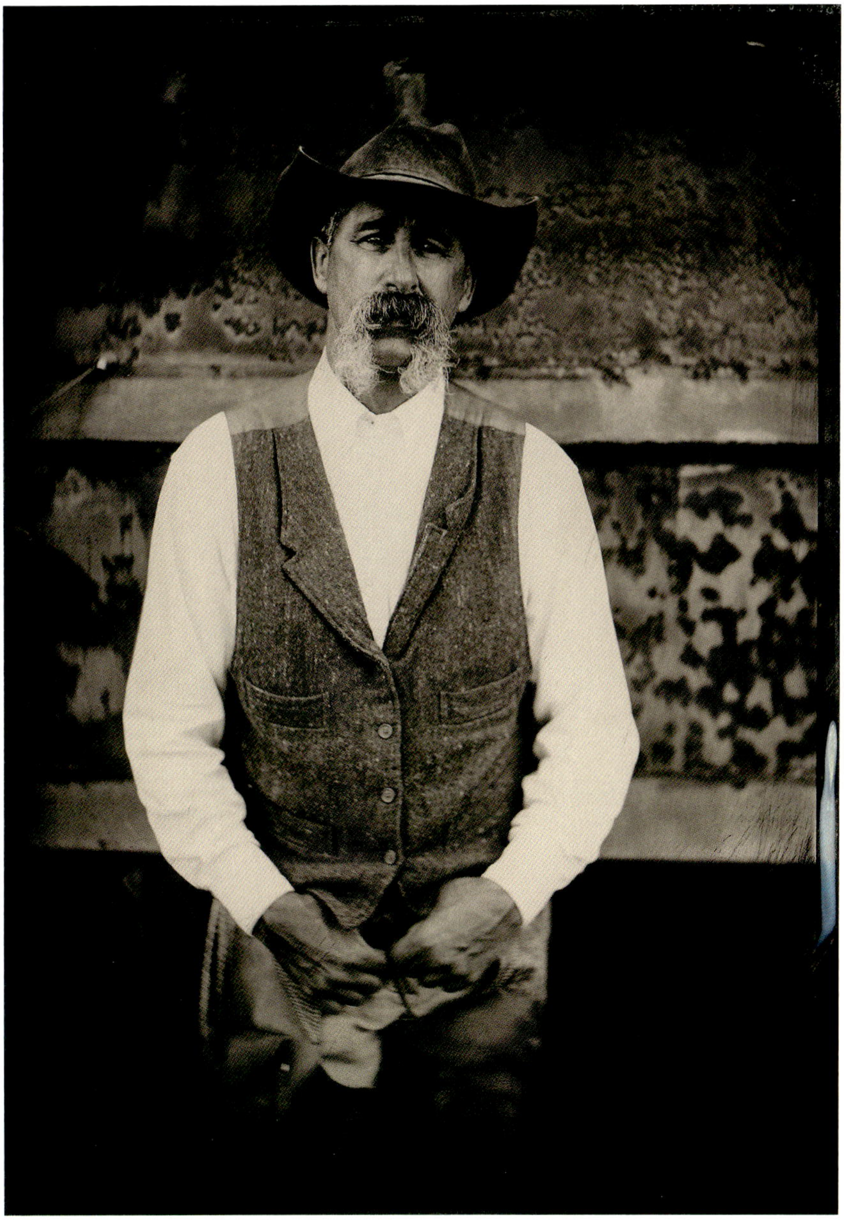

PLATE 101

Tim Belt

MEIER RANCH, COLORADO

Actually, the only place I've ever lived is on the Moorhouse Ranch. When I was a kid, I worked for the Sixes [the 6666 Ranch], and stayed out there wagon [living in a range teepee] and then I went to college at Sul Ross [in Alpine, Texas], but other than that I lived in the same house, or the bunkhouse next to it, all my life. And, so, that's how I started cowboyin'. I didn't actually start; I was just—in other words, before I remember, that's what I was doin' because that was the way I was raised. I had three brothers and we all were raised like that. I don't remember the first time I rode and I don't remember the first time I smelled burnin' hair from a brandin' calf, and I couldn't tell you how to ride a horse because it just seems to me that anybody could ride a horse, because it—that's the way it was for lots of cowboys. They was just born around horses and rode before they were old enough to remember.

And, so, I went to college, but, I set in those college classrooms and all I was thinkin' about was punchin' cattle and I'd tell my dad that I didn't really want to go to college, that I wanted to go to cowboyin', and he says there'll be plenty of cows to punch when you get out of college. Well, now that I've got a little older, I found out that that's the truth. There's still plenty of cows to punch, and I might've been a whole lot better off if I took goin' to school and studyin' a little more serious, but I don't regret cowboyin' all my life. Still like to smell a little mesquite wood burnin' and still like to get up before daylight and catch horses and make a pretty good round and come in and be awful tired and roll my bed out and go to sleep. It's a good way of life and I don't guess I'm quite as fired up about it as I used to be, but I do still like it.

I have a son that's sixteen named Gage who follows in my footsteps. He's caught the disease and he probably won't ever get rid of it, and he likes cowboyin'. I couldn't help from bein' sort of tickled with him because he's pretty much like his old dad, but I hope he does take education a little more serious, and cowboys, too.

I do remember, when I was a kid, and I worked at the Sixes, and I'd just gone there, and it was a cold fall mornin' and mistin' a little, and we came in from makin' a big round that mornin' and turned our horses loose and walked up the wagon, and I walked inside that big tent which they call the fly and they had a wood stove goin' and you could smell that mesquite wood, and the biscuits were cookin' and it was warm in there, and they had lanterns in there, it was just sort of a dim light. I thought I was in heaven.

TOM MOORHOUSE
MOORHOUSE RANCH, TEXAS

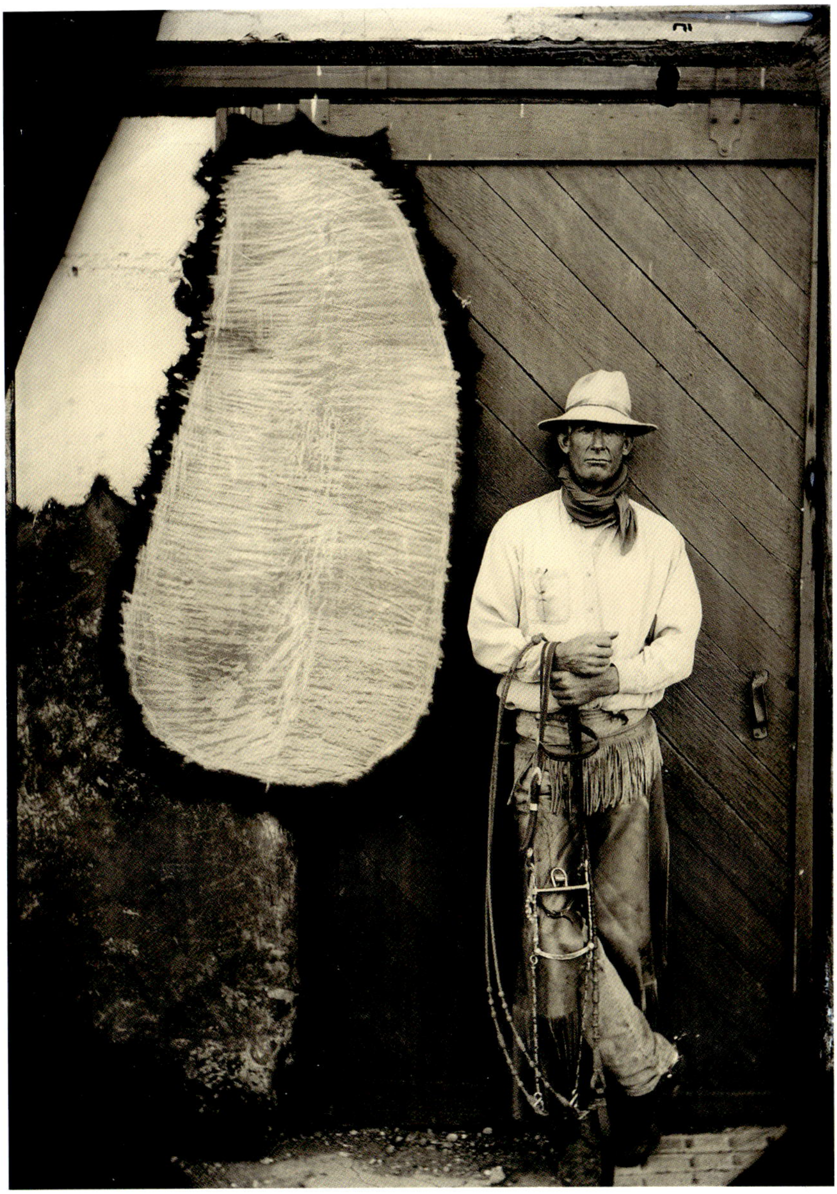

PLATE 102

Terry Riggs

MAGGIE CREEK RANCH, NEVADA

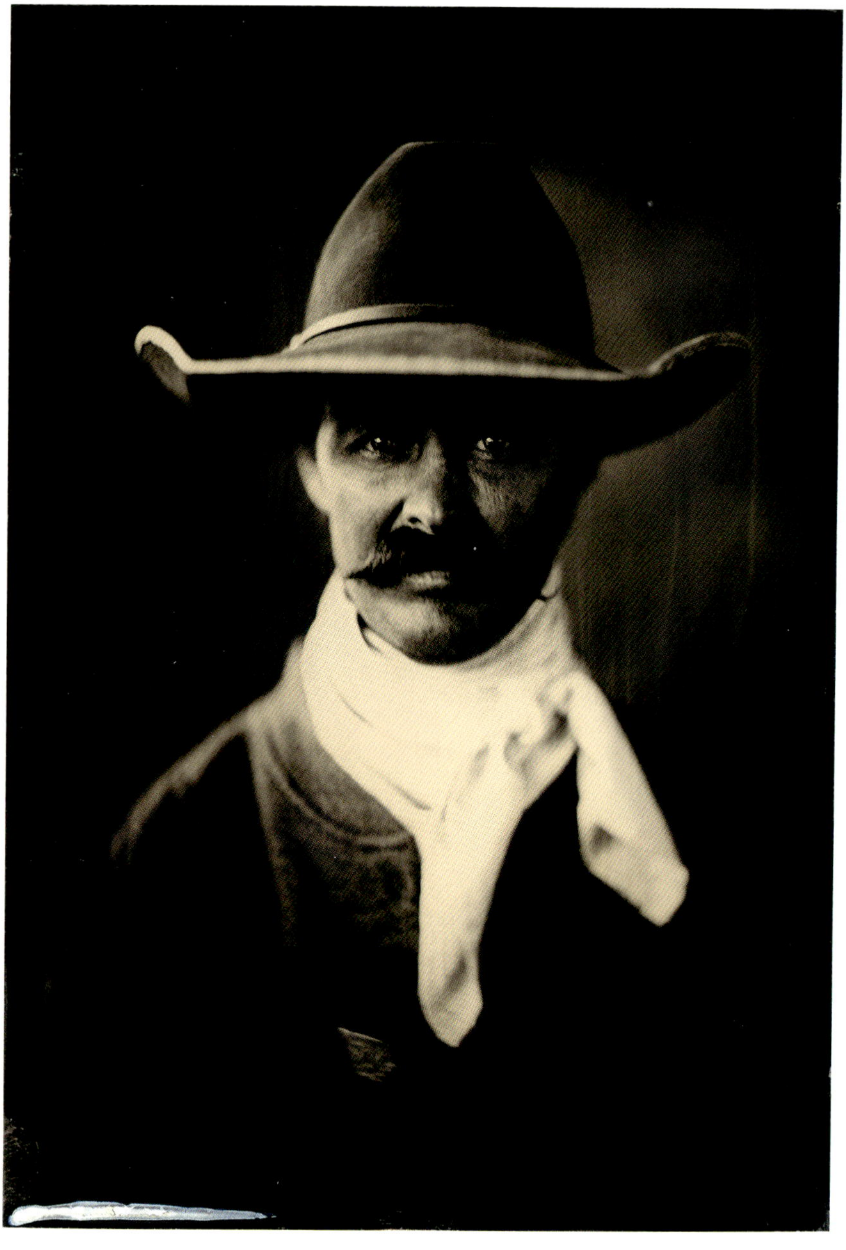

PLATE 103

T. J. Thompson

KINGS RIVER RANCH, NEVADA

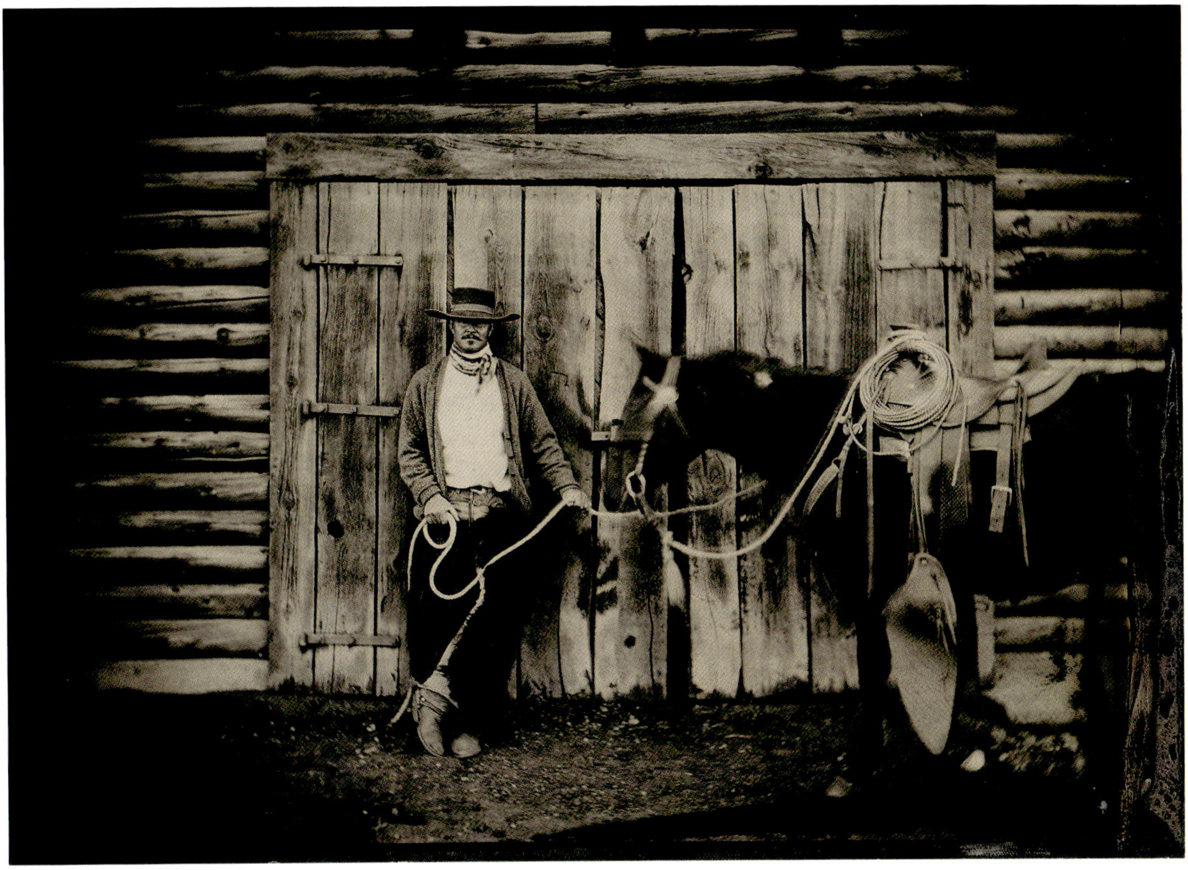

PLATE 104

Jake Brown

YP RANCH, NEVADA

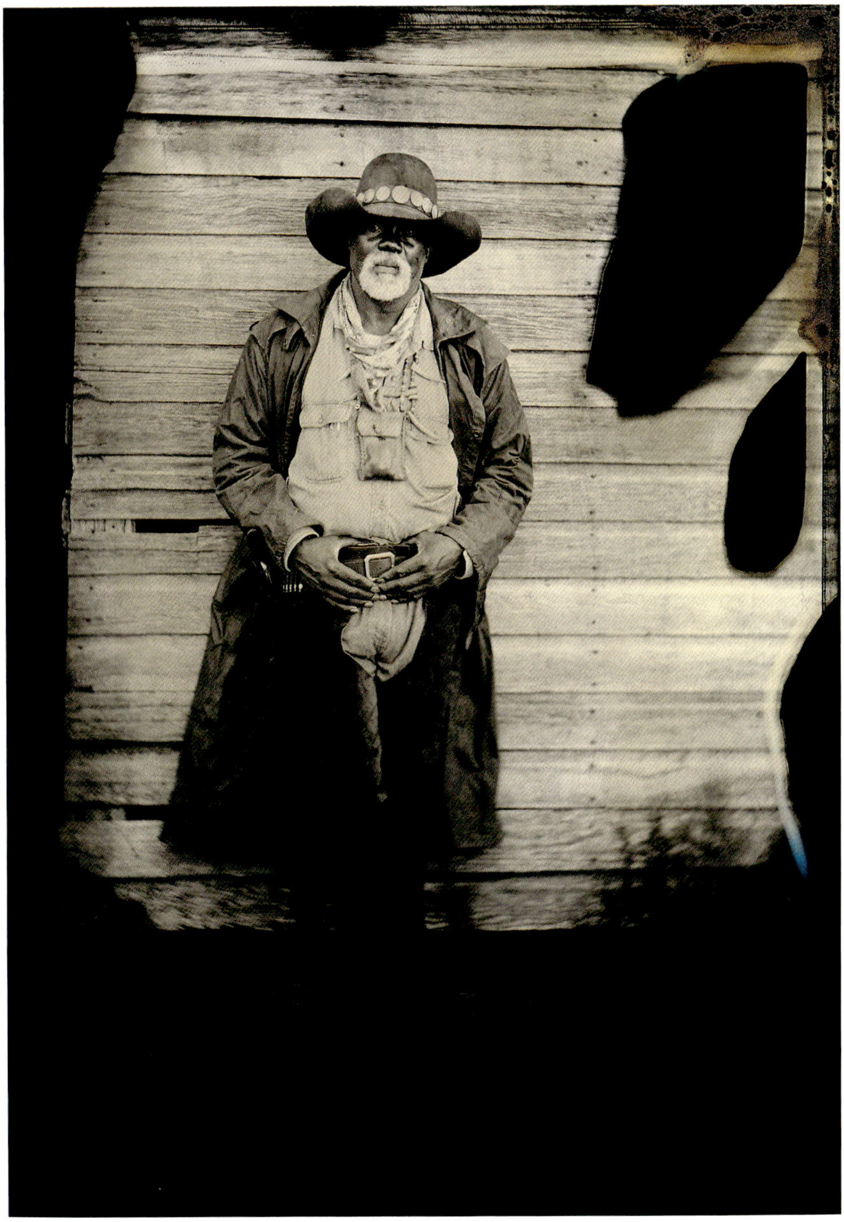

PLATE 105

Jim Myrick

BROKEN ARROW EQUESTRIAN, NEBRASKA

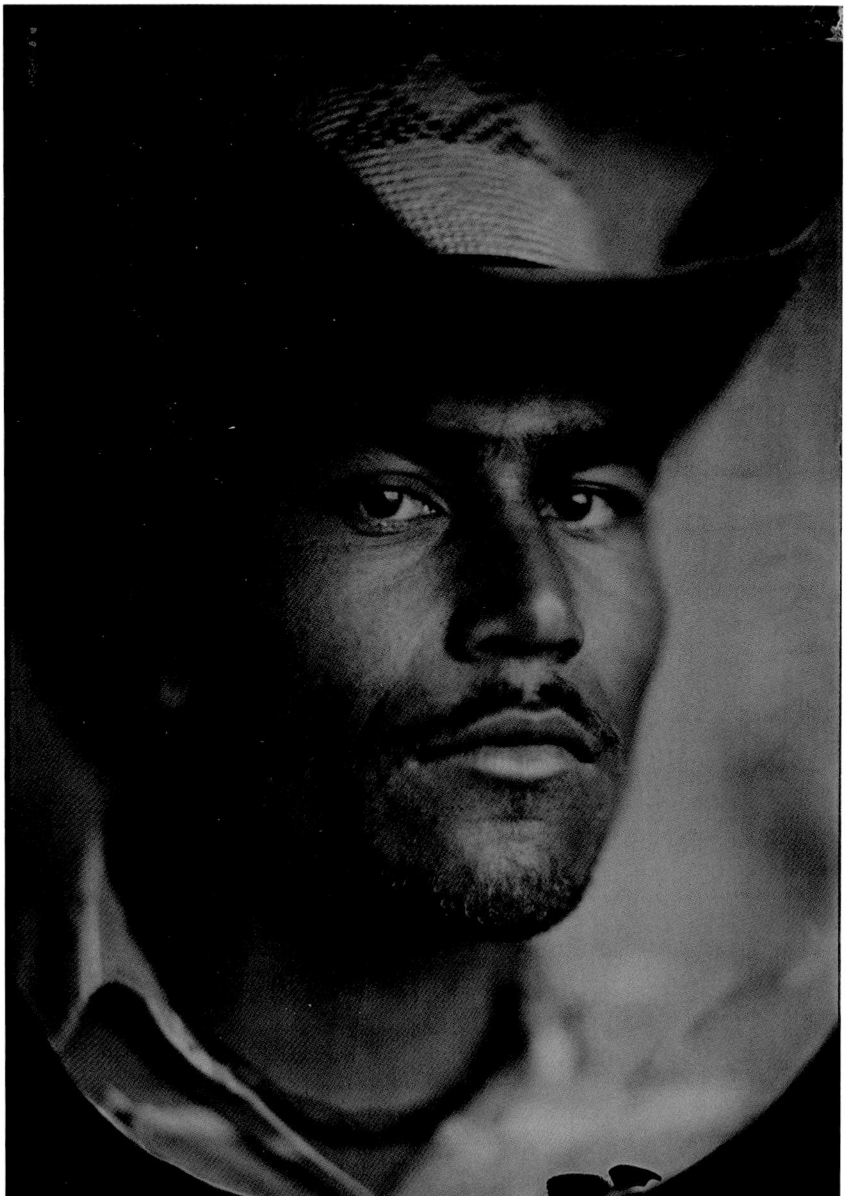

PLATE 106

Manuel Rodríquez Franco

EL RANCHO LA MORA, COAHUILA, MEXICO

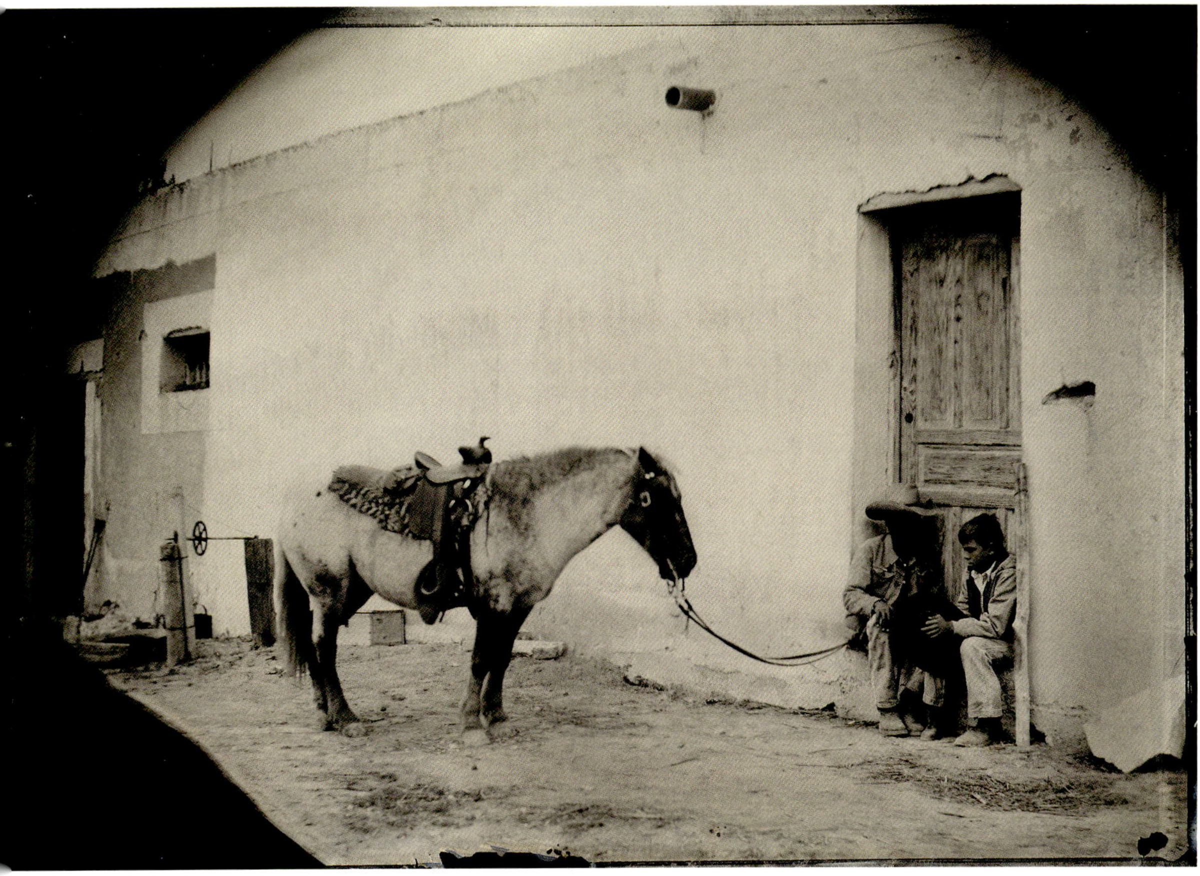

PLATE 107

Fidencio Escobedo Vega, Manuel González Vera

EL RANCHO LA MORA, COAHUILA, MEXICO

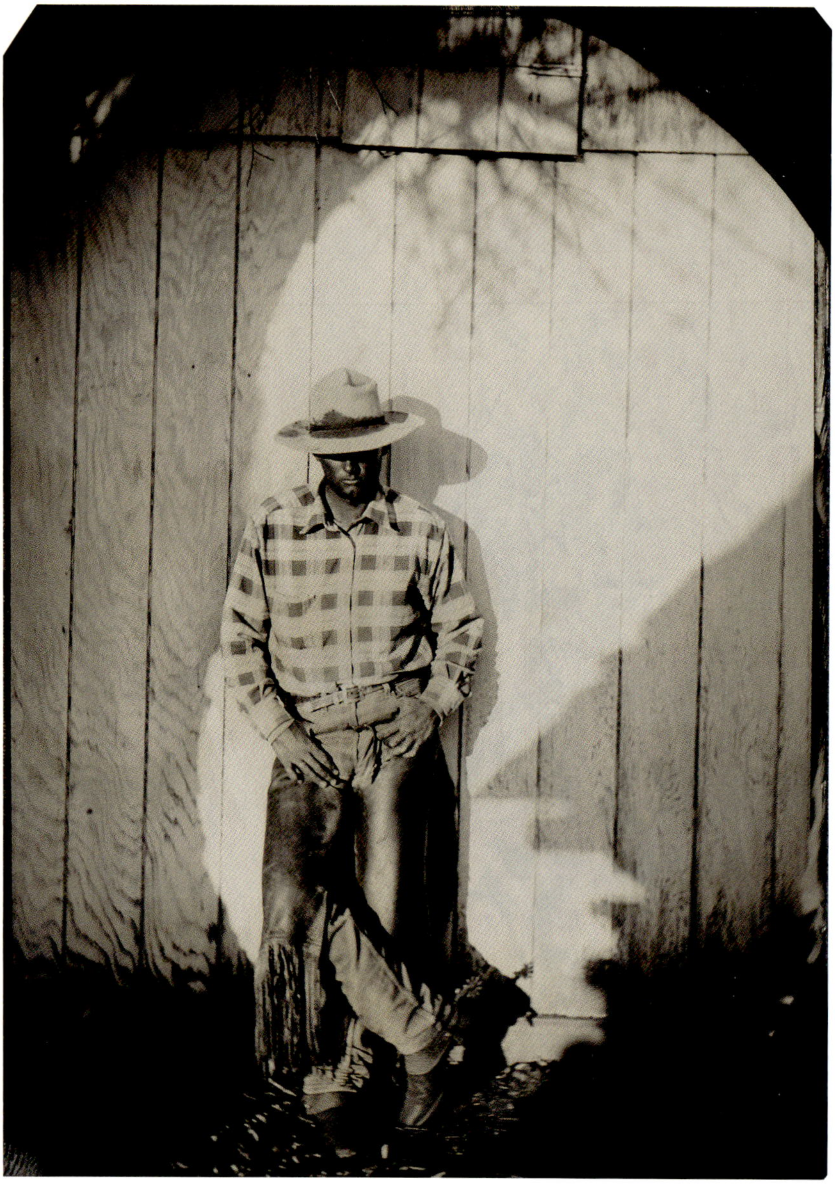

PLATE 108

Will Neal

SPANISH RANCH, NEVADA

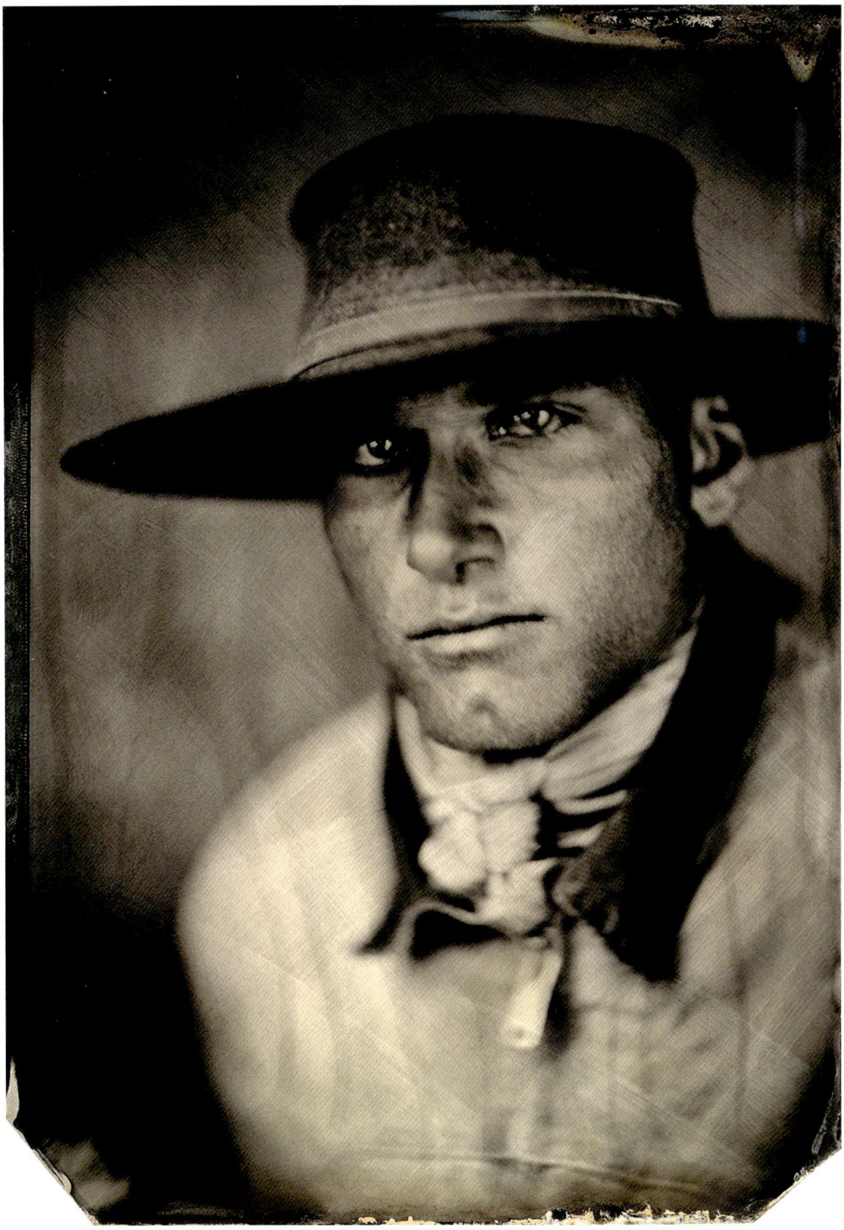

PLATE 109

Will Neal

SPANISH RANCH, NEVADA

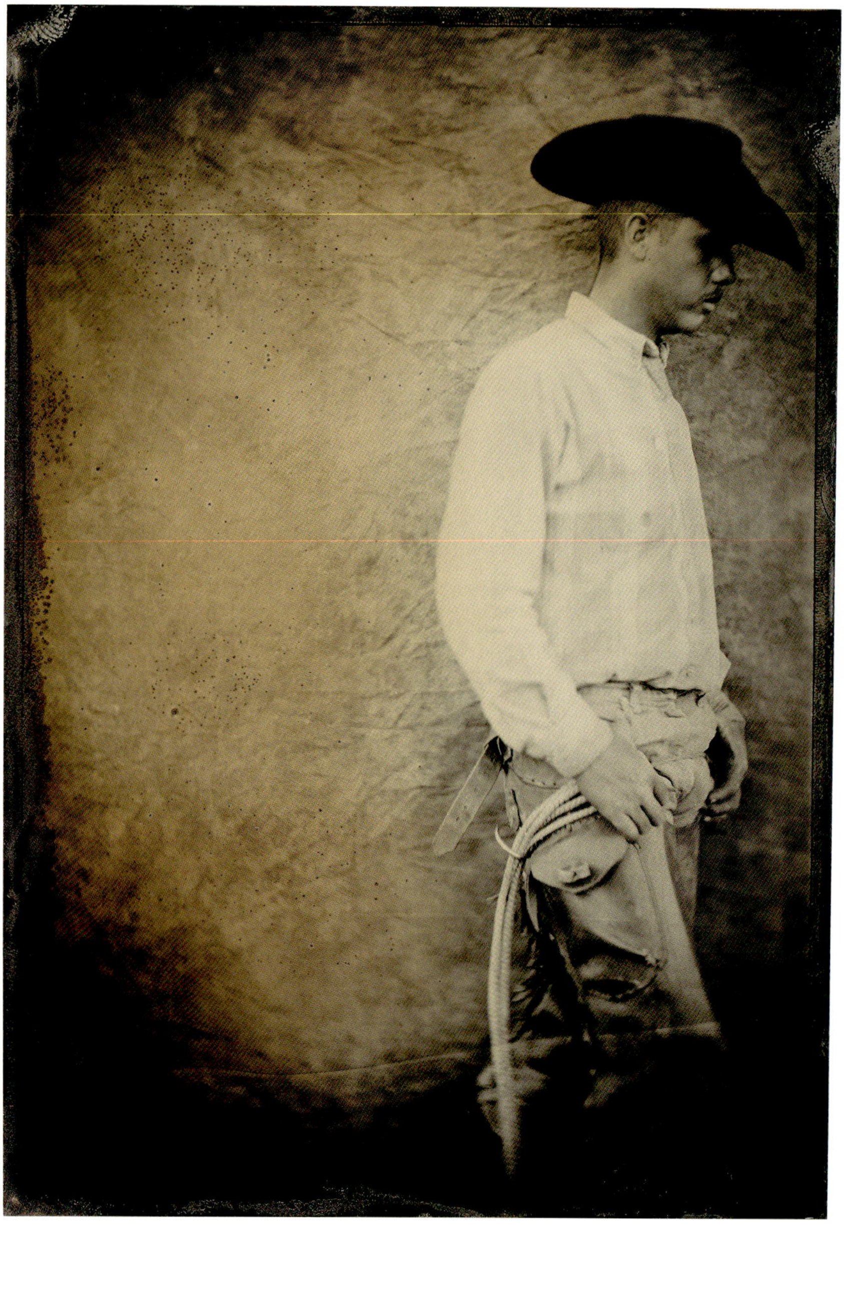

PLATE 110

Clay Rodgers

BABBITT RANCH, ARIZONA

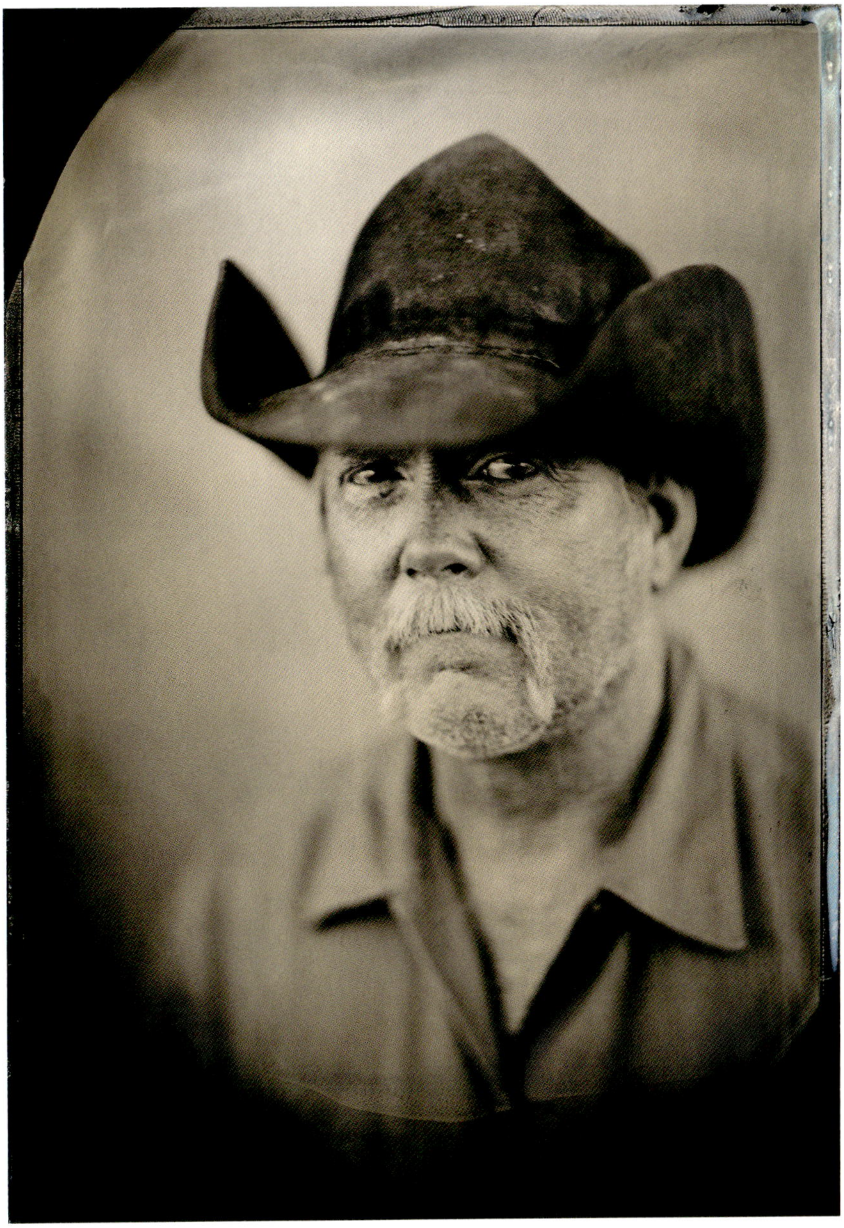

PLATE 111

Jack Rodgers

BABBITT RANCH, ARIZONA

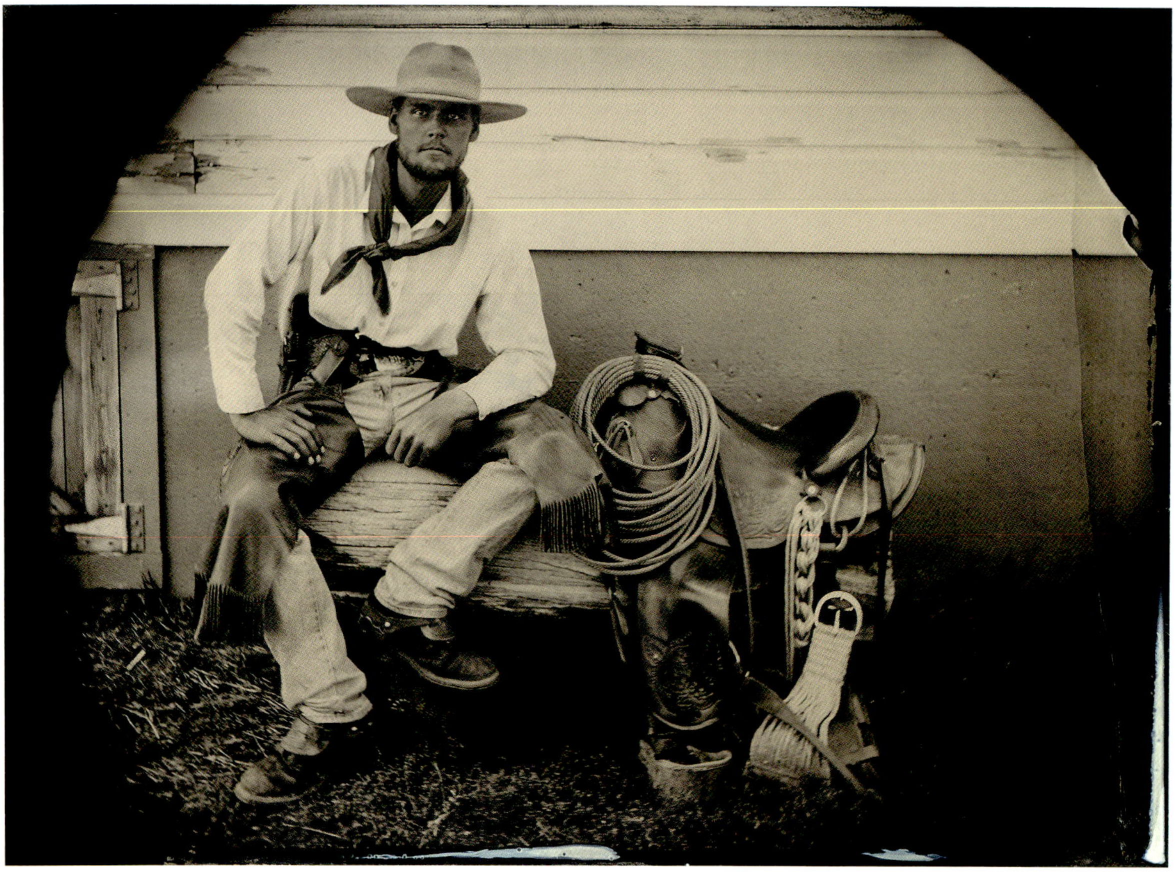

PLATE 112

Wesley Busenitz

DENNY LIVESTOCK, MONTANA

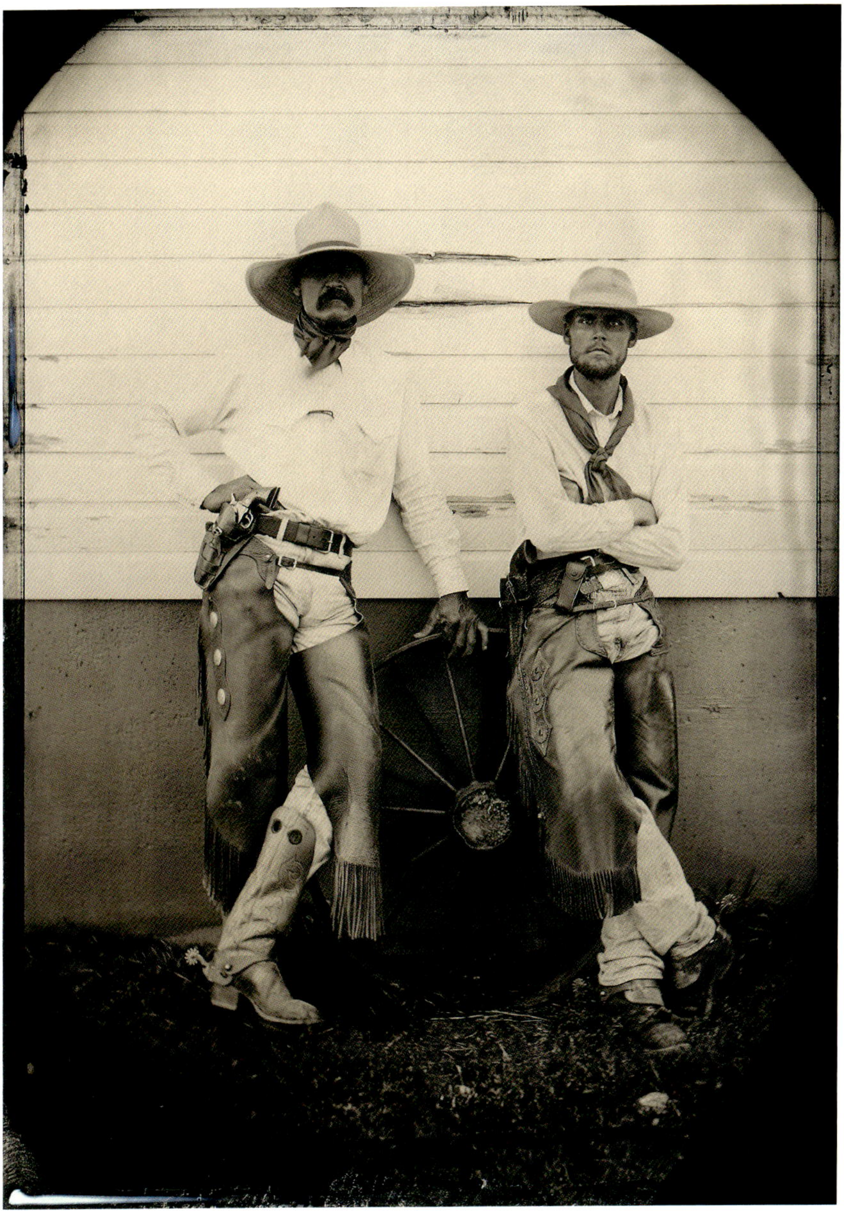

PLATE 113

Reuben and Wesley Busenitz

DENNY LIVESTOCK, MONTANA

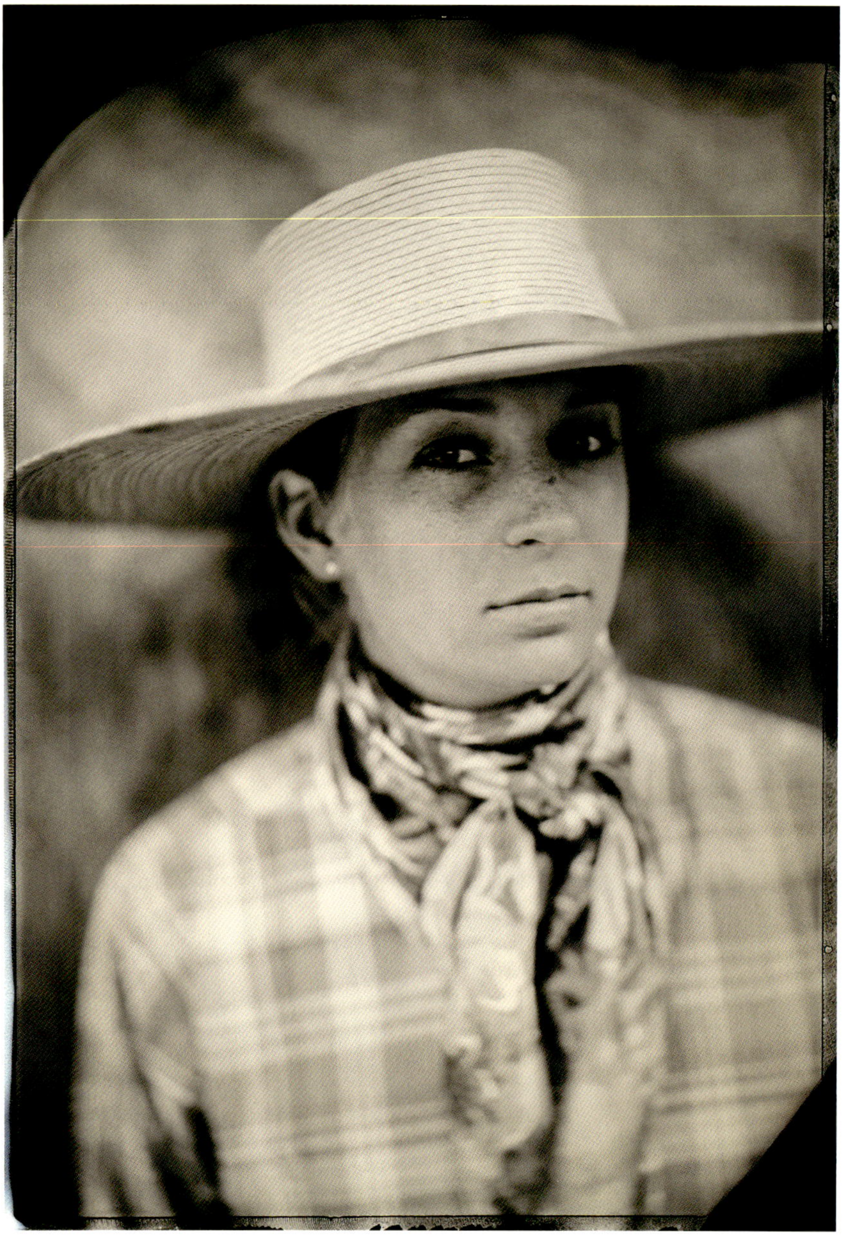

PLATE 114

Katie E. Groves

TS RANCH, NEVADA

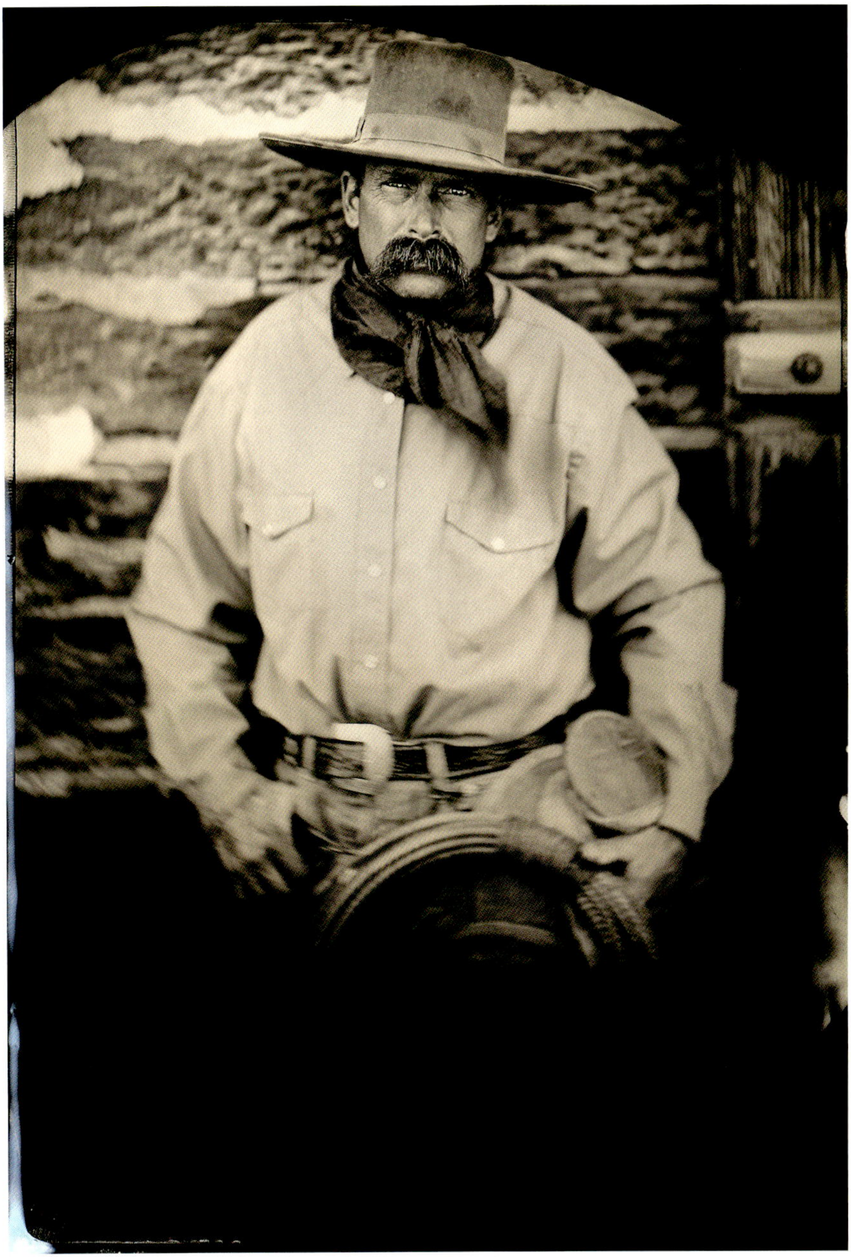

PLATE 115

Doug Groves

TS RANCH, NEVADA

I'm a Shoshone Indian, and how I got into ranchin' was my great-granddaddy, he had a pretty good outfit set up, cattle-wise and horse-wise. He ran pretty good herds on 'em and that was my goal from a very young age. They gathered a lot of horses and a lot of cattle, big brandings that I loved to see, and that's what I wanted to be.

I mainly love the outdoors, the hills, everything out there, and it gives a man time to think and time to see places that no one else has ever seen other than the buckaroo and the Natives. And the reason I choose this way of life is I feel it makes you do your share in all of nature's cycle on earth—by utilizing the land, taking care of the streams. You're out there on horseback and your dog and your cattle, and what I love about it is there's no slackin' on day-to-day work. A lot of times it's hard work. You needed to try to be one day ahead, but all along you're about a week behind on the regular process of taking care of the ranch. But the smells and the sights and the sounds of the cattle and livestock—ain't no better sound than that. I'd rather hear that than horns honkin', sirens goin'.

Traditions and history-wise, my kids pretty much was raised in our traditional ways, our culture, heritage. All our history's been handed down orally to where nothing's really written down and it's really important to know. And bein' on the Native side, we're close to nature. We were taught that, after all, God created everything, before he created the man to take care of all the creation that he's done to keep that cycle goin'. I feel I'm meeting my goals and taking the footsteps of my ancestors. Just northeast from here, a place called Hagerman, Idaho, they had a theory going on that in the 1500s, Spaniards brought the horses to America, but then, from what we know, is all our people—the Shoshone people—before they learned how to use the horse, they ate him, just like they did with the deer and the buffalo. Then after a while they figured that, well, they can tame him and pack him and ride him. So therefore they were the Lords of the Plains, the Shoshone people. They'd dominate, they'd raid the other tribes, and they was rulin' with the horse.

I have uncles that are gettin' close to their seventies and they're still ridin'. So I want to follow suit. And my maternal grandfather, he was eighty-seven years old and still breakin' colts, so that's my goal . . . is I wanna keep goin'. And that's pretty much what I have. I have a little girl now that is four years old and that's all she dreams about every day is, "Dad, let's go saddle up and ride a horse."

REGGIE SOPE
DUCK VALLEY RESERVATION, NEVADA

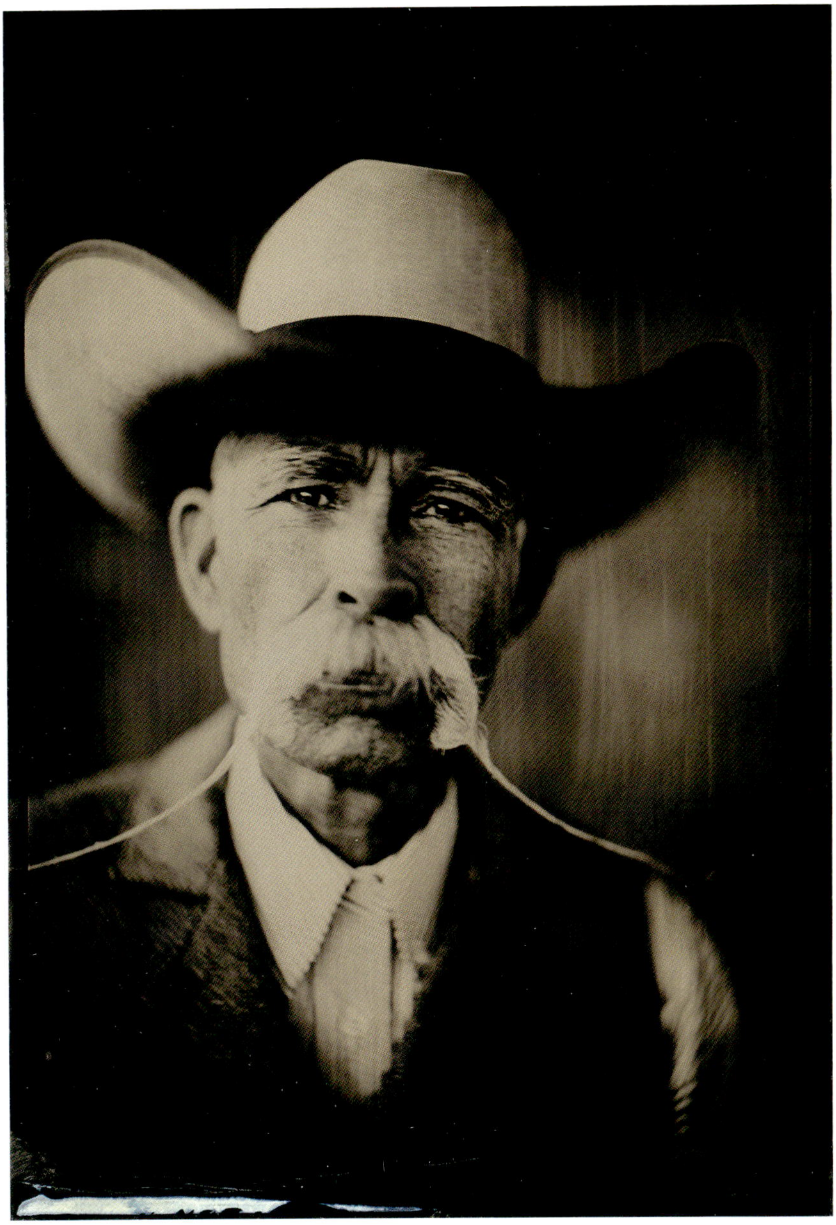

PLATE 116

Robert Chaison

CINCH RING RANCH, TEXAS

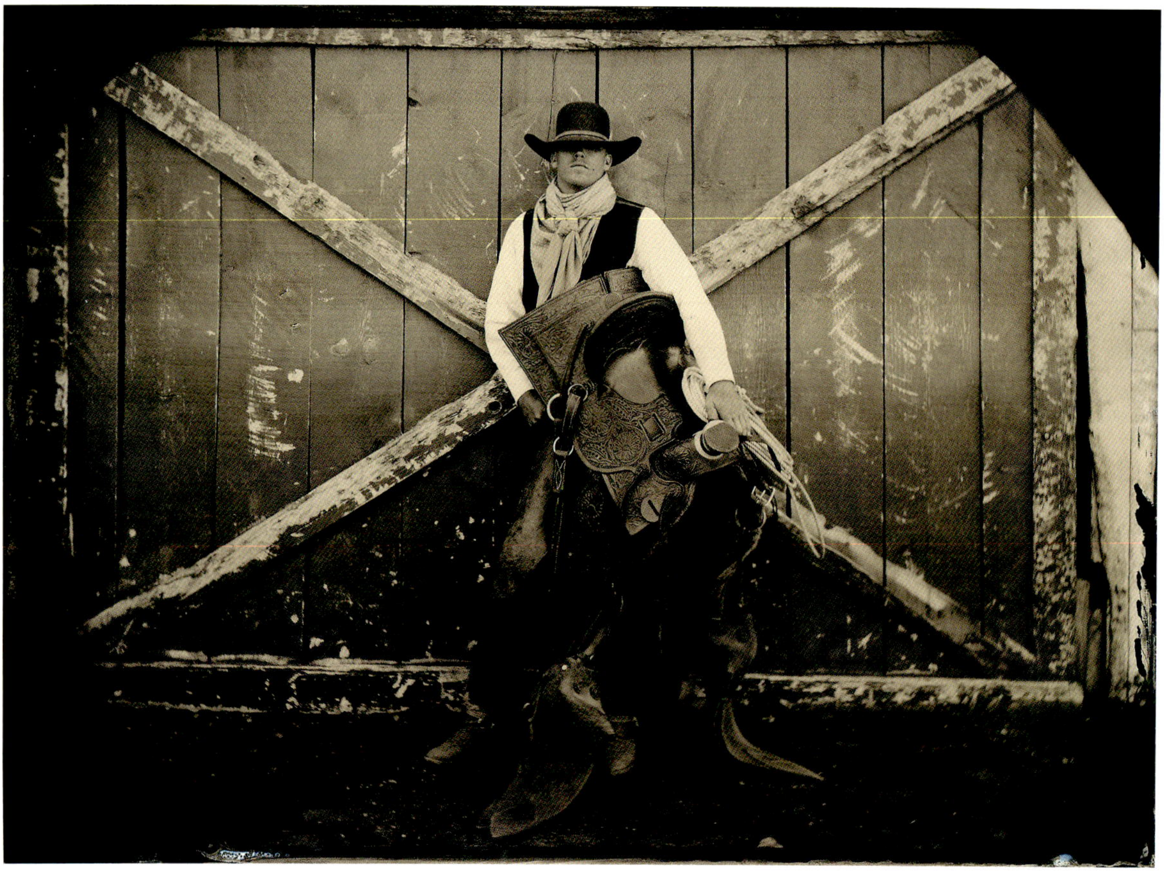

PLATE 117

Clint Damewood

ZX RANCH, OREGON

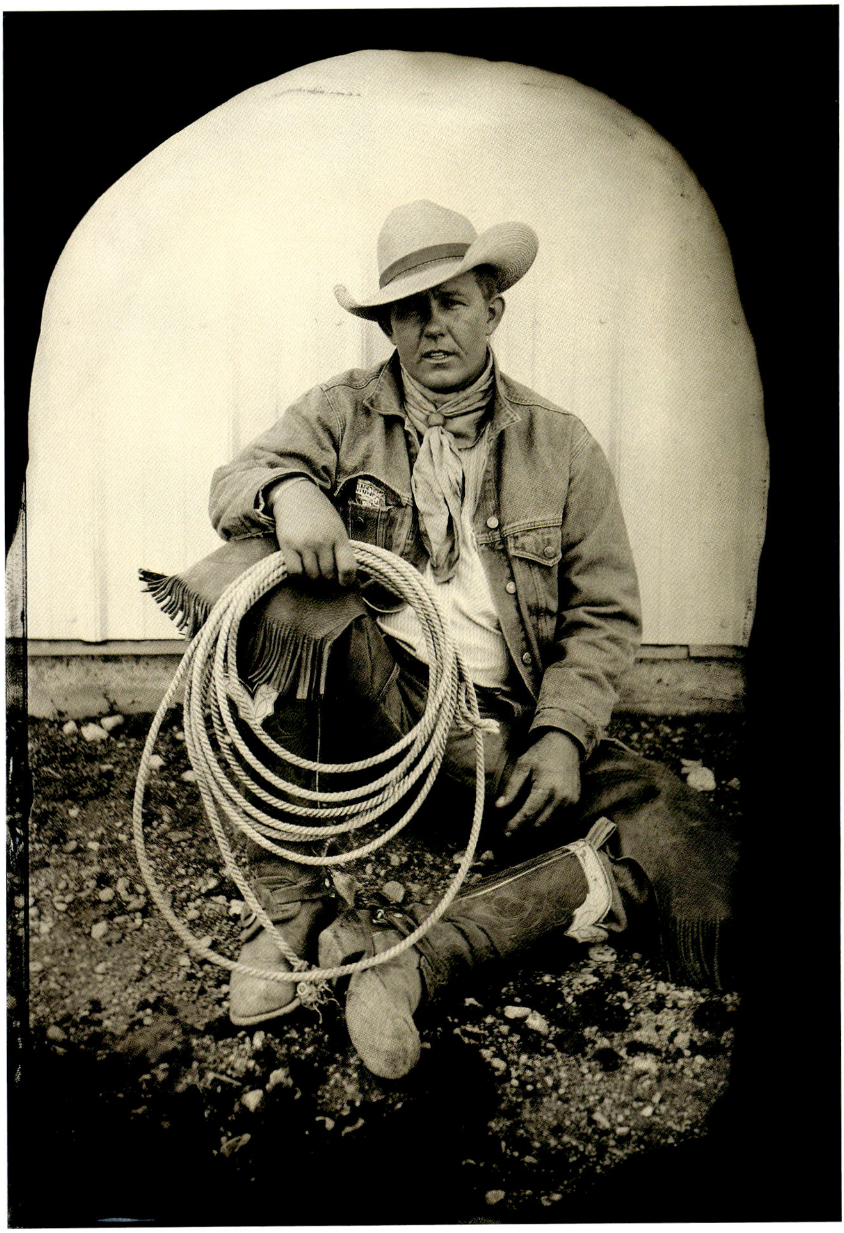

PLATE 118

Justin Rogers

PADLOCK RANCH, WYOMING

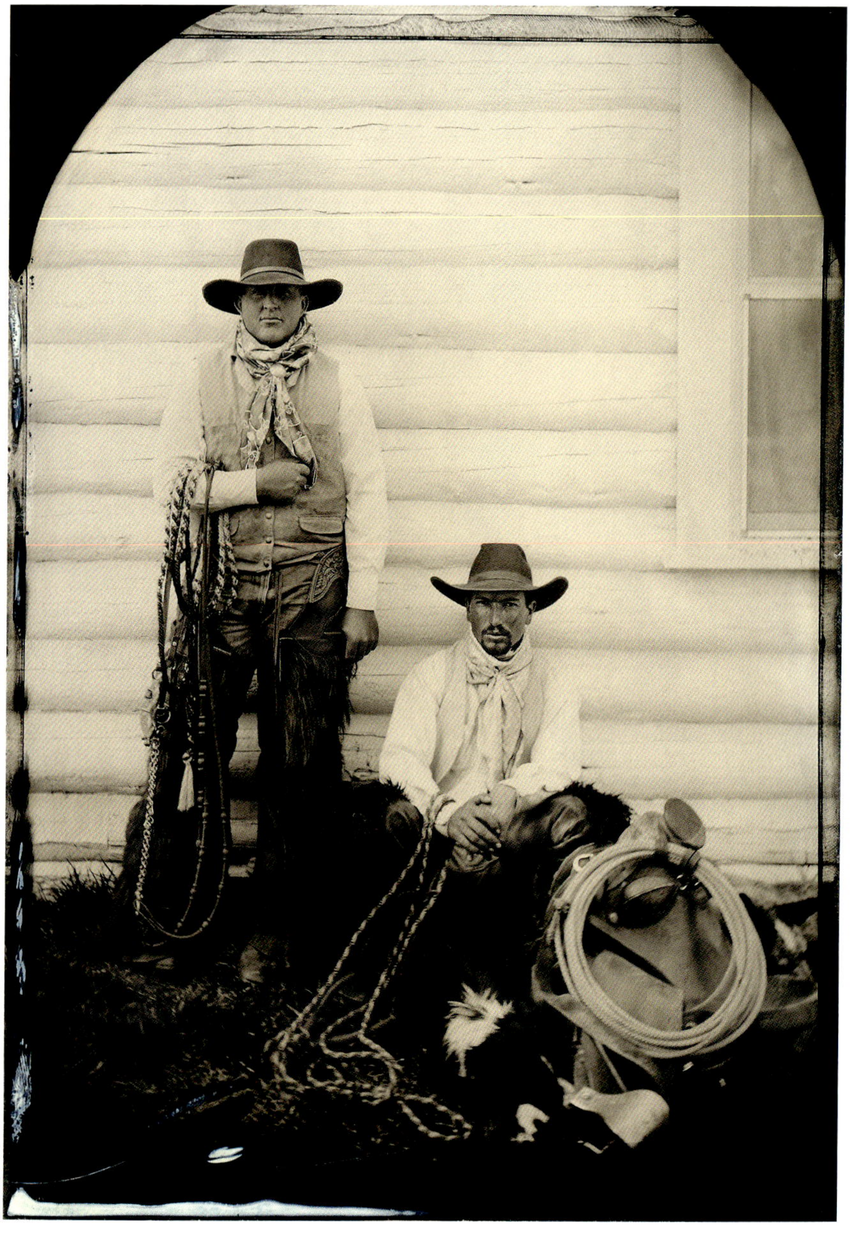

PLATE 119

Kirk Lohof, K. C. Verhelst

SUNLIGHT RANCH, MONTANA

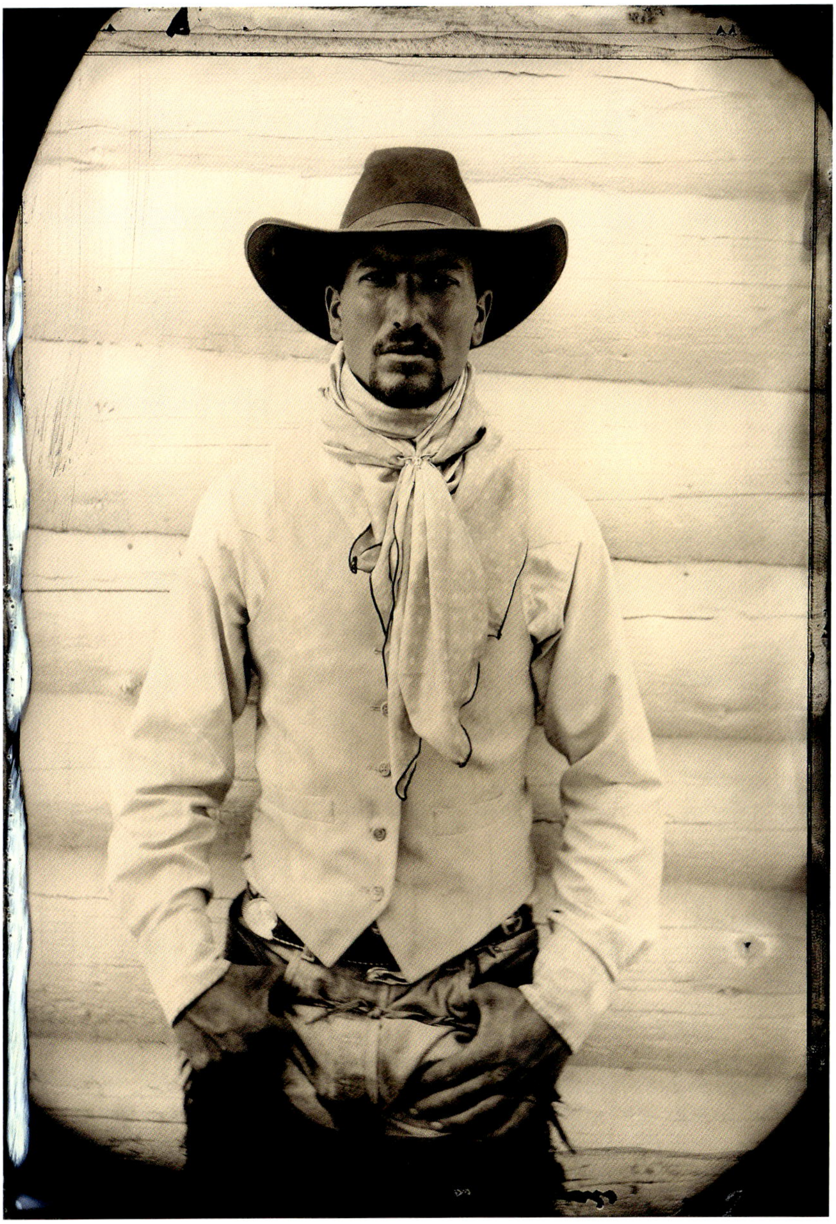

PLATE 120

K. C. Verhelst

SUNLIGHT RANCH, MONTANA

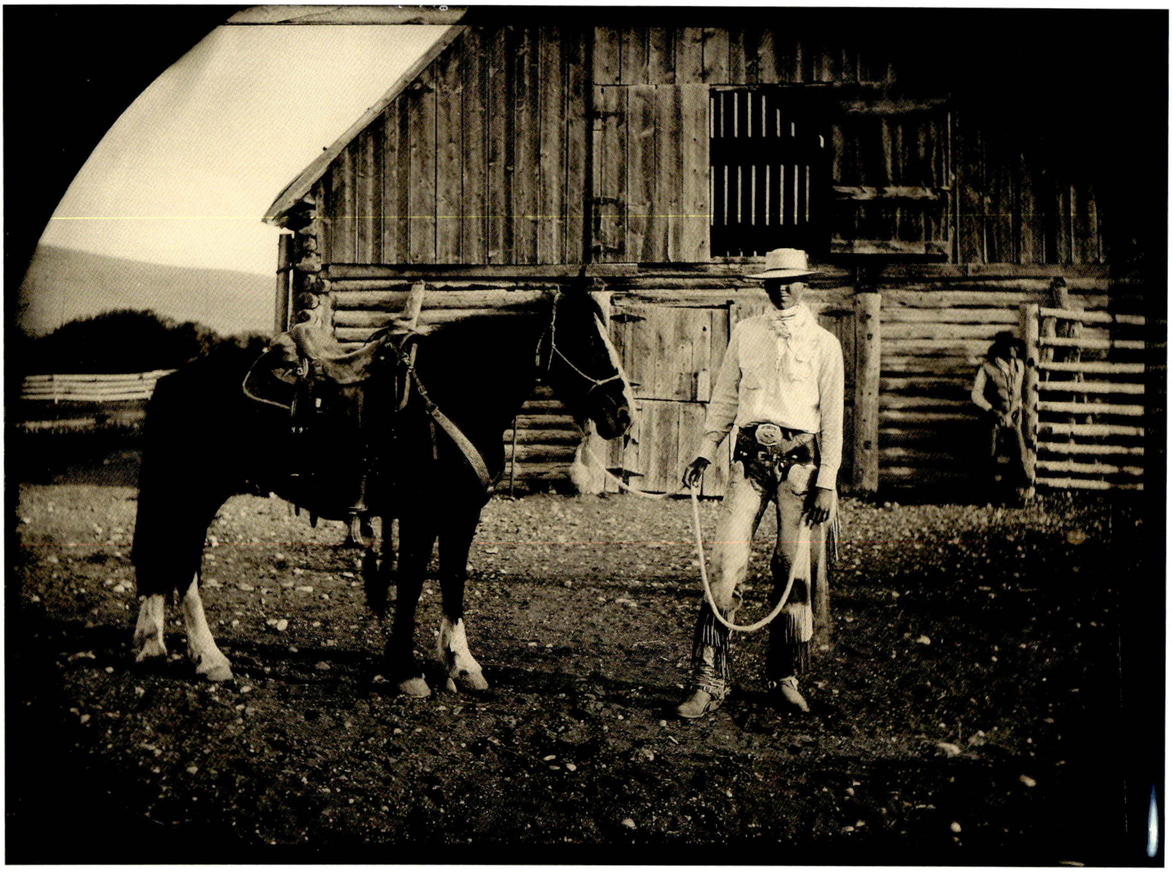

PLATE 121

Eric Johnson (front), Art Robinson

SNOWLINE RANCH, MONTANA

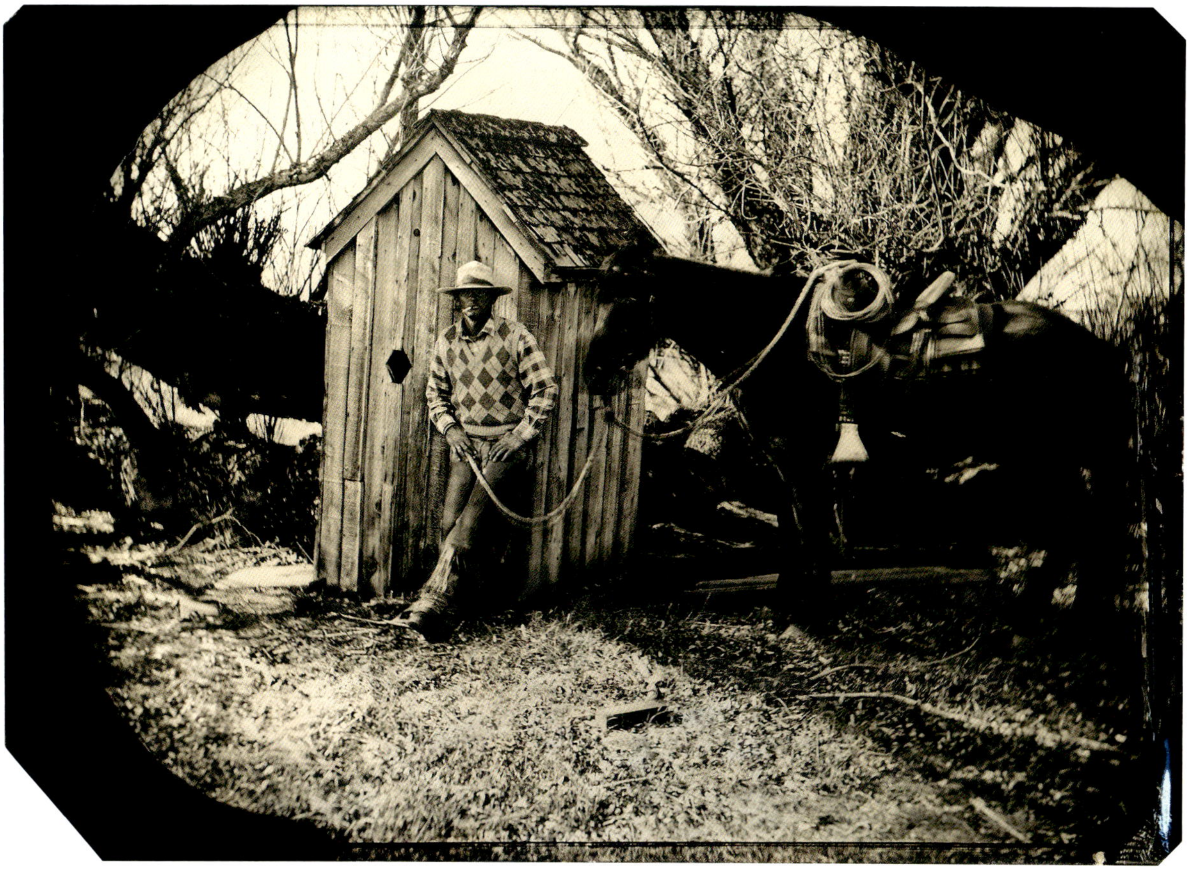

PLATE 122

Will Neal

SPANISH RANCH, NEVADA

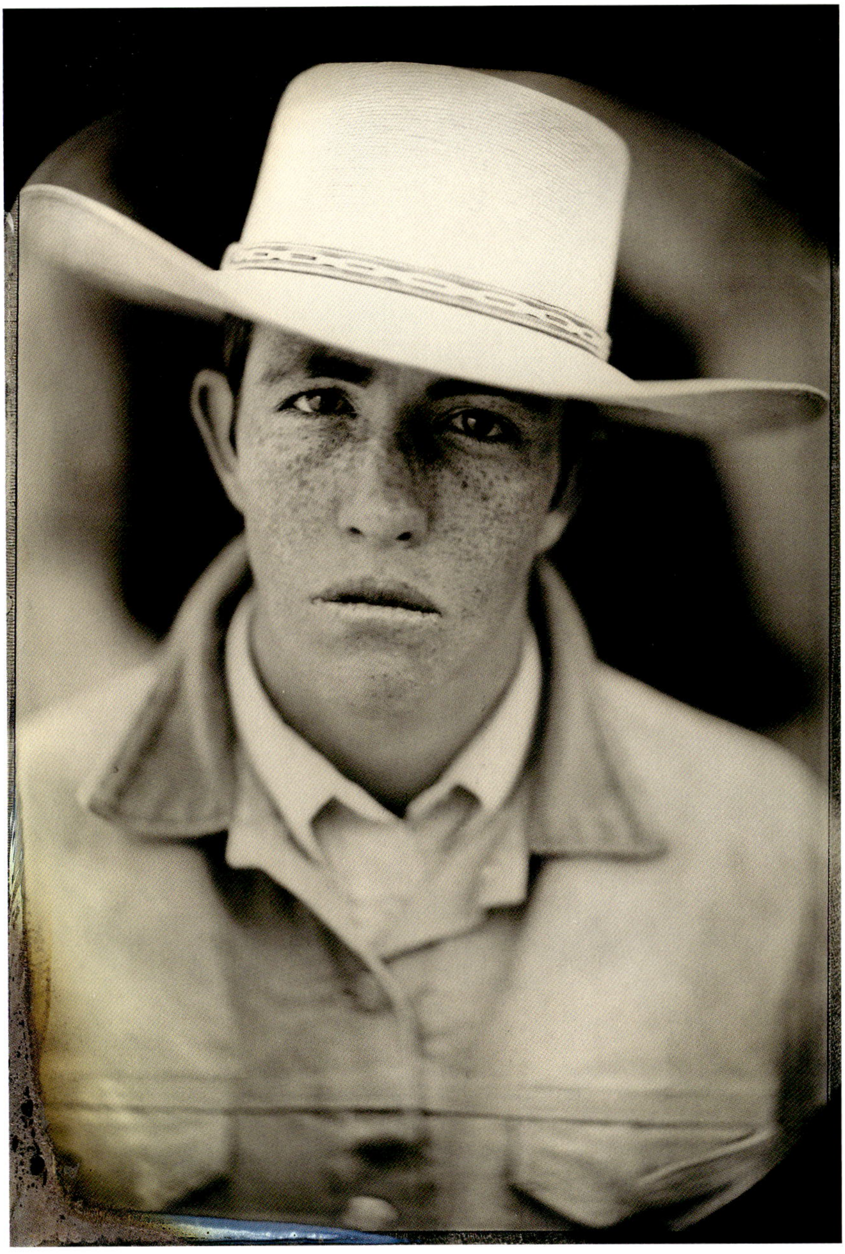

PLATE 123

Seth Franklin

BUTTE CREEK RANCH, OREGON

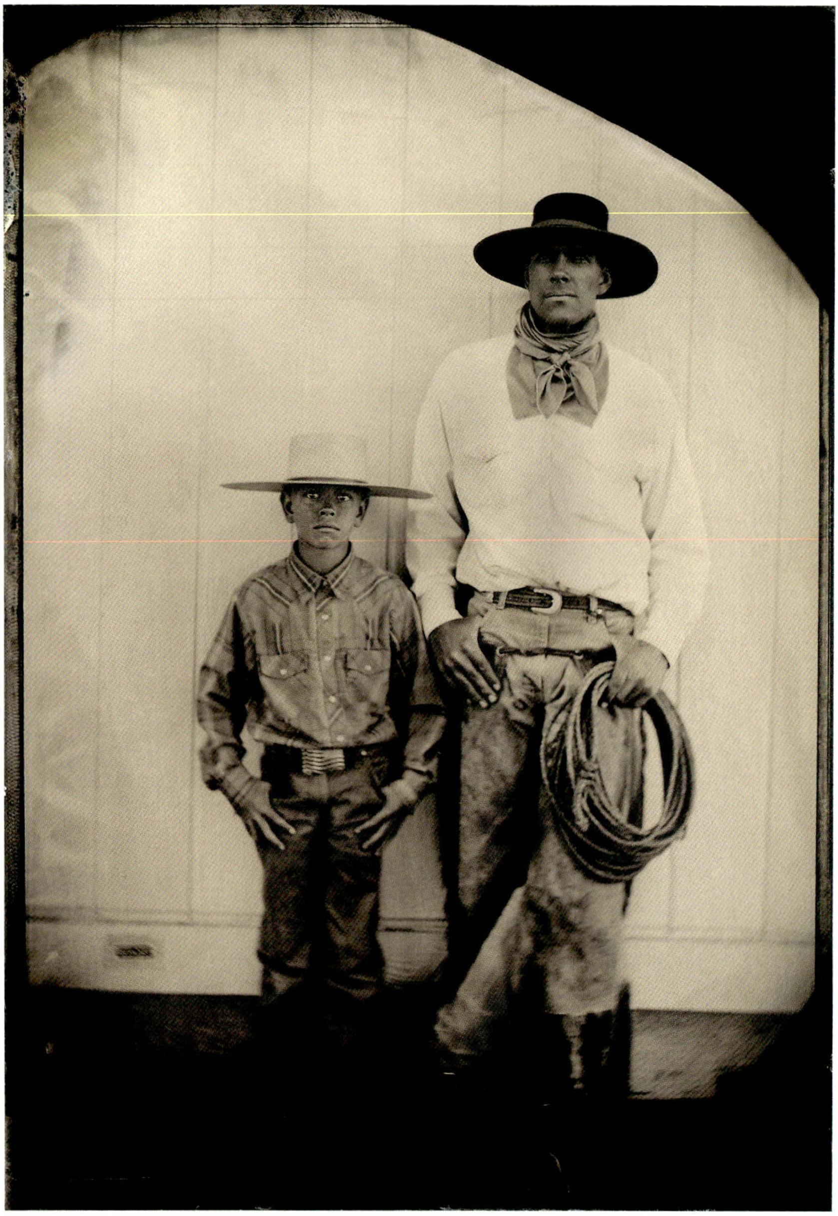

PLATE 124

Jerry and Mat Carter

CROWN RANCH, OREGON

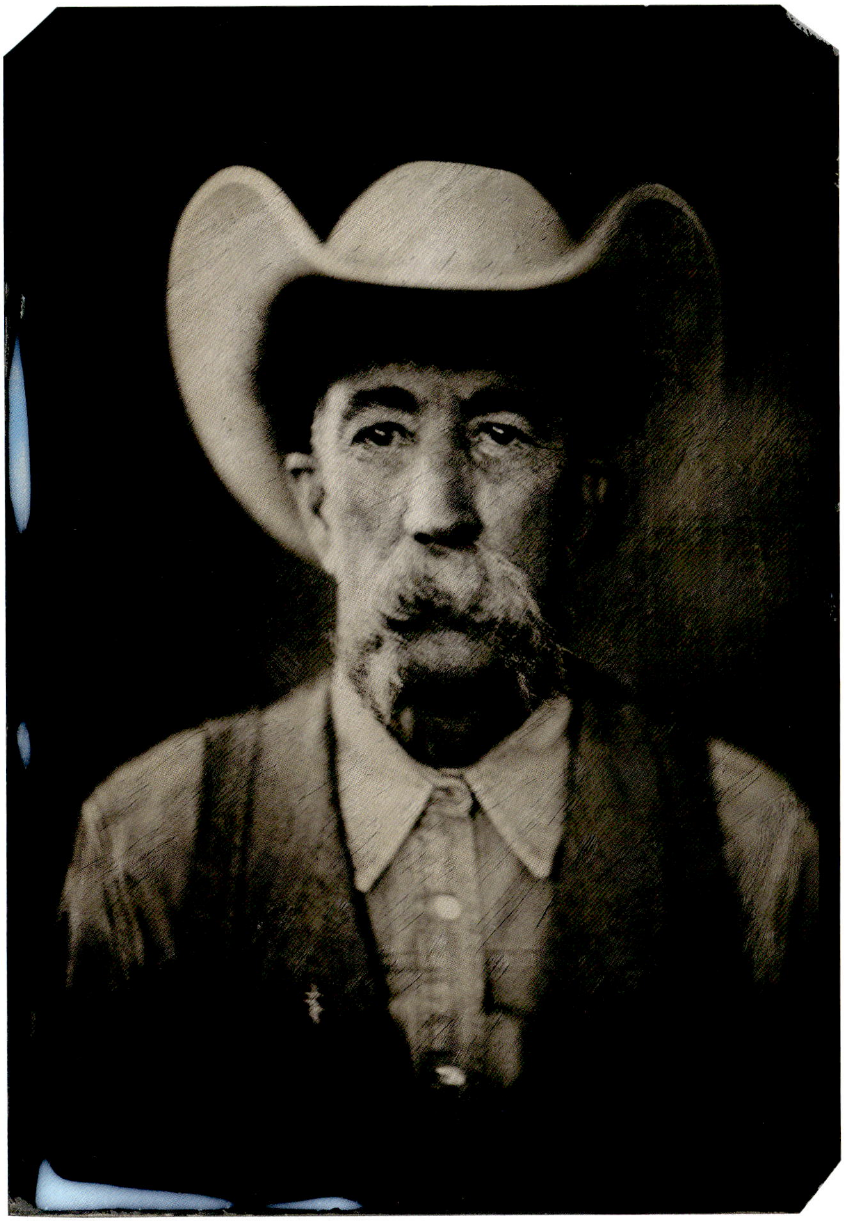

PLATE 125

Charles Ellis

ELLIS CATTLE CO., TEXAS

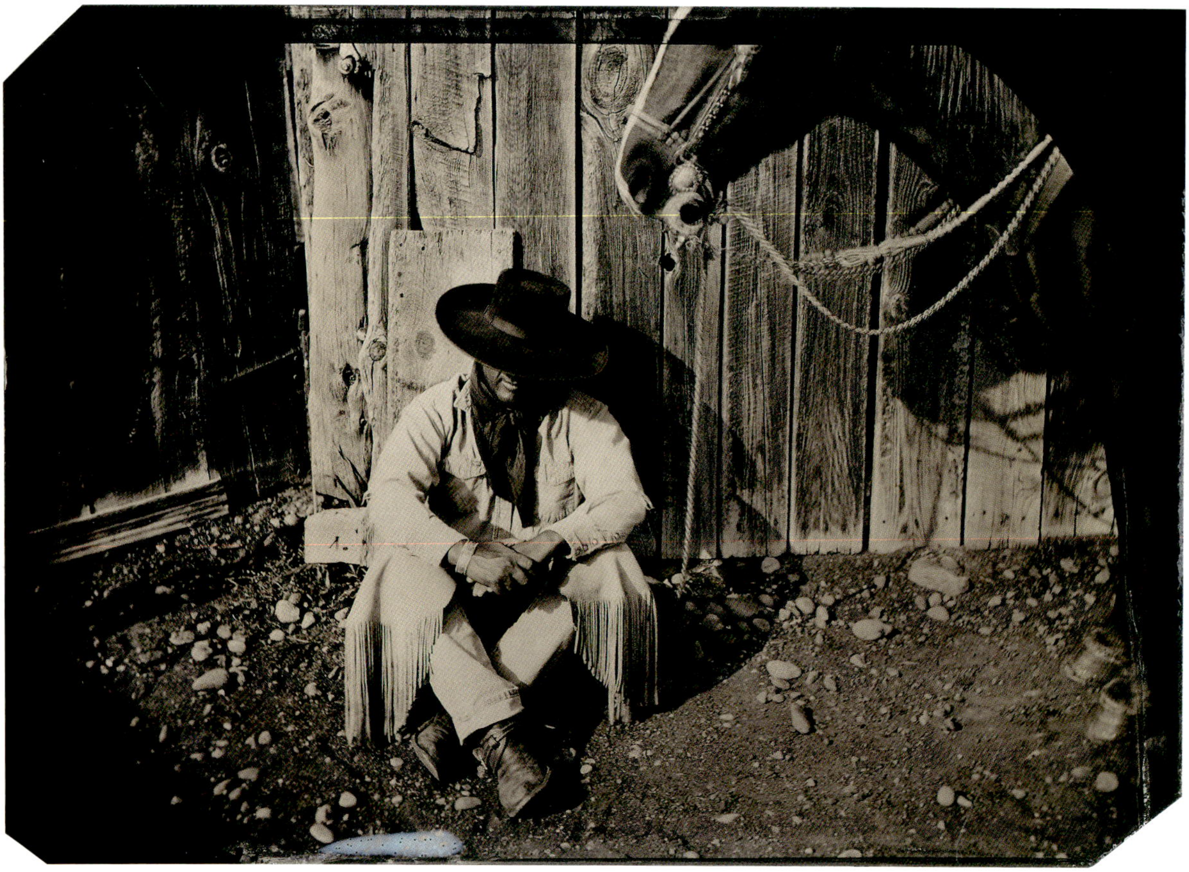

PLATE 126

Pedro Márquez

RANCHO DEL CORAZON, COLORADO

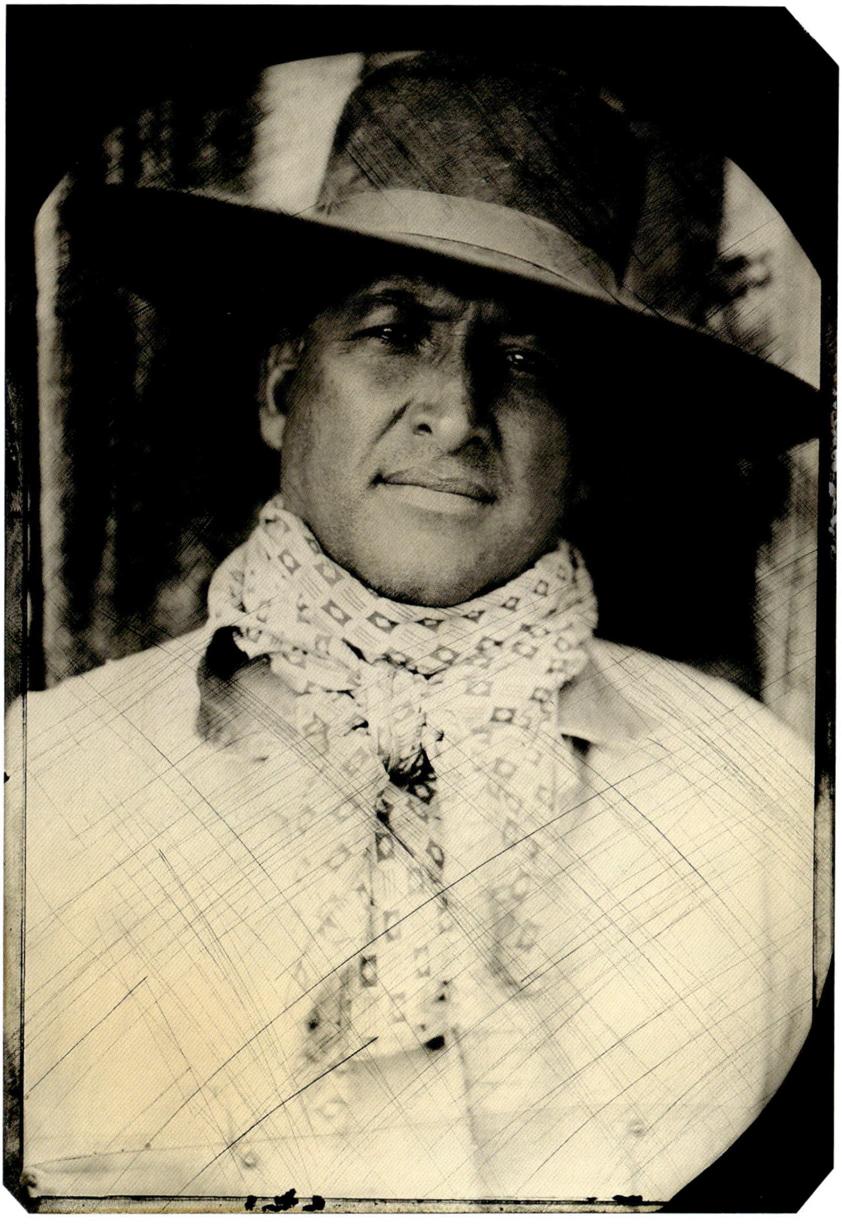

PLATE 127

Pedro Márquez

RANCHO DEL CORAZON, COLORADO

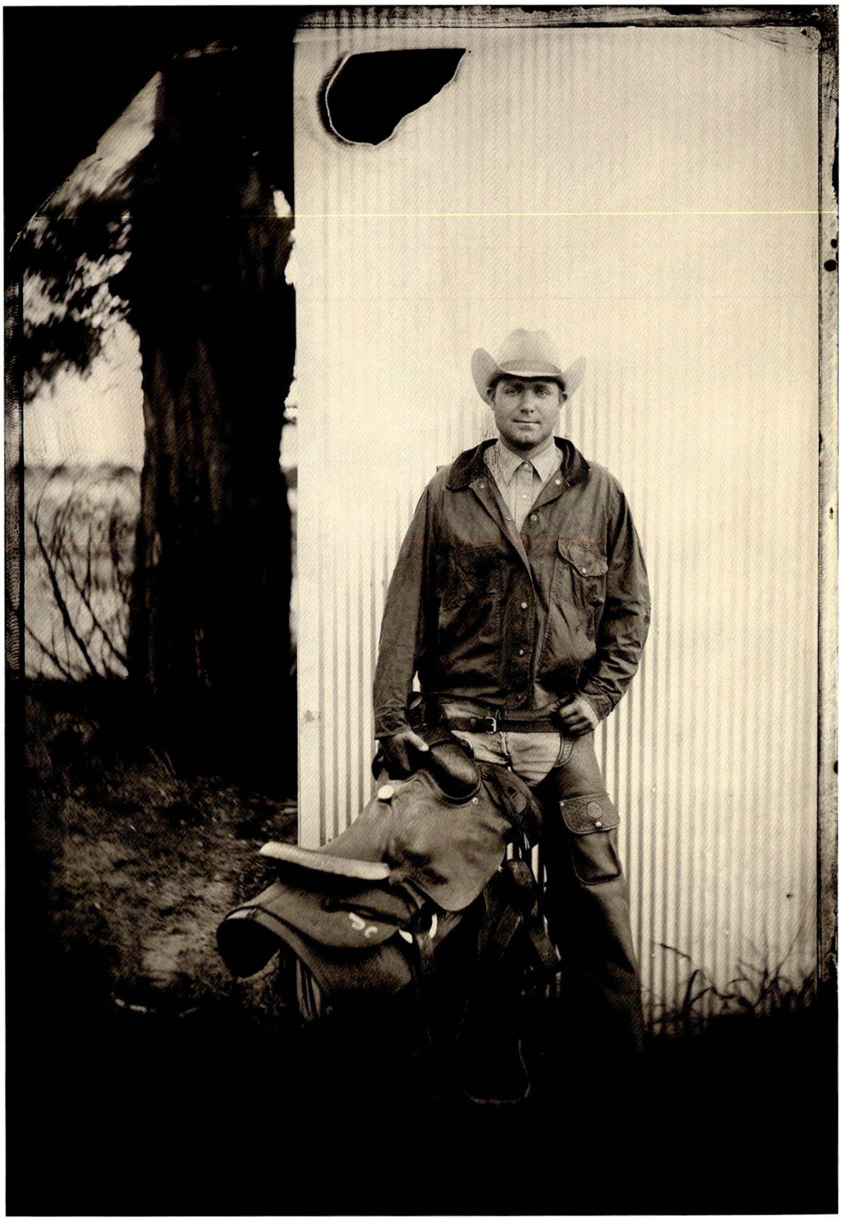

PLATE 128

Morey Hutchison

CHAIN RANCH, OKLAHOMA

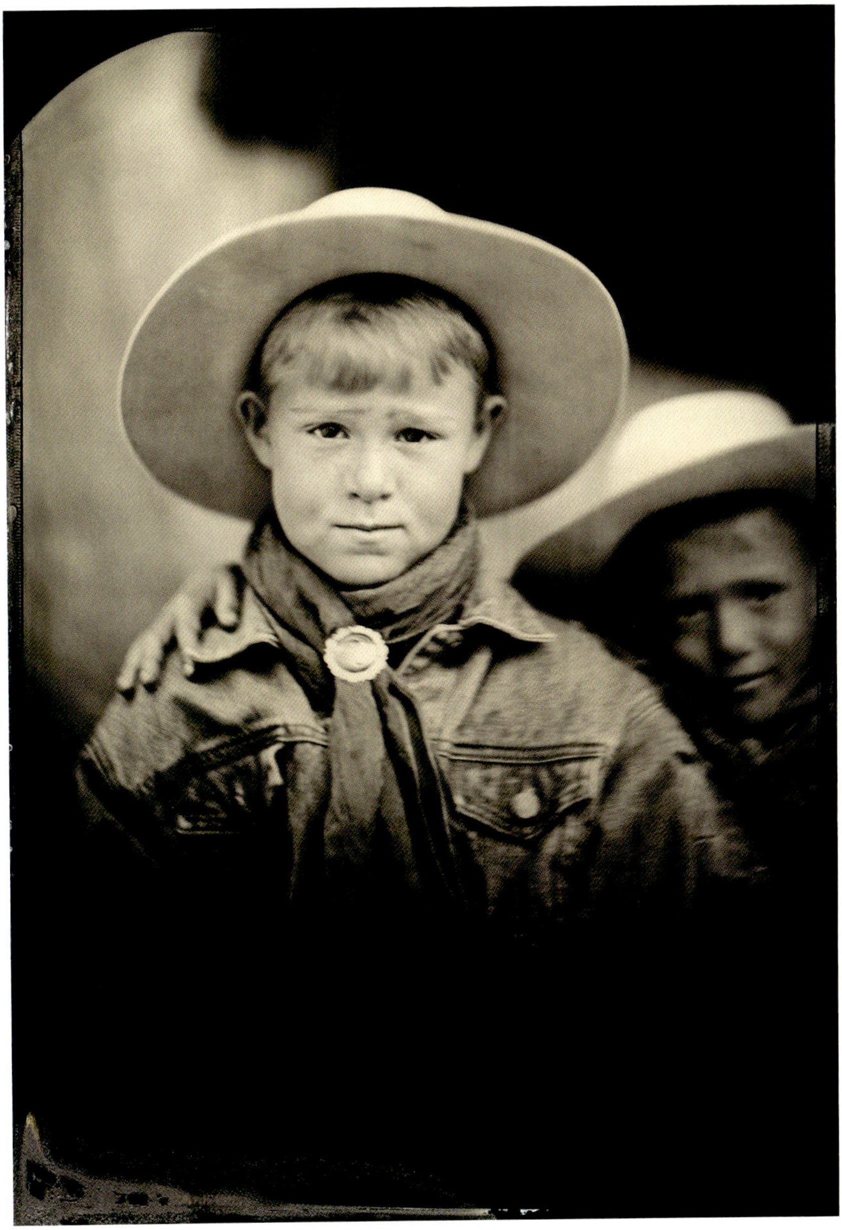

PLATE 129

Trey and Conner McGowan

NEVADA

My family had a small ranch in northern Colorado and got kinda pressured from population there so we moved up here in 1972. Now we see people startin' to move to Montana, but I don't know where we'd find any more open country, so this is probably where we'll stay. We've raised seven kids on the ranch. That was our big goal because kids learn a lot of responsibility and initiative workin' around livestock and takin' care of little calves that kinda depend on you for everything.

We run kind of a cowboy outfit. We don't use four-wheelers; we do everything horseback and run lots of cattle in big rough steep country; go horseback every day. We get a lot of ridin' in. I've had a lot of fellas come and apply for a job. They wanted a job that had a little more ridin' and a little less tractor-driving. A lot of them, after about two weeks, they come back and say "Well, I didn't mean that damn much ridin'."

So we tend to stay outside all day every day, and if things get tough around this part of the world, all you gotta do is look up at the mountains and gaze around you a little bit and it sure makes you happy to be here. I tell everybody I never worked a day in my life; it's all been fun.

We raise horses and there's sure a lot of pleasure. You go out there amongst the mares in the summer and see a little colt and you kinda keep your eye on him and that fall when you wean them colts you kinda look at them and watch the way he moves and kinda put him away in a special place in your mind and later on, a couple of years maybe, you start ridin' that colt and when he gets to be a good broke horse that you're usin' every day, there's a lot of pleasure in ridin' a horse that you raised and doin' your work on him.

There's not a lot of money, but there's always a lot of pleasure in workin' outside in this beautiful country. God made some of the most beautiful on earth, I think, here in the mountains of Montana and workin' with cattle and horses every day it's always an adventure. Do something different every day. About the time you get tired of one thing, it's time to start doin' somethin' else.

I had a pretty good old horse I rode for a lot of years, and the kids named him Root Beer, and I started ridin' him when he was just three. Old Root Beer was just honest and kind and there was one time when we had a big old yearling that needed doctorin' and I pursued him as fast as I could, a little further than I should have. About the time I got him roped, he went over the edge of a cliff, and I had dallied up [tied up] and the dallies was stuck and I thought, man, we're in trouble now, cause that big old yearling's gonna jerk me and Root Beer right over that cliff and it ain't gonna be pretty. By golly, Root Beer just knew what was up and he just braced

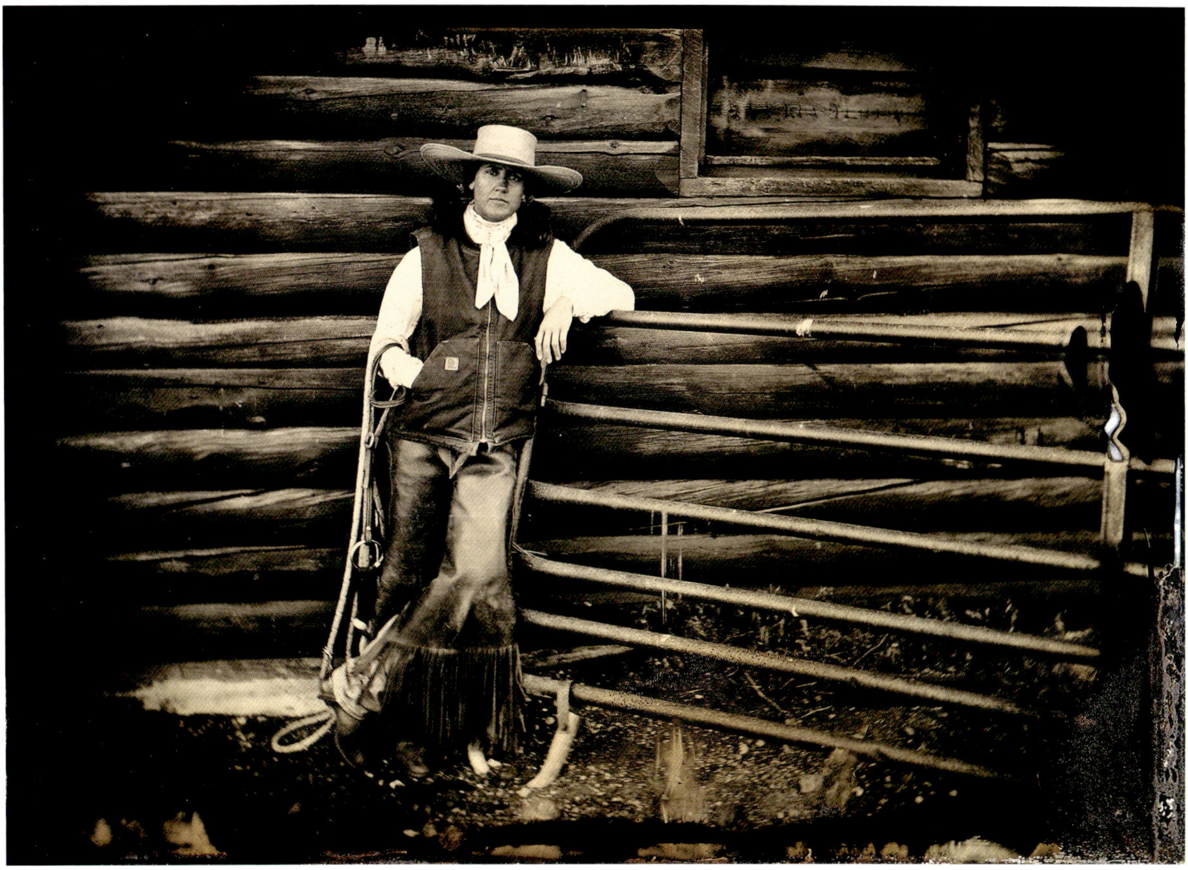

PLATE 130

Tilly Van Norman

VAN NORMAN RANCH, NEVADA

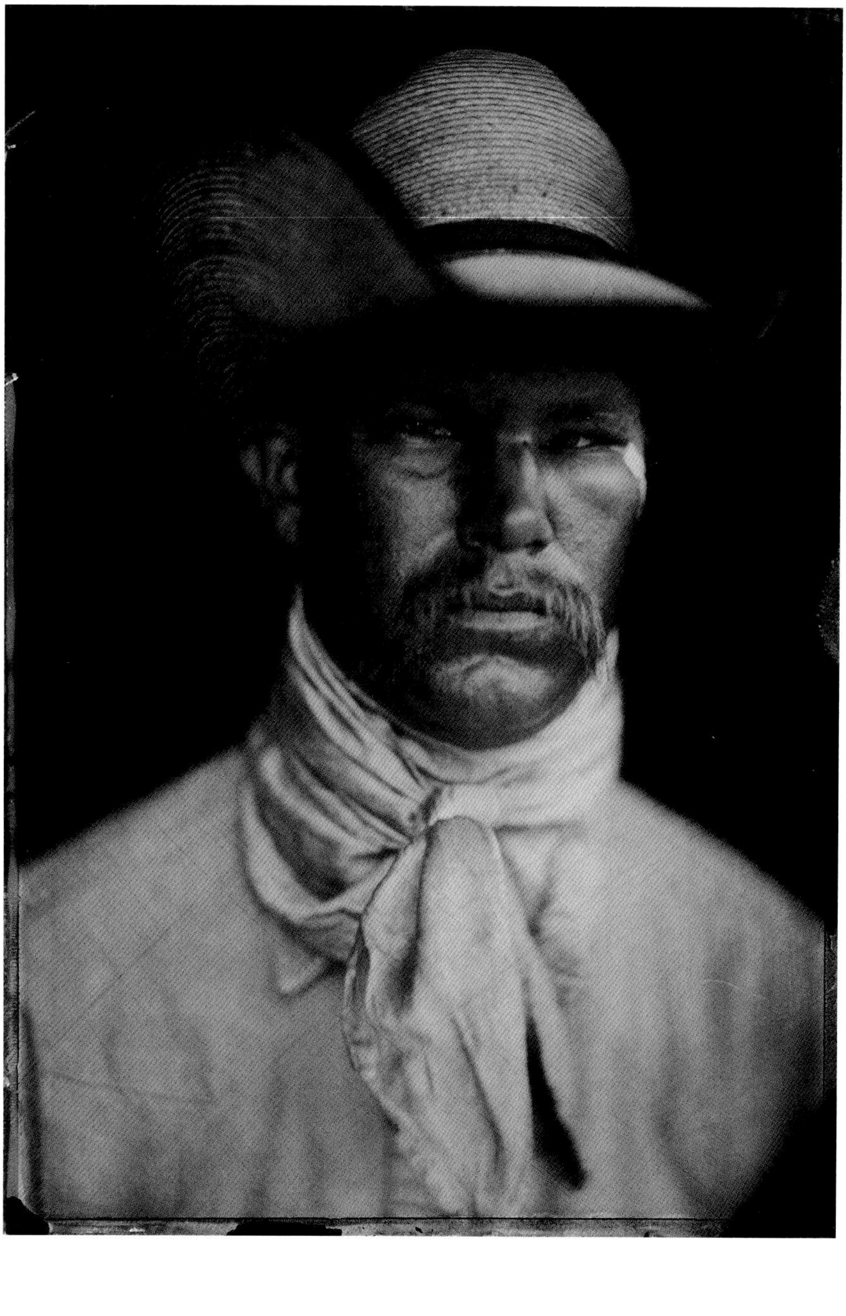

PLATE 131

R. D. Horn

JA RANCH, TEXAS

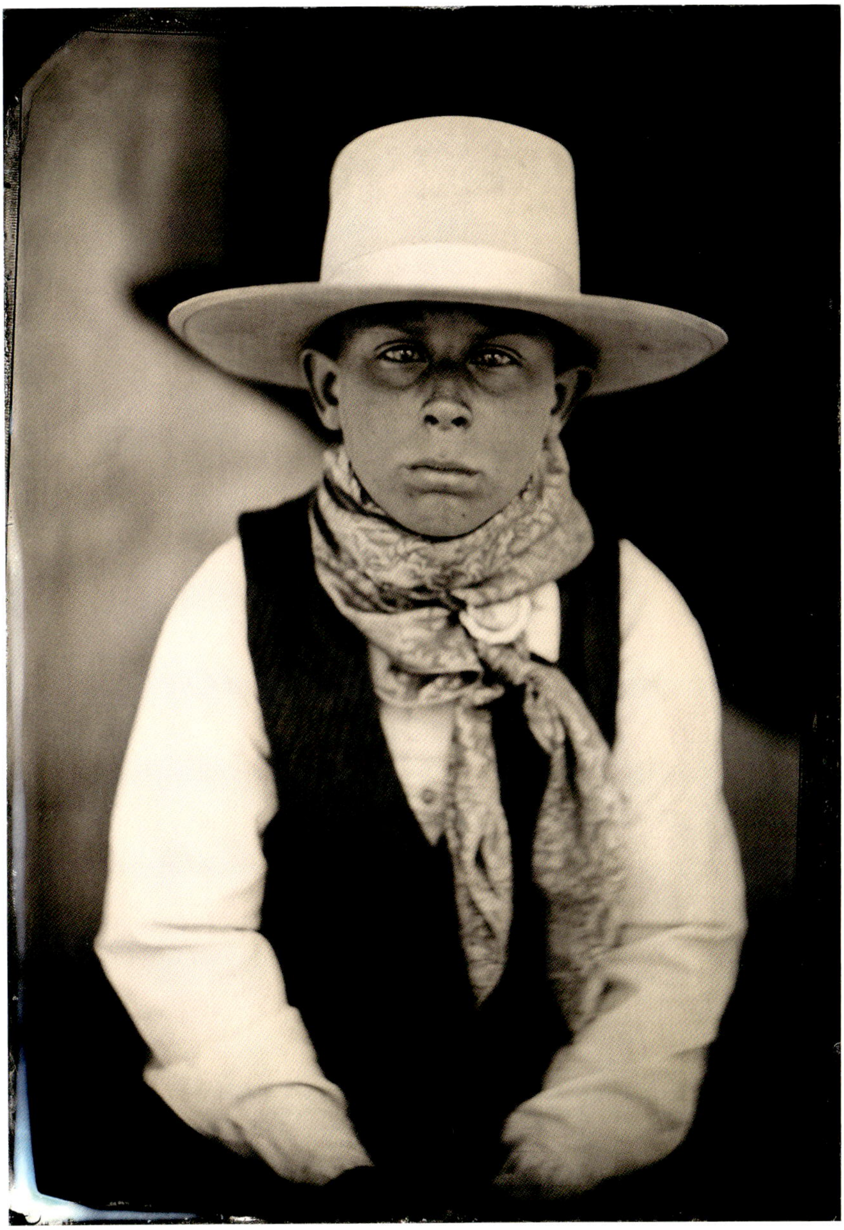

PLATE 132

Ray Allen Baird

HITT MOUNTAIN CATTLE ASSOCIATION, IDAHO

himself up there and stood there hangin' with that 850-pound yearling hangin' off the end of that rope, and I thought, ya know, that's just about as honest and true and big-hearted as you'll ever get and whenever I think about what we've done and spent a lifetime doin', I guess bein' around them kind of horses is probably really the thing that would come back to me.

But I tell my kids that if you love horses that's great, and if you like cattle that's great, but if you're gonna be in ranchin', you gotta have a love for the land because that's the one thing that really stays, and you gotta be able to appreciate that land and take care of it and cherish it and nurture it. The love for the land is really what carries you through from one generation to the next. Cattle come and go and horses come and go and people even come and go, but the land stays there.

ROGER PETERS
DRAGGIN Y RANCH, MONTANA

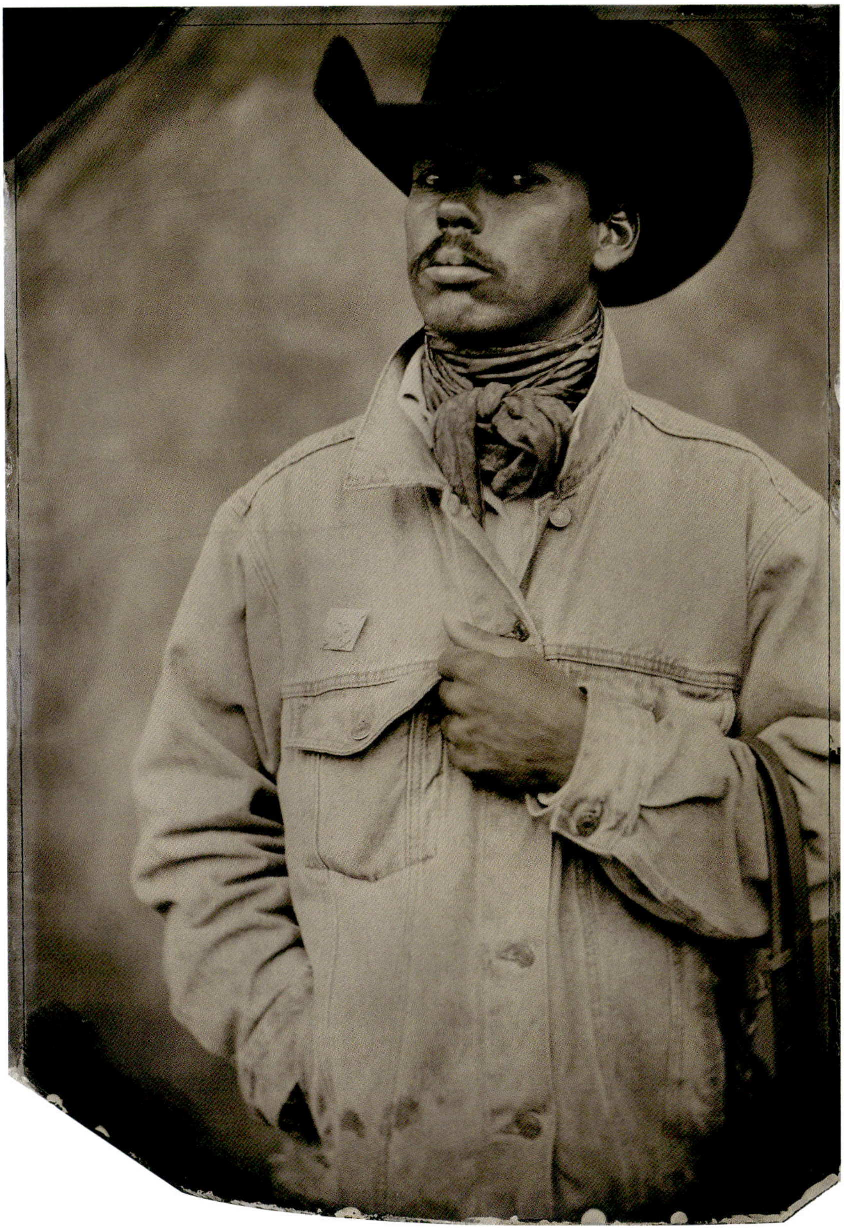

PLATE 133

Efraín Corrales

SANDHILL CATTLE CO., TEXAS

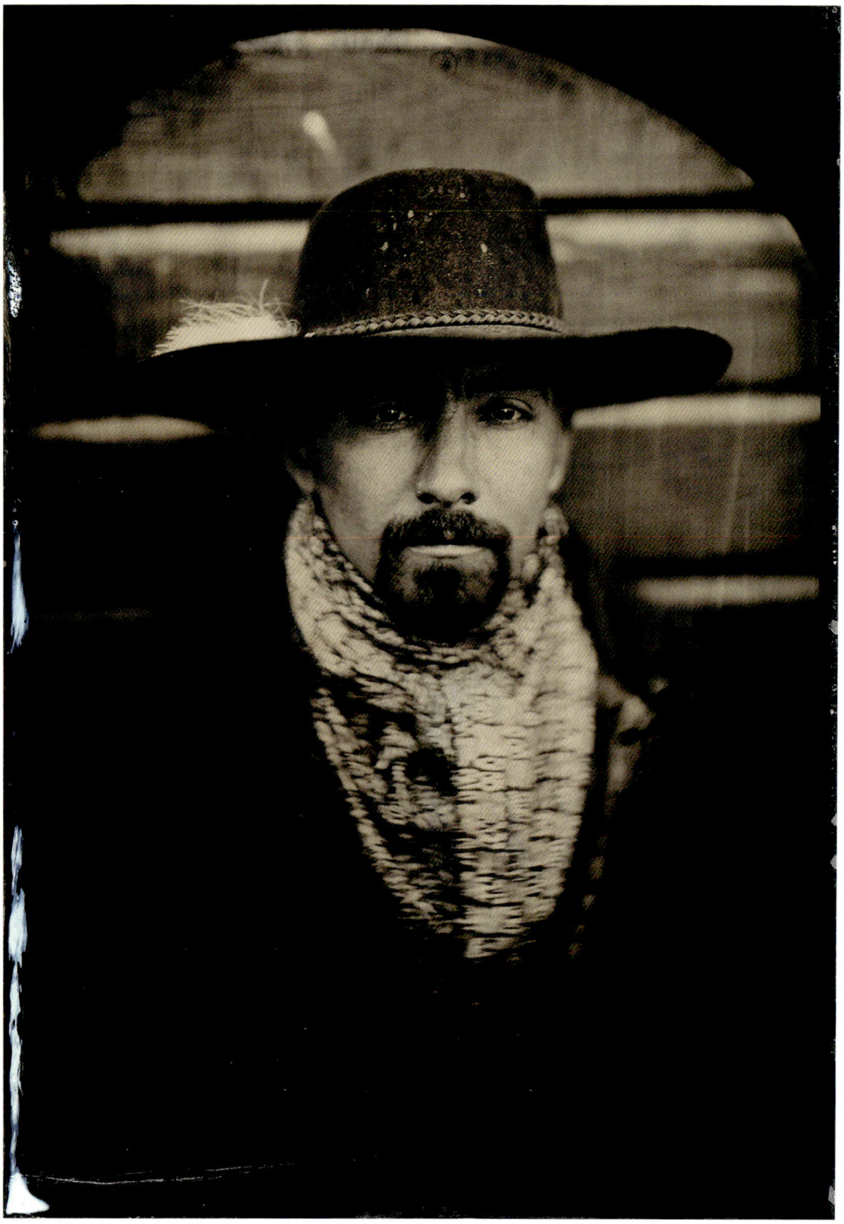

PLATE 134

Maxime Gauthier

GANG RANCH, BRITISH COLUMBIA, CANADA

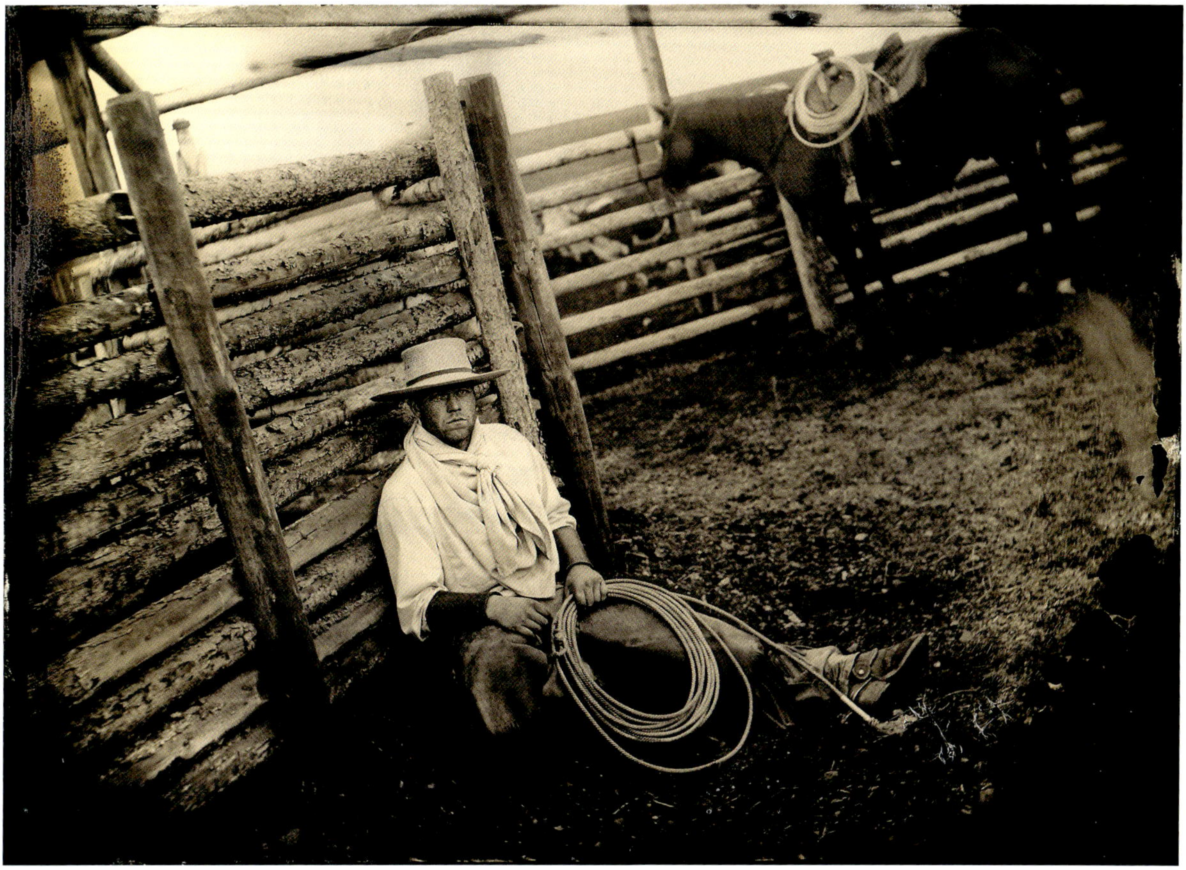

PLATE 135

Mike McCormick

DOUGLAS LAKE RANCH, BRITISH COLUMBIA, CANADA

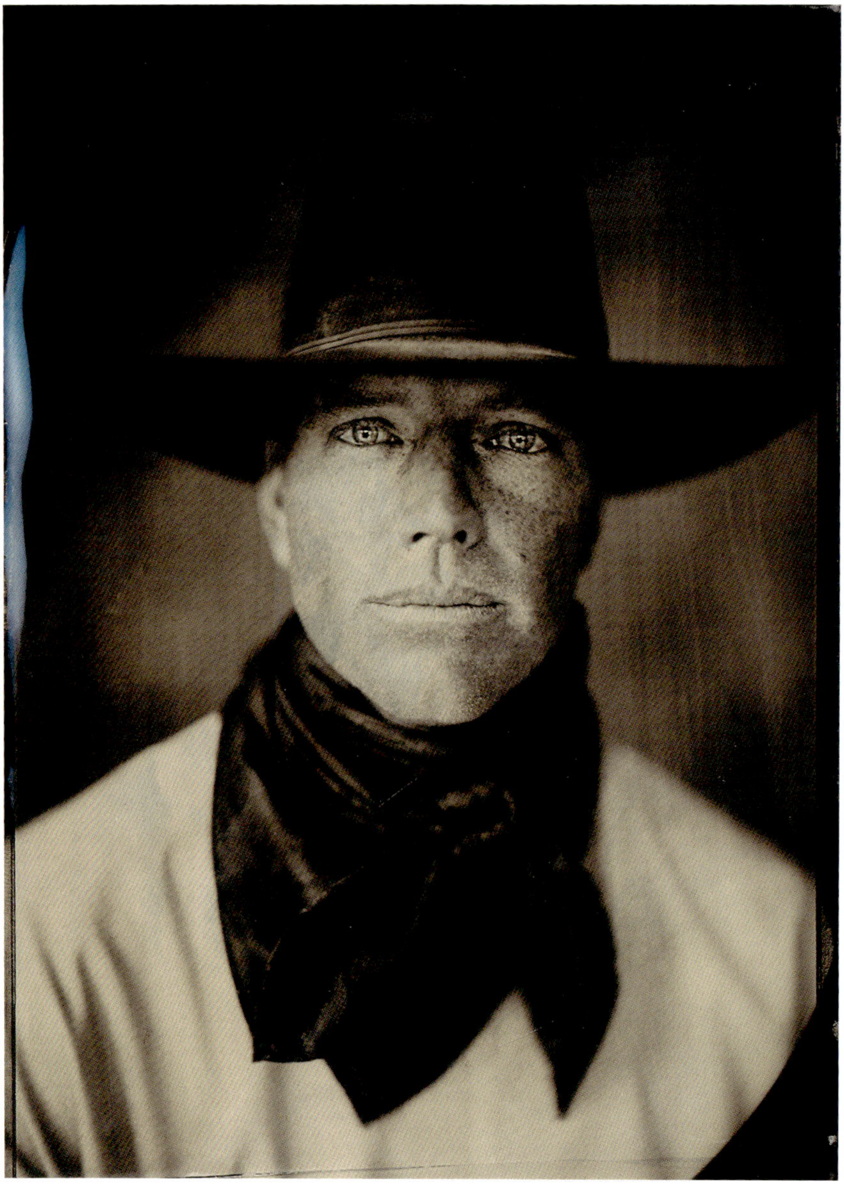

PLATE 136

Kacy Wachob

WACHOB RANCH, NEBRASKA

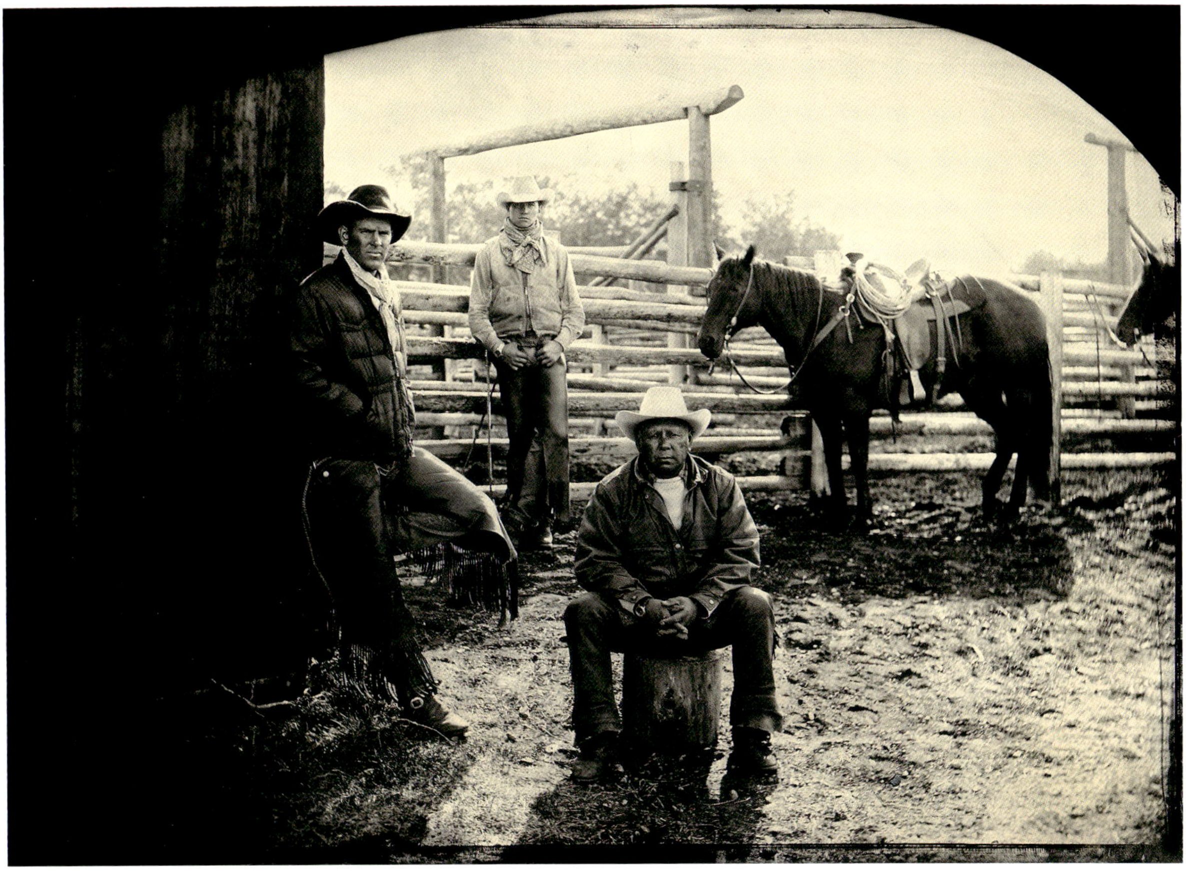

PLATE 137

Nolan Eek, Cameron Jacobs, Jesse Coutlee

DOUGLAS LAKE RANCH, BRITISH COLUMBIA, CANADA

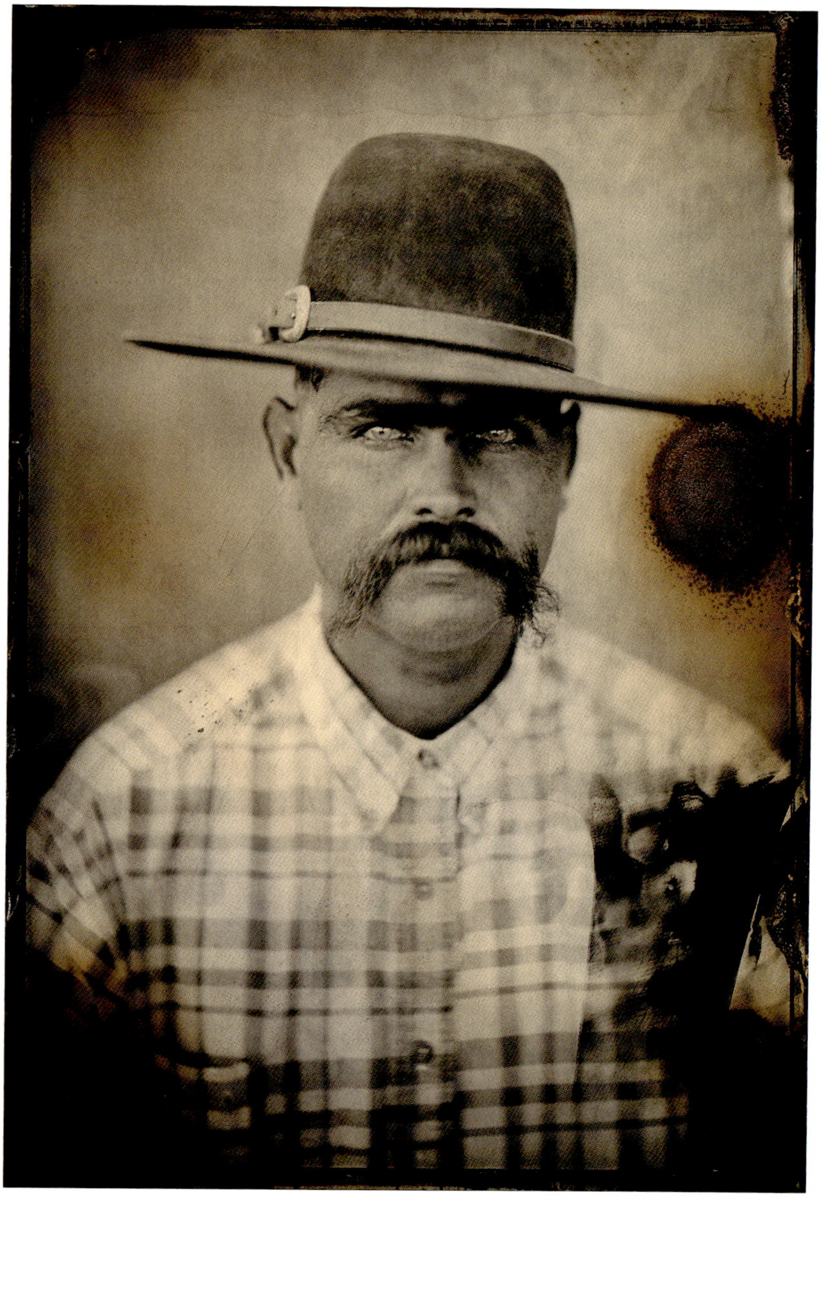

PLATE 138

Jim Youngblood

NEVADA

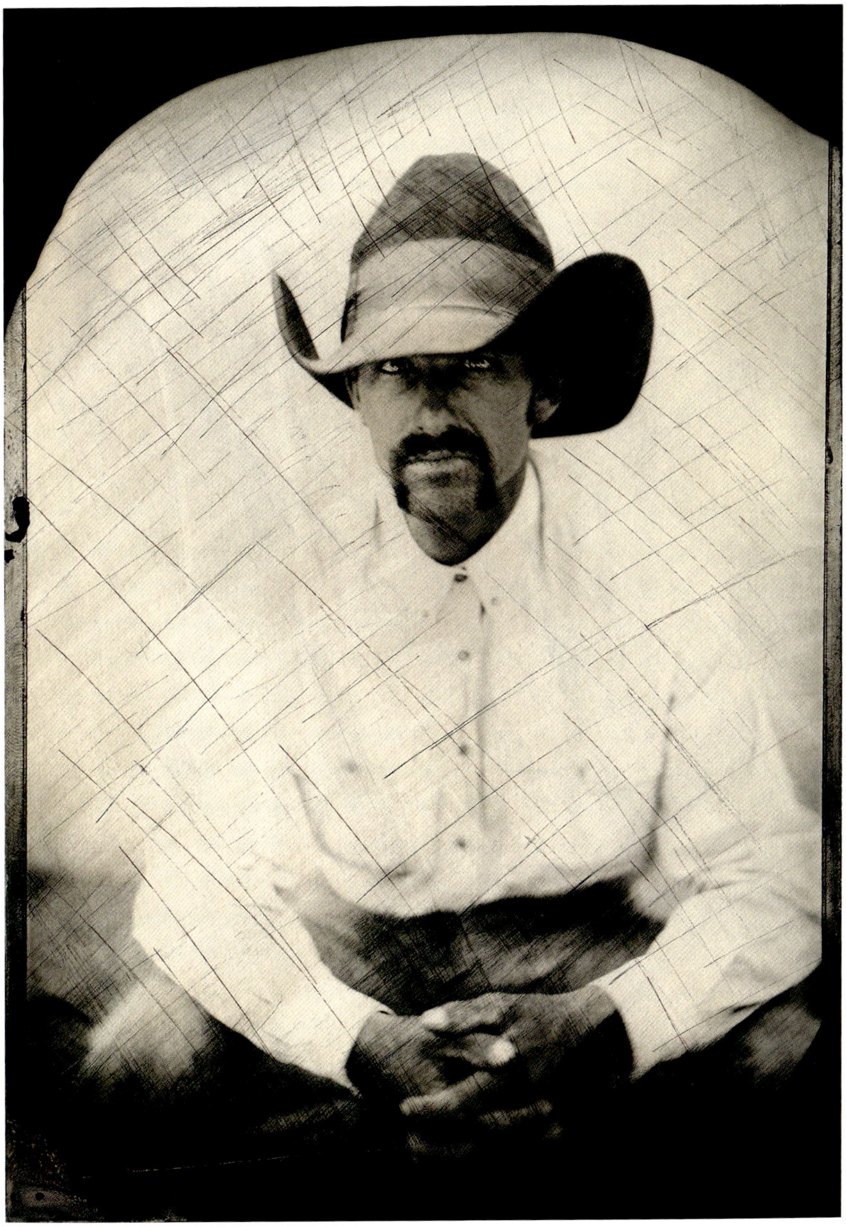

PLATE 139

Linc Bundy

ORO RANCH, ARIZONA

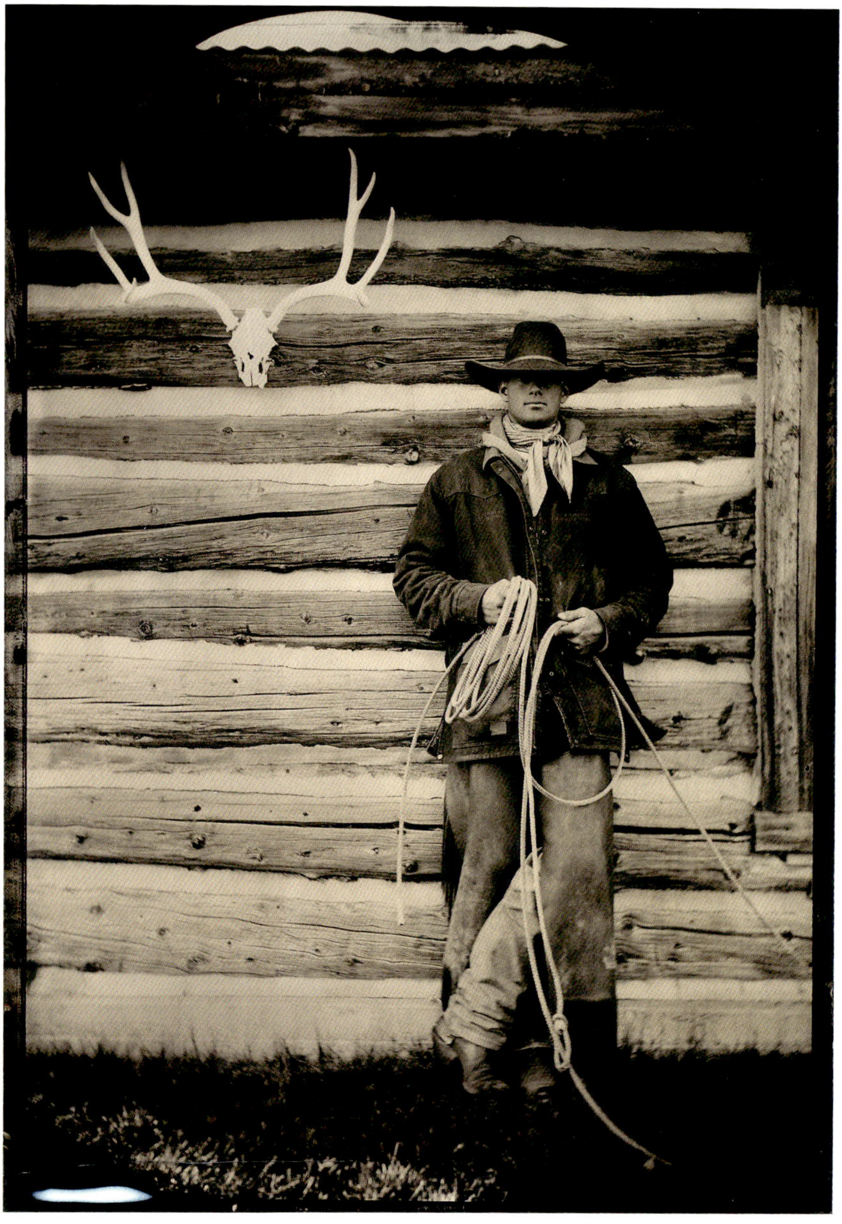

PLATE 140

Hanes Holman

PX RANCH, NEVADA

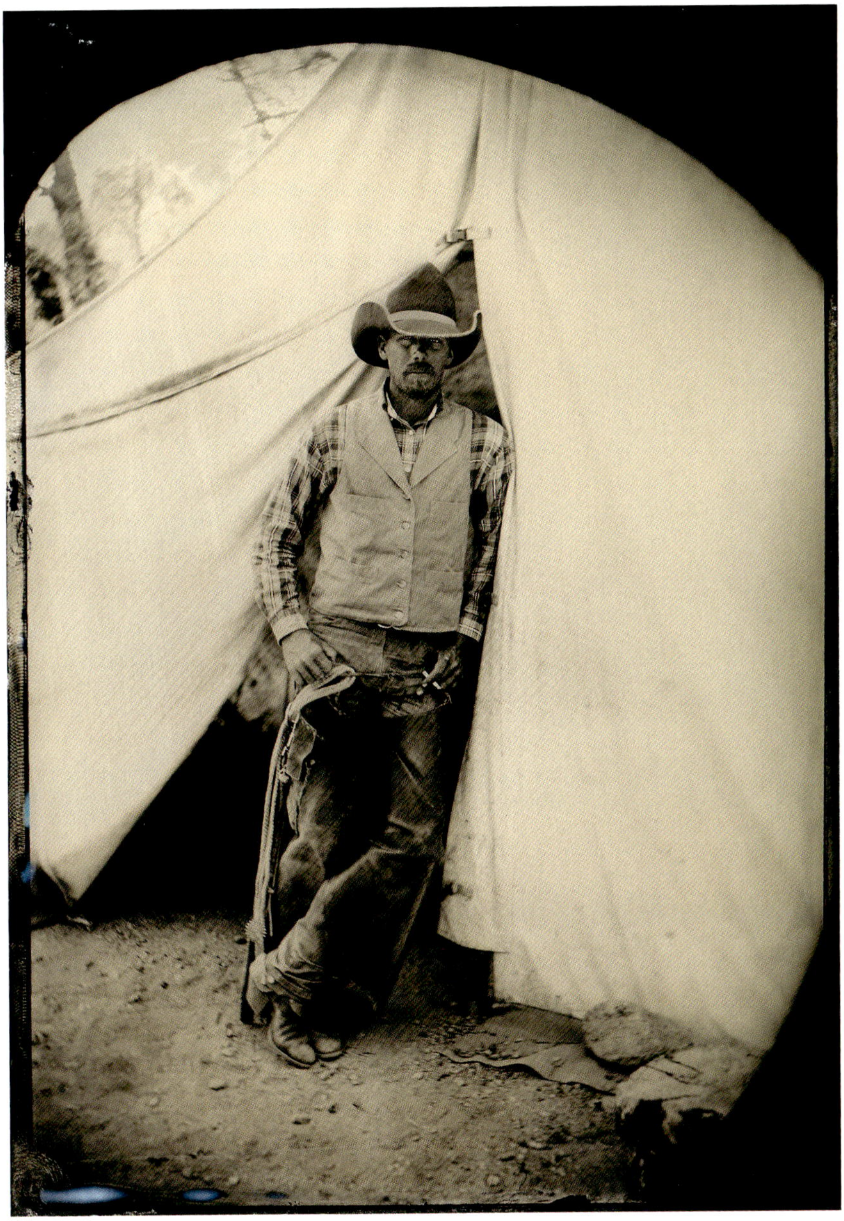

PLATE 141

Brandon Muncy

ORO RANCH, ARIZONA

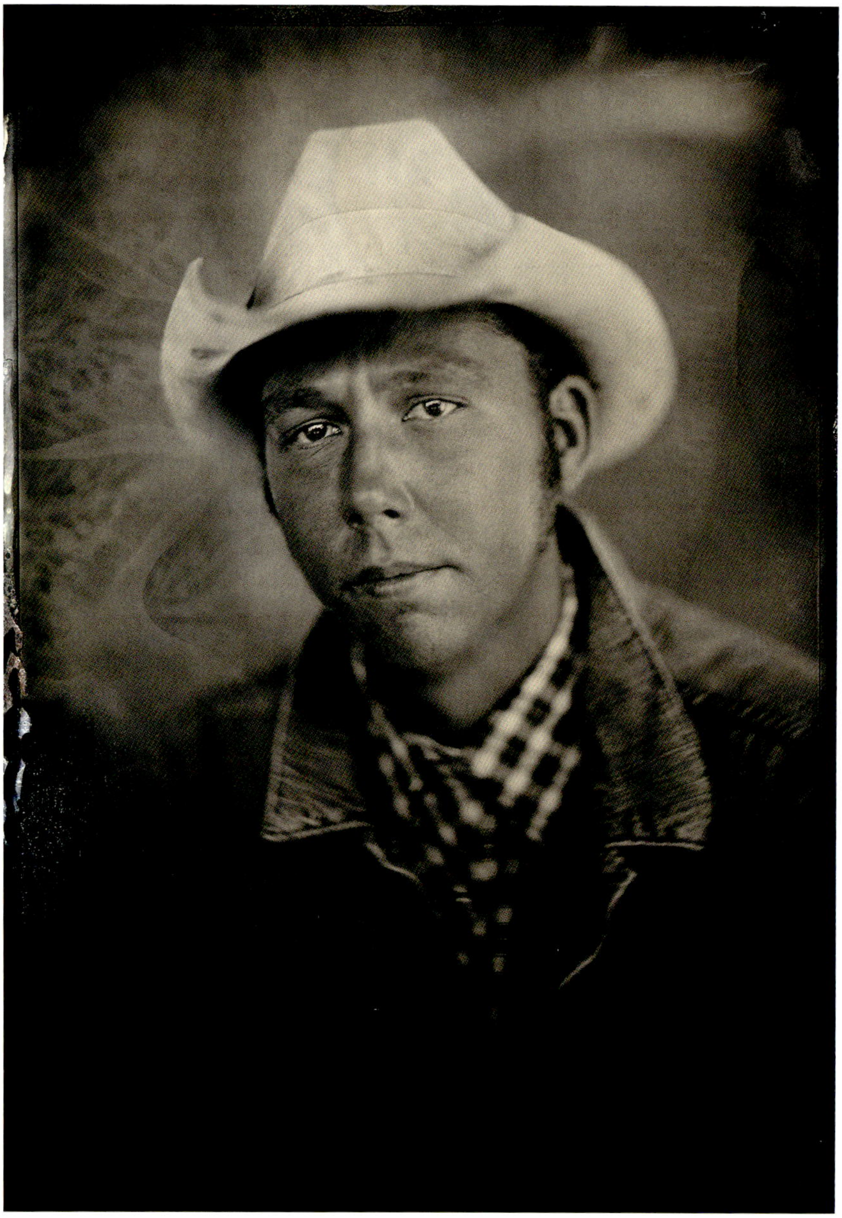

PLATE 142

Andrew Dean

NEW MEXICO

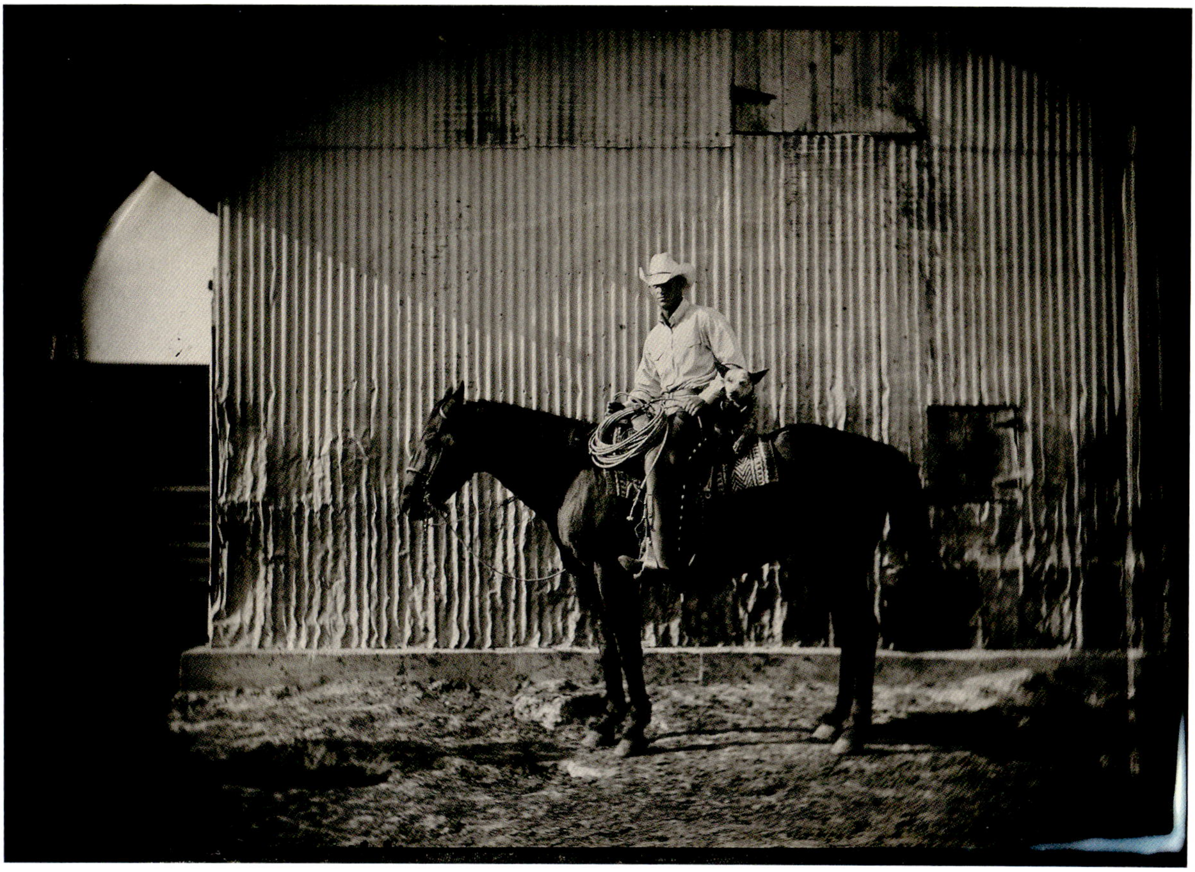

PLATE 143

Cooper Adams with Ruby (dog)

XI RANCH, KANSAS

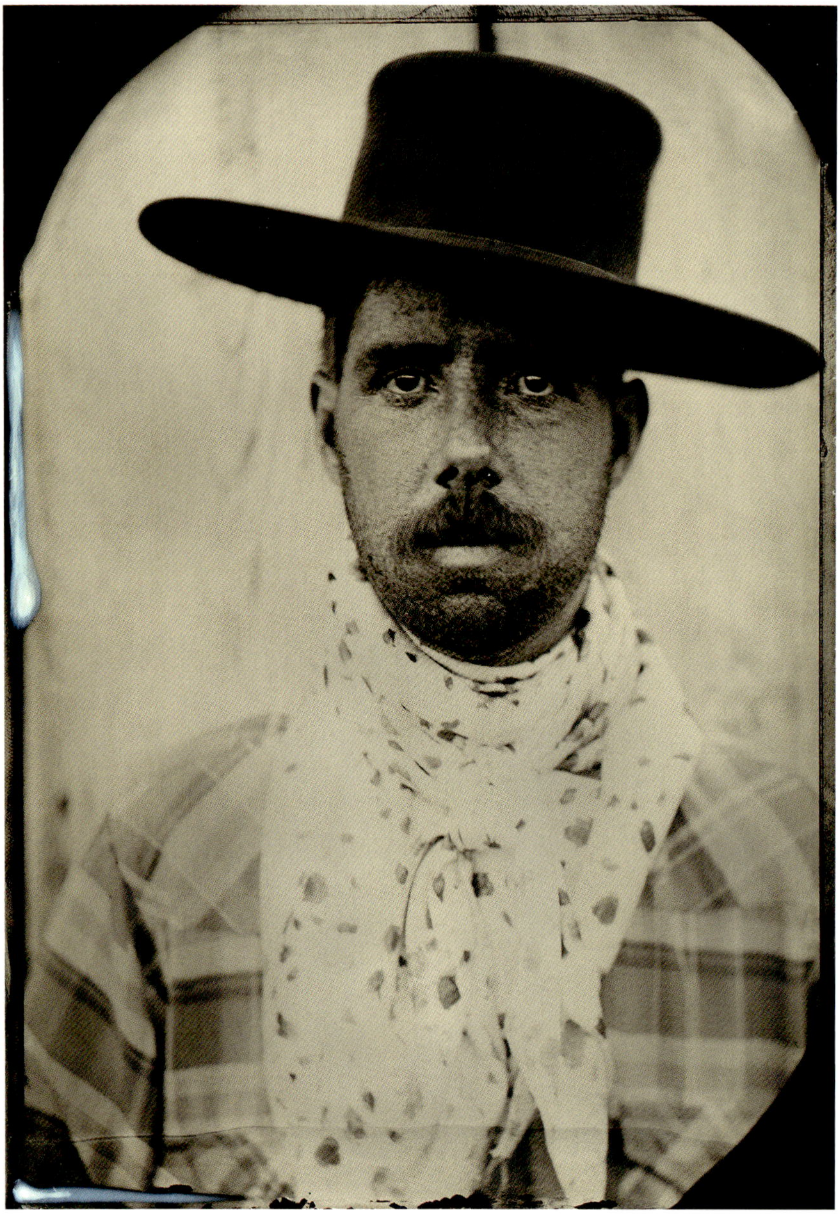

PLATE 144

Wes Miner

SNOWLINE RANCH, MONTANA

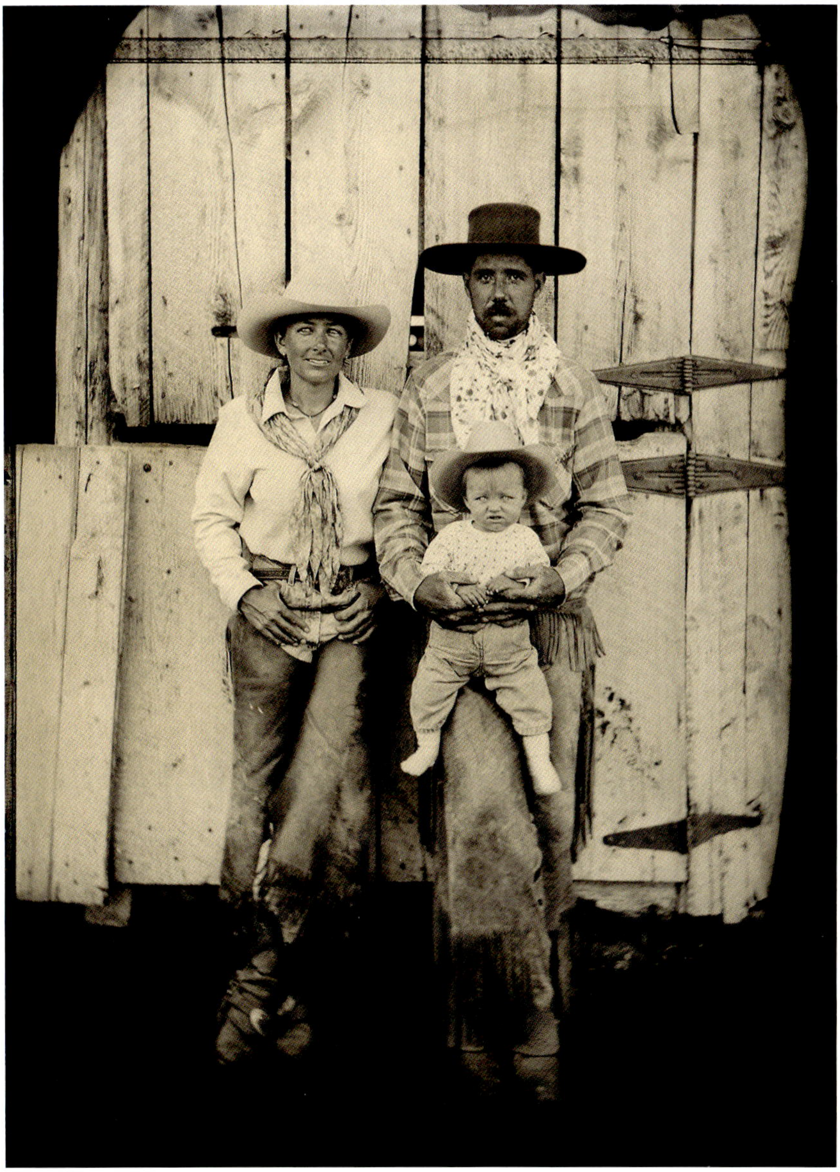

PLATE 145

Jodi, Wes, and Myla Miner

SNOWLINE RANCH, MONTANA

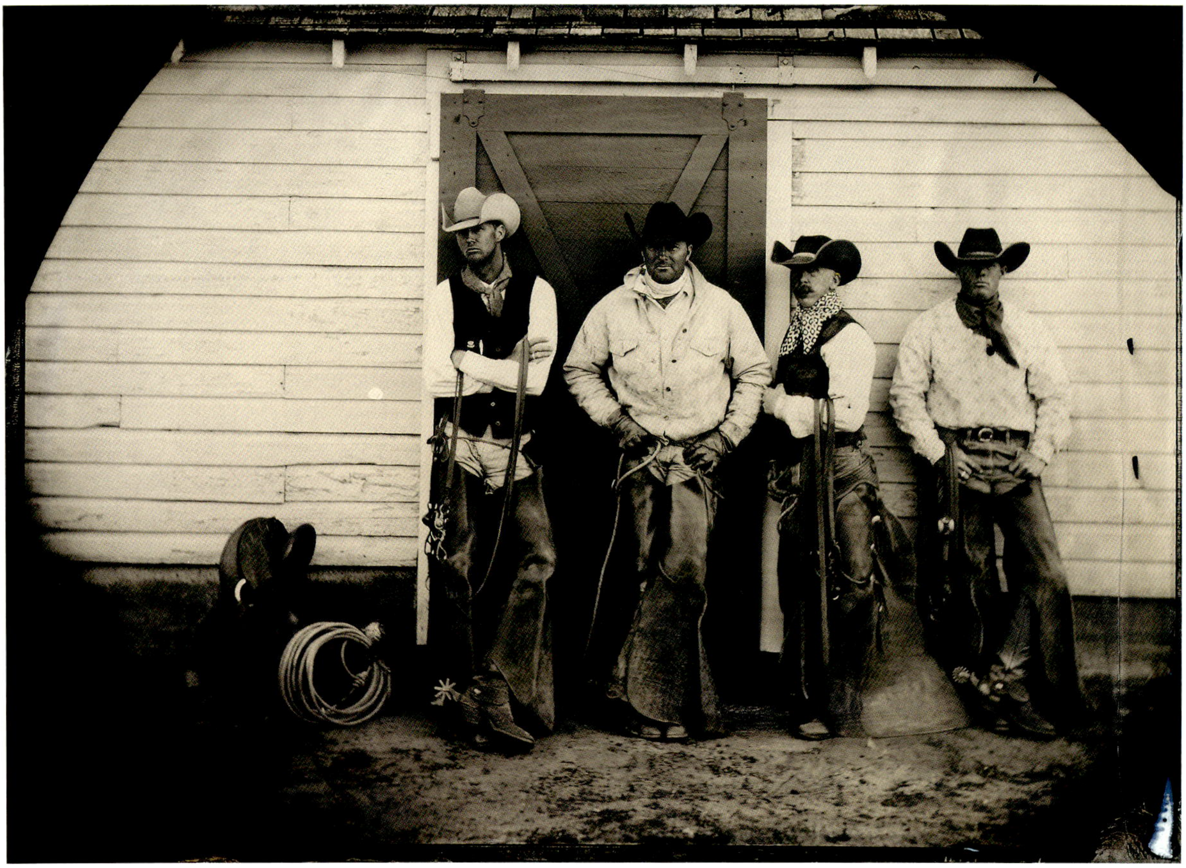

PLATE 146

Quentin Marburger, Tim Stout, Cliff "Frosty" Foster, Steve Eytcheson

JA RANCH, TEXAS

PHOTOGRAPHER'S NOTES

GROWING UP IN THE TEXAS PANHANDLE, I often visited a cousin who worked at the 6666 Ranch, one of the old historic outfits in Texas, so I am quite familiar with the cowboy lifestyle. Though I've never been drawn to doing the actual work of a cowboy, I do connect with some of the essentials they hold dear: raw land, solitude, self-reliance, trusting those you work with, earning respect, and being your own boss. Many of them might laugh at my comparison between common threads we share, since their work is so much more physical, dangerous, and less rewarding financially, but I think some of the ranching men and women I've gotten to know over the years would understand.

I have been drawn to photograph cowboys for twenty-five years—in tintype for the past six years. The tintype process takes me even closer to the cowboys in important ways, I believe. It requires more patience, and making each plate by hand has shown me that I'm not always in control—environment, weather, and chance always play a part in the final product. In this world of yesterday deadlines and "perfect digital photography," I find a renewed awareness that patience and serendipity are important gifts. I would like to thank all those who gave me time and tolerance, allowing me to photograph them in this arcane style of photography that slowed us all down so we could get to know each other a little bit better.

People who have seen my cowboy photos often ask if I have "styled" the cowboys. Did I tie their scarves just so? Did I ask them to put the leather brush cuffs on their arms? Did I turn up their shirt collars like that? The answer to all these questions is a clear "no." I did not have to do anything to their clothes or their look. I photographed the men and women exactly as I found them. These are their ordinary, workaday outfits—not costumes, not dress up. Every piece and feature serves a purpose in their jobs. It's amazing and refreshing that in the early twenty-first century there are still people who get to go to work dressed like this.

In Minden, Nebraska, I met Tom Kelly and his two daughters on their small family ranch—one of the increasingly few family ranches left in the West. I made my first mistake with Tom by inadvertently running my trailer tires about a foot off the driveway onto his grass. Tom was visibly upset, but he gently informed me that he considered grass absolutely precious. It was hard to grow and keep in the dry plains of Nebraska and it was the thing that kept his ranch going, the thing that fed his cattle, from which the family earned their living. I felt terrible, but Tom quickly forgave me and made me feel very welcome at his home. When it was time to leave the Kellys, Tom, who's raised his daughters to be excellent horsewomen and ranchers, pulled me aside and said, "Robb, please promise me one thing. That you'll get it right." I knew exactly what he meant. His way of life is misunderstood in many ways. Cowboys are sometimes thought of as a brutish, drinking lot with little respect for the environment. The truth as I saw it was that these are kind, family-centered people with great respect for nature, animals, and God's gifts and for a hard day's work. I'm sure Tom will let me know if I succeeded or not.

At the TS Ranch in Battle Mountain, Nevada, is a stunning collection of timber outbuildings redolent of leather. It's here that braided leather ropes and worn saddles of the buckaroo style are put away, and also where cowhides are stretched, scrapped, and cut in preparation for braiding into new gear. After a long day of shooting tintypes, ranch manager Doug Groves called us in to dinner. The big surprise was that Doug is a lover of lamb. I had expected steak, but a lamb dinner at a cattle ranch was a welcome and wonderful deviation from the script. We shared a beer after dinner, had lively talks about politics, religion—all the things you're not supposed to bring up, especially with those you don't know well. At the end of the evening Doug showed me some of his braided rawhide—a craft that fills his winter months. The reatas and hackamores were stunning in their workmanship and artistry. The attention to detail and the nimble fingers it takes to be a great braider does not seem to fit with the kind of rough work those same hands have to perform over miles of wide-open sagebrush range.

Cookhouses all have their own form of protocol. When Holly and I arrived at the Gang Ranch cookhouse at 5:30 a.m., we were met with a silence unlike any we had experienced on any other outfit on this trip. The six cowboys bent over their breakfast plates didn't say a word to us, didn't even acknowledge us. Trying to break the ice I asked a cowboy seated by himself at a table for six if we could join him. "No," he said flatly, barely looking up. "Seat's taken." As we awkwardly backed off from the table, a young cowboy kindly told us that the table in the corner was for visitors. After our quiet breakfast, we uneasily began setting up for the photos, hoping we could establish a better rapport with the cowboys.

The 12' x 7' trailer I take on these trips and the bulky camera equipment I use definitely catch the attention of those being photographed. It is a very long process, one that requires total concentration and dedication from those being photographed as well as from the photographer. The trailer is not only a practical tool, but also a way to share the amazing experience of tintypes with those I photograph. Once the cowboys at the Gang Ranch saw how I worked and joined me in the trailer to see the photos develop, their attitude changed completely. They were talkative and curious. They wanted to know about the history of tintypes and see more examples. At one point, I had up to five broad cowboys in the small trailer watching the process. The next morning at the cookhouse, it was quiet again—I guess no one wants to talk much at 5:30 a.m.—but there was eye contact, quick waves and smiles. We felt like part of the "gang" at Gang Ranch.

At the end of our first day at the Gang Ranch, Holly and I were exhausted. We had worked thirteen hours straight on four hours' sleep. Ready to call it a day after what we thought would be the last shot, Holly was putting away my camera equipment, but when I stepped out of the darkroom trailer I saw Colter Schlosser leaning on the wall with his head down. Though I was tired, I couldn't resist taking the shot. Wrapped around his neck was a gorgeous print scarf and over his chaps, he wore what is called an *armita*—a leather fringed, apron-like piece of gear that offers extra protection. Holly moaned at the idea of setting up the camera again, but we ended up making two exposures of the scene and the result is on the cover of this book. "You were right," Holly actually said after she took down the equipment a second time. "It was worth it."

Having spent a lot of time around cowboys, I knew that the way they express themselves is unique and very colorful. That's one of the reasons I decided to tape interviews with almost everyone I photographed. To capture the essence of their lives in their own amazing words. Another reason is I wanted a record of what it's like to be a cowboy today. I'm not one of those who believe that cowboys are a dying breed. I think, instead, cowboys are adapting to a new world and have been for decades, but still it is important to document what cowboy culture is like at this very specific point in time. I especially was happy to get insight and reminiscences from the older men—the links to the past in this world. When we interviewed Ralph Chain, the eighty-year-old owner of the Chain Ranch in Oklahoma, he got teary-eyed. He had been working for years himself interviewing old-timers for posterity, and as we talked, it became clear to him that he was now the old-timer sharing his memories and anecdotes. The quotes and stories you see throughout the book are taken directly from the tapes we made during our six-month project. Cowboys talking cowboy.

Trying to get to the fall camp on the ORO Ranch north of Prescott, Arizona, was like going on an obstacle course on the moon. At the headquarters, the ranch manager, Wayne Word, showed me on a map where the cowboys were doing fall work and shipping cattle and warned us that it might take us five to seven hours to get back there towing my trailer. After explaining that the primitive road we would be taking wasn't marked, he threw up his arms and said, "Hell, I don't know really how to tell you how to get there, when you come to a decision on which turn to make, look at which way looks more worn and head that way." I didn't feel very confident, but off we headed south—staying on ORO property the whole way—looking for Wes Foote, the "jigger boss," and his group of cowpunchers.

At one point on our drive, we came up on a rise and when we crested the top we were looking down a steep grade of a road with a 700-foot drop if you failed the curve. I stopped my truck and trailer to take a photo, since the view was simply stunning. I secured the parking brake and put the truck into park and leaped out. However, on the steep incline, the truck and trailer started sliding down the loose dirt road under their own weight. I immediately jumped back in, threw the truck into low and eased down the steep hill. The picture was lost but we were safe, though our hearts had a run of it. After five hours, we finally arrived at a beautiful campsite where eight range teepees were set up next to a creek lined with cottonwoods. This was home to eight men and a cook for six weeks of fall work.

After shooting some photos, I saw some large semis pulling up to the campsite. They were there to load cattle that would be shipped out. "How did they get here?" I asked one of the guys. "Surely they didn't go over the same road we did." I learned there was another road in, from an interstate to the west.

When it was time to leave we were grateful for the shortcut, and even more grateful that the cook had packed us a meal, which he miraculously had made over the campfire. Leonard McNabb was the cook's name and he was a true artist and a throwback to another time. He had to shoot and dress a cow every eight days to feed himself and the eight cowpunchers. He made a notch on his pistol for every cow he had to slaughter while at the camp. On the road, we unwrapped Leonard's meal—a rare, well-seasoned steak wrapped in a huge homemade tortilla with homemade salsa. And for dessert, a mincemeat pie made of cow's tongue and wild fruit picked from the trees around the campsite. The crust was delicate and as beautifully fashioned as anything you'd see at a Manhattan bakery. He'd dusted the outside with cinnamon and confectioner's sugar, and biting into that treat after the long day we'd had, I couldn't remember anything tasting so good. "Never a trust a skinny cook," Leonard told me, and I never will.

In the old Westerns, it was the cowboys versus the Indians. But real life is more complicated of course. Indians can actually be cowboys. I had the pleasure of visiting forty-five of them at the Duck Valley Reservation on the Nevada-Idaho border. All of them were dashing Shoshone buckaroos, running several hundred head of cattle on the reservation. Native American cowboys actually shouldn't be a surprise since Native Americans have long been horse people. The Shoshone were the ones who gave Lewis and Clark the horses they needed to cross the Rockies. I was thrilled to photograph these wonderful people who have such deep connections to the land, cattle, and the history of the West.

I didn't know what to think when my wife, Jeannie, who was making my schedule for the trip, told me she had booked me at Uncle Buck's Lodge in Brewster, Nebraska. But when I drove into town and saw that the town's population was only eighteen, I expected the worst—some type of fleabag motel. How nice it was to be wrong. The owners of the beautiful lodge—Justin and Tracy Bradley, who I was going to photograph the following day at their other business, Sandhills Ranch—told me that the whole hotel had free wireless Internet. At the hotel restaurant, we had one of the finest steaks on the entire trip, cooked rare just like I love it, and had a choice of a great selection of wines. Later that night, Bosnian guests checked in and took over the kitchen, cooking food from their motherland and insisting that we "eat eat eat." The couple, regulars at Uncle Buck's, had brought liquor from Yugoslavia and told stories about escaping during the war and relocating to Lincoln, Nebraska. Here I had worried about being stuck in Podunk, but instead we had a surprisingly sophisticated and very international couple of days in the Sandhills of Nebraska.

So many great names on the trip: Frosty, Rooster, Chance, Sage, Stretch, Skeeter, Silas, Chase, Merlin, Bear, Rock, Beau, Rowdy. But probably my favorite name was Beano—the cowboy boss at the Diamond A Ranch in Arizona.

I met Pete Wagner at the Big Loop Rodeo in Jordan Valley, Oregon, which is the big event for buckaroos. When we started talking I noticed his strange accent. Pete was born and raised in Heilbronn, Germany, and decided to become a cowboy when he was four years old, after listening to stories his grandfather read him about the West. When he left school at eighteen, he bought a one-way ticket to Arizona where he worked as a stable hand for one of the big outfits. The cowboys took a liking to him and taught him to rope and ride, and two years later he hired on as a cowboy. That was thirty-nine years ago. Pete picked up the buckaroo ways and now lives in Oregon. The mystique of the cowboy reaches far.

Pete wasn't the only international cowboy I met. At the same Big Loop Rodeo, I photographed Nathan Fluter, a young buckaroo with a great face and a beautiful dark complexion. I asked Nathan about his nationality. When he asked me to guess, I said India or Bangladesh. He was surprised at my answer, which was correct. At age three, he was adopted from an orphanage in Calcutta by an Oregon couple, and he grew up riding and ranching like any good cowboy child. He knows no other way of life. The diversity of those involved with ranching never ceases to amaze me.

David Ross of the Pitchfork Ranch in Texas is known to his co-workers only as "Ross." I started photographing Ross nineteen years ago, and he really hasn't changed much other than his long, droopy moustache is a bit whiter now. Certainly his outfit isn't any different. He wears only white shirts, brush cuffs, suspenders, and Levi 501s, which he refuses to wash. He puts on a new pair and when they start to fall apart from wear and tear he'll replace them. Ross spends the winters alone in a 12' x 12' range teepee next to fields of winter wheat. His job is to scare the geese away with gunfire. Over those four months, he only sees another person every three to four weeks when his supplies are dropped off. Ross likes the time alone in the cold. "It's good for a man to be alone," he says. "It clears your mind."

When I photographed John Edwards, a cowboy at the Douglas Lake Ranch, I asked him how he liked the winters in British Columbia. I expected him to tell me how he toughed out the cold or had learned to bear it, so his answer surprised me. "I can't winter very well anymore," said John, who is in his fifties. "So I go to Baja from December through March to windsurf."

Here was this burly man in leather chaps and the whole cowboy regalia. I couldn't picture him any other way. "John," I said, "I just can't imagine you in floral print surf shorts on your board."

He laughed. "It's a good time, let me tell you."

Most any ranch that respects the traditional ways of working has a place in every real cowboy's heart, but some ranches have more mystique than others. The YP Ranch in Nevada is one of those. It's known as a premier buckaroo outfit, where things are done "right." When I was at the Spanish Ranch—a wonderful outfit itself—I met Chase Sligar, an eighteen-year-old whose father was a buckaroo on the Spanish. Chase had just landed a job at the YP and it was as if he'd just been accepted to Harvard, or the cowboying version of it. The excitement in Chase's eyes and the pride in his mother's were palpable. Not only would Chase be continuing in the family business, but he was starting at the top.

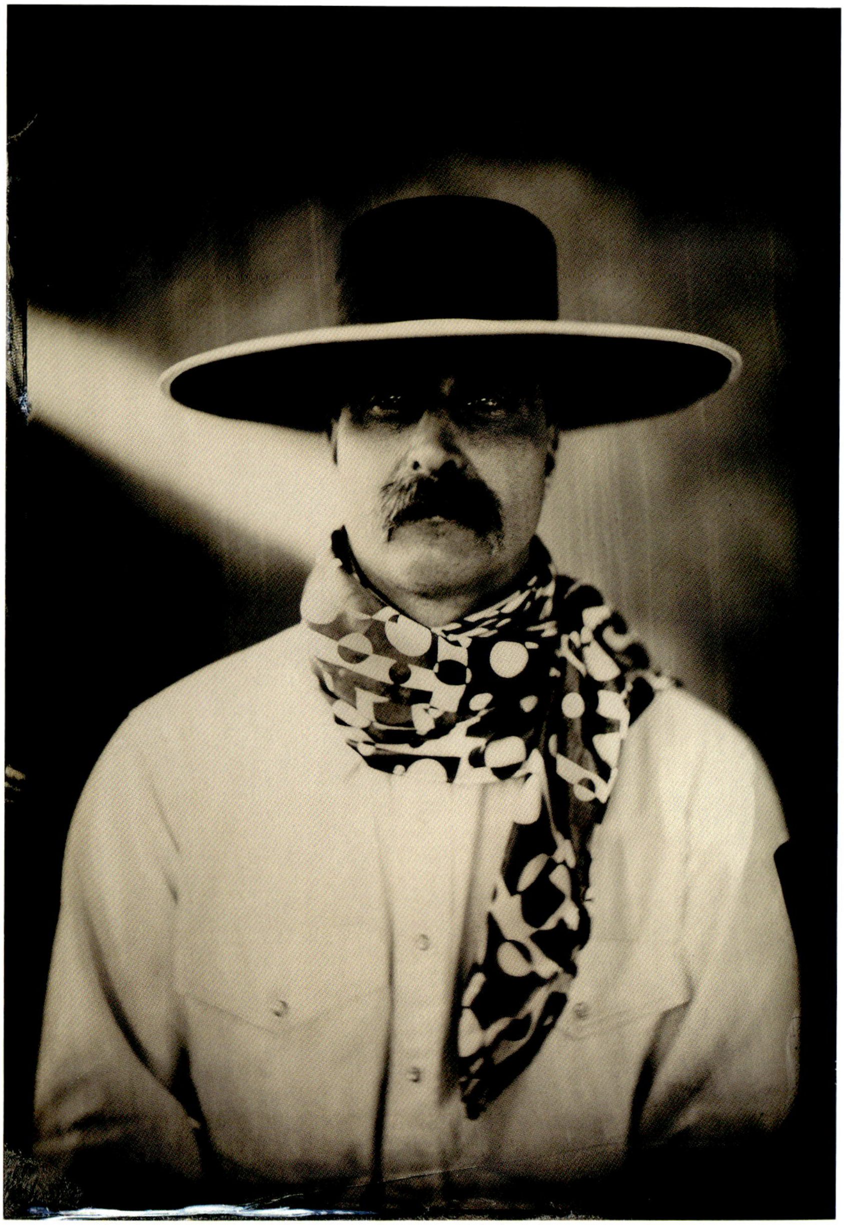

PLATE 147

Travis Castell

TC OUTFIT, SOUTH DAKOTA

AFTERWORD

Jay Dusard

Robb Kendrick has delivered to us a remarkable suite of compelling images. Beyond the fixed gazes that appear to emanate from a much earlier time, certain details may begin to stand out to the viewer. Shirts, vests, jackets all seem to be buttoned backwards. Everyone holding a catch-rope appears to be a lefty. Could it be that Robb Kendrick cornered more southpaws than have ever occupied the ranks of major league baseball pitchers? Check out all the ropes attached to the forks of saddles on the left side; no detective agency needed here. The four backward sixes branded on the back of a cowpuncher's hat (Plate 55) confirm that all these pictures are backwards.

Well, dear friends, you haven't been hornswoggled. Reverse-reading images are the product of the tintype direct-positive process, so while up doesn't become down, right *does* become left.

Tintype (a.k.a. ferrotype or melainotype) was patented by Professor Hamilton Smith of Ohio in 1856 and is considered America's first major contribution to the art of photography. Not exactly what America is best known for.

Now, the COWBOY! That's your bonafide high-rimmin', wide-loopin', double-hockin', silver-plated, E Pluribus ICON that the entire planet recognizes and admires. Even Brother Kendrick savvied this. After all, he grew up in Texas.

But, back to the tintype. It is fitting that Robb chose to portray his working cowboy subjects in the eminently affordable medium that peaked in popularity after the Civil War—during the ascendancy of Anglo ranching and cowboying in North America. One could argue that photographing contemporary workers in such an unrefined, archaic medium overly romanticizes them. I know that the subjects don't feel that way. Robb's vision simply anchors them in the traditions that they respect and cherish.

What Robb's cowboys practice is contemporary reality, not nostalgia. The varied, sometimes harsh, landscapes that these folks inhabit and work in are distinctly more suited to the raising of livestock than to most other uses. The horses they raise, train, and partner with are as essential to the craft as they were a century and a half ago. A modicum of mechanization notwithstanding, fine horsemanship, skill with a rope, and finesse in the handling of cattle still rule the range.

In different decades Robb and I have traveled some of the same trails and visited some of the same outfits. Photographically, we have had certain aspects in common. In the early 1980s my approach was thought to be cumbersome, antiquated: 8" x 10" view camera, huge tripod, a dozen lenses, too few film holders. Plenty of film, but not always a clean, dark place for unloading and reloading. A quarter-century later, along came Kendrick with his penchant for further antiquity and all the burdensome trappings of his *modus operandi*: 8" x 10" view camera adapted to 5" x 7", big tripod, an assortment of period lenses, boatloads of 5" x 7" metal plates. Plus towing a darkroom trailer with counter space, trays, chemicals (some rather toxic), water, safelights, hot plates, storage racks and bins . . . the beat goes on.

I have watched Robb at work, as he photographed cowboy friends of mine (Warner Glenn, Plate 30, and Monk Maxwell, Plates 82 and 83). For openers, Robb is friendly, engaging, respectful. Once he has decided upon the portrait location, usually determined by architectural features and the nature of the light, he expedites the setup of the darkroom trailer, tripod, and camera, then preliminarily positions his subjects in a composition. Entering the trailer, he mixes his potions and prepares a sensitized metal plate, then loads it into its holder. Back outside, he refines the composition and focus, makes an educated guess as to exposure time, and informs his subjects of how many seconds he desires them to hold still. With an opaque bag over the lens, Robb loads the plate holder into the camera, pulls the darkslide, removes the bag for the predetermined number of counted seconds, then re-covers the lens.

Time is of the essence here, since the exposure must be made and the development process begun while the plate is still moist. So, the maestro must hustle back into the trailer. Often the little darkroom draws a crowd, as cowboys are invited in to witness the emergence of their images in a tray illuminated by a dim amber safelight.

Cowboys make circles. A man or woman may ride out from headquarters or cow camp to inspect the cattle, to rope and doctor a sick one, or check on the availability of water and forage. The distance and duration of the completed circle is often dependent upon the unforeseen. Stray cattle from a neighboring ranch may need to be returned and breached fencing repaired. A pipeline leak in arid country may require some ingenious patchwork. The return ride may be in the dark, on a tired horse.

The outside circle is the longest, widest-ranging path that a cowboy travels in rounding up cattle. Here one usually goes for the longest periods of time without seeing one's comrades. The cowboy assigned to ride the outside circle is invariably the most competent and experienced member of the crew.

Here, at the beginning of our overly populous, overly conflicted, heartburn-inducing twenty-first century—on the toe of the curve, a photographer might say—Robb's timely images give me comfort and hope. A recent plane flight angled me across western New Mexico, over remote country that I had been horseback in, helping various rancher friends gather cattle. That nothing appeared to have changed made me think of Robb in his rig somewhere between British Columbia's Chilcotin River and the Sierra de la Encantada in Coahuila, traversing the cow country of three nations. He proved (perhaps only to himself and to me) that cowboys, old-timers and new recruits alike, may be threatened, but they're far from vanishing.

Robb Kendrick rode the outside circle and returned with immense revelations.

COCHISE COUNTY, ARIZONA
JUNE, 2007

ACKNOWLEDGMENTS

MY GRATITUDE TO SO MANY PEOPLE. Susan Welchman who has always believed. Chris Johns who took a chance when tough decisions were called for. Bob Moorhouse, Chuck Guildner, Jay Dusard—all talented photographers who opened doors in parts of the West where I had no connection—thank you for trusting me to carry your good names. Also thanks to Jay for writing the afterword; your acknowledgment of my work means the world. Tom Bowerman, Jon Griggs, and the many others who also provided connections to cowboys and ranches that always welcomed me with warm receptions and generosity of time. Craig Buck, Holly Wilmeth, and Derek Rankins, who traveled at different times with me on the project. Your positive attitudes meant a lot during the eighteen-hour days. Bill Allard, for your words of praise. Bill Wittliff, for your support of my work and your enthusiasm for this project. J. P. Bryan for your support in producing the limited-edition book. Byron Brauchli for your beautiful gravure work, and Jace Graf for pulling together all the elements of the limited-edition book and for fifteen years of friendship. The University of Texas Press for doing this book right. Teresa Wingfield for your elegant design—your patience with me is appreciated. David Cavazos for overseeing production. Though you were on the verge of retirement, you took this book on with great enthusiasm. Thanks Marianne for bringing your beautiful words, which add so much richness and meaning to the photos. You were busy, but you made the time. Jeannie, thanks for keeping me connected and on schedule during this complex trip. Last, I have to thank all the cowboys and cowgirls who made me feel so welcome during my visits at these great ranches across the West. You led me to other ranches, you shared your homes and time and selves with me, and without you this work would not be possible. Thanks.

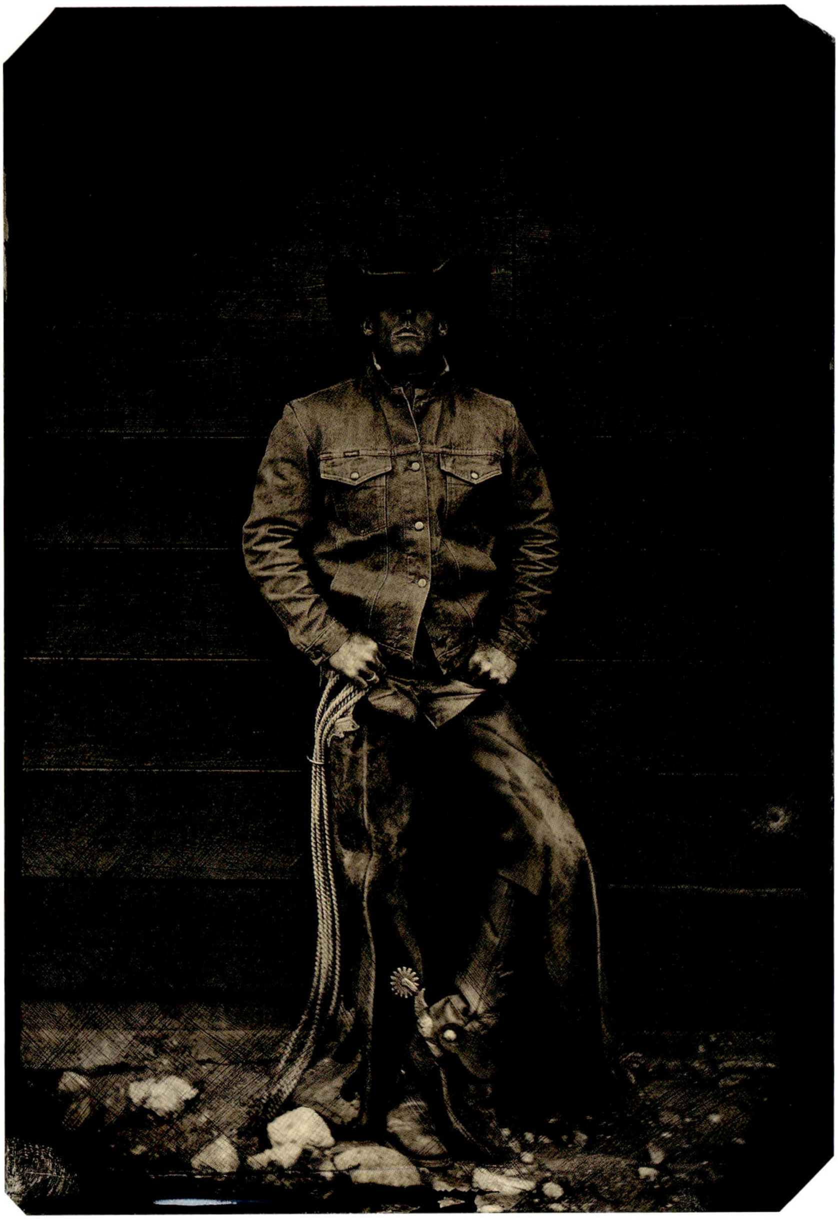

PLATE 148

Steve Eytcheson

JA RANCH, TEXAS